PRESENTED TO

....

BY

....

DATE

....

The
GREAT
LIVES
DEVOTIONAL

The GREAT LIVES DEVOTIONAL

DEVOTIONAL

365 MEDITATIONS
ON THE
MEN *of the* BIBLE

BARBOUR
PUBLISHING

GREET LIVES *of the* BIBLE PROVIDE GREAT EXAMPLES *for* CHRISTIAN MEN TODAY

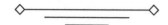

As iron sharpens iron, the Bible says, so one man sharpens another (Proverbs 27:17). This newly-compiled devotional features scores of important biblical men who will sharpen today's readers by their important examples, both good and bad. God thought their lessons were important enough to capture in His Word.

The 365 daily readings include Bible characters such as:

- Moses
- Daniel
- David
- Peter
- Paul
- John the Baptist
- and, of course, Jesus,

providing both biographical background and inspiring, challenging spiritual takeaways.

Featuring contemporary devotionals and "classics" from the likes of Charles Spurgeon, D. L. Moody, Andrew Murray, and Matthew Henry, *The Great Lives Devotional* is perfect for men of all ages.

ADAM: MADE IN GOD'S IMAGE

Then God said, "Let us make mankind in our image, in our likeness, so that they may rule over the fish in the sea and the birds in the sky, over the livestock and all the wild animals, and over all the creatures that move along the ground."

GENESIS 1:26 NIV

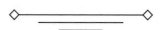

God made Adam—and every human after him—in His own image. That can mean a lot of things, but it doesn't mean Adam was like God in that he possessed all knowledge and power, or that he was perfect in his love and holiness. Adam was a created being, and though he would live eternally, he had a beginning. God, on the other hand, always was and always will be.

First and foremost, "created in God's image" means that the Lord made humans as the only living things on earth with a true consciousness of their Creator. While all created things owe their existence to their Creator, only humans can truly know and love the One who made them.

God spent the first days of creation making the cosmos, the earth, the plants, and the animals. All of those things, in their own ways, reflect God the Creator. That's because God wanted people to see Him in all creation. But what He wanted most was a loving, personal relationship with the only beings He created in His own image—us!

MOSES: A PATTERN OF CHRIST

By faith Moses, when he was come to years, refused to be called the son of Pharaoh's daughter; choosing rather to suffer affliction with the people of God, than to enjoy the pleasures of sin for a season.

HEBREWS 11:24–25 KJV

How wonderful is the place Moses occupies in the kingdom of God. A pattern of Jesus as a prophet, as a mediator, as an intercessor, in his meekness and his faithfulness, there are few of God's servants that stand higher. And what fitted him to take this place? Just this—the choice to give up everything for the reproach of Christ.

Christian, wouldst thou live in the favor of God and enter into His tent to meet Him as Moses did? Wouldst thou be an instrument and a power of blessing, a man strong in faith? Seek to be perfectly separate from the spirit of the world, refuse its pleasure and honor and riches; count the contempt of God's people and the reproach of Christ thy treasures. Ask for the enlightening of the Holy Spirit to teach thee what true conformity to Christ is, in thy relation to the world, its culture, its possessions, its friendship.

Beware of judging of what is lawful by any human standard: Christ alone can teach thee what it means to forsake all. . .and follow Him.

MARK: GROWING IN FAITH

Now Barnabas was determined to take with them John called Mark.
ACTS 15:37 NKJV

Whether he's called John, his Hebrew name, or Mark, his Greek name, this is the man who wrote the second Gospel, which reports the apostle Peter's outlook on Jesus' ministry.

Mark's mother was a believer who had a prayer meeting in her house. Peter went there after he was freed from prison. The apostle seems to have been close to the family, because he refers to Mark as his son. Another of Mark's faithful family members, his cousin Barnabas, took Mark on a missionary journey with the apostle Paul. But at Perga, Mark left the missionary work, returning to Jerusalem. Paul didn't appreciate Mark's vacillation, and when a second missionary journey was in the offing, he refused Barnabas's suggestion that they give Mark another chance.

The disagreement became so fierce that it caused a rift between the two missionaries. Paul and Barnabas split up and spread the Gospel separately. But by the end of his life, Paul had forgiven the errant missionary and let Mark again join him. The apostle even asked Timothy to bring Mark from Ephesus because he was "useful."

From useless to useful, Mark's life is a picture of a believer who grows in faith and consistency. He who draws near to God again, as Mark did, may become a valuable tool in the Lord's hand.

TIMOTHY: LEARNING, APPLYING, TEACHING

Timothy was well thought of by the believers in Lystra and Iconium, so Paul wanted him to join them on their journey.

ACTS 16:2–3 NLT

Timothy started with credentials, became an intern, and ended up a leader in the church at Ephesus. The apostle Paul trusted his protégé enough to allow him to instruct the Ephesians on the Christian life.

The young missionary was told to tell the Ephesians "not to teach false doctrines. . .or to devote themselves to myths and endless genealogies." Why? "Such things promote controversial speculations rather than advancing God's work" (1 Timothy 1:3–4 NIV).

With each step Timothy took, Paul passed along more responsibility. Timothy became a master learner. As Paul instructed, Timothy applied the learning to his teaching.

Paul's final direction to Timothy was as strong as what he'd given throughout the young man's training, and it makes sense for us as well: "Continue in what you have learned and have become convinced of, because you know those from whom you learned it, and how from infancy you have known the Holy Scriptures, which are able to make you wise for salvation through faith in Christ Jesus. All Scripture is God-breathed and is useful for teaching, rebuking, correcting and training in righteousness, so that the servant of God may be thoroughly equipped for every good work" (2 Timothy 3:14–17 NIV).

Timothy's job is also ours: Learn, apply, teach.

SOLOMON: A HOPE AND A FUTURE

*"King Solomon will be blessed, and David's throne
will remain secure before the LORD forever."*

I KINGS 2:45 NIV

He was the son of the most famous king of Israel. He would succeed his father on the throne, but his pedigree wasn't without controversy. His parents, David and Bathsheba, had committed adultery at the beginning of their relationship. David, a man after God's own heart (Acts 12:22) actually resorted to murder in an unsuccessful attempt to cover up this indiscretion.

Despite the sins of his parents, though, Solomon was judged faithful based on his own relationship with God. He was not the oldest of King David's sons nor was he the most cunning. But he was the son both David and God chose to take the throne.

Solomon stood before his father to receive both instruction and blessing. David also supplied Solomon with materials he would need to construct God's temple. When David died, Solomon knew he lacked the experience to lead his people, but he did possess a desire to rule well.

No one is doomed by his personal or family history. Let's take encouragement from Solomon's story, which shows grace in action. God will redeem, cleanse, and use any man willing to humble himself and obey.

SILAS: SHINING IN THE SHADOWS

The crowd joined in the attack against Paul and Silas, and the magistrates ordered them to be stripped and beaten with rods.

Acts 16:22 NIV

Silas was a prophet, missionary, and prayer warrior, one of the apostle Paul's most trusted ministry partners. If we read what's written of Silas in scripture, we'll gain a great deal of respect for this faithful man.

One of Silas's most compelling stories is set in prison. He and Paul had been jailed after casting a fortune-telling spirit out of a slave girl. Her owner thought this made her less valuable, so he accused the missionaries of breaking the law. They were arrested and beaten.

At midnight, Paul and Silas were still awake—not complaining and demanding release but praying and singing in their cell. A miraculous earthquake set them free, and the two men then led their jailer to faith in Jesus.

It's likely that Christians in the first century well knew the character of Silas. Perhaps his name evoked thoughts of faithful leadership.

Can the same be said of us? If so, wonderful! Keep up the good work. If not, ask God to make you more like Silas, ready to shine in the shadows of an increasingly dark world.

JOB: ASKING WHY

There was a man in the land of Uz, whose name
was Job; and that man was perfect and upright,
and one that feared God, and eschewed evil.

JOB 1:1 KJV

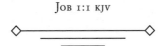

Woe upon woe upon woe. Job lost his herds, his children, and his health—all in a short time. Few human beings have ever suffered like he did.

Job was a wealthy man in a time when wealth was measured by the sheep, goats, camels, and oxen a man owned. He lost a fortune in Satan's attacks. Then he lost an even greater treasure—his ten children. Before long, Job couldn't even say, "At least I still have my health."

Though many have spoken of "the patience of Job," he did not accept his losses meekly. To his credit, Job did not follow his wife's early advice to "curse God, and die" (Job 2:9 KJV). But over time he complained to God, challenged the Lord to show him his sin, and argued that he should never have been born.

Job's response is entirely understandable from our human point of view. We want to believe that if we live well, good things will come to us. While we know that every human being is sinful, scripture does identify Job as "perfect and upright." When bad things happen to good people, we ask "Why?" When bad things happen to us, we ask "Why me?"

In the end, God answered Job's "why" questions with other, larger questions—questions that clearly implied that God knows far more than we as humans do. Job ultimately accepted that truth with humility. May we do the same.

BOAZ: MAKING AN IMPRESSION

Just then Boaz arrived from Bethlehem and greeted the harvesters,
"The LORD be with you!" "The LORD bless you!" they answered.

RUTH 2:4 NIV

When we're first introduced to Boaz, a key character in the beautiful redemption story that is the book of Ruth, we get a pretty good idea of what kind of man he is. He greets his workers with a hearty, "The LORD be with you!" They respond with an equally enthusiastic, "The LORD bless you!"

Talk about a strong first impression. Right away, we see that Boaz is a godly man who treats his servants with kindness and compassion. We see that the workers know him as a man who loves God and others.

Someone has rightly observed that you have only one chance to make a first impression. What impression do your words and actions make on those you meet? Do the people who encounter you know right away that you're a man who loves God and loves other people—whatever their position in life. Can they see that you want to bless them?

As followers of Jesus Christ, we are called to love both our fellow Christians and the unsaved world, even our enemies. Let's commit to treating others the way Boaz did. At the very least, we'll make our world ever so slightly more peaceful. Even better, we may lead some people to faith in our Lord.

GIDEON: GOD WORKS THROUGH US

*But the Lord said to him, "For sure I will be with
you. You will destroy Midian as one man."*

JUDGES 6:16 NLV

Throughout the book of Judges, the people of Israel habitually turned from the Lord. At one point, God gave His rebellious people into the hands of Midian for seven years. The Midianites destroyed the Israelites' food supply and left no sheep, cattle, or donkeys, leaving the people "very poor" (Judges 6:6). When the Israelites cried out to the Lord, He sent a prophet, followed by an angel (identified as Jehovah Himself in 6:14) to remind the people that God was with them. And He would make Gideon their deliverer.

Gideon wasn't so sure about that. "O Lord, how can I save Israel?" he asked God. "See, my family is the least in Manasseh. And I am the youngest in my father's house" (Judges 6:15 NLV).

It's understandable why Gideon would feel that way. Our world views people's importance based on status, experience, and age. But the Lord operates differently, often choosing weak people to display His awesome power.

Maybe you don't come from money, or you're not particularly popular, or you're new in the faith. None of that matters. God stands ready to work *through* you—to empower you to do exactly what He wants. Surrender to His will and watch Him work.

CLASSICS: CHARLES SPURGEON

JESUS: WISE MEN WORSHIP HIM

*Now when Jesus was born in Bethlehem of Judaea in
the days of Herod the king, behold, there came wise
men from the east to Jerusalem. . . . When they saw
the star, they rejoiced with exceeding great joy.*

MATTHEW 2:1, 10 KJV

Beloved friends, if wise men of old came to Jesus and worshipped, should not we come also? My intense desire this morning is that we all may pay homage to Him.

Let those of us who have long worshipped worship anew with yet lowlier reverence and intenser love. And God grant—oh, that He would grant it!—that some who are far off from Him spiritually, as the Magi were far off locally, may come today and ask, "Where is he that is born King of the Jews? for we have come to worship him." May feet that have been accustomed to broad roads, but unaccustomed to the narrow path, this day pursue that way till they see Jesus and bow before Him with all their hearts, finding salvation in Him. These wise men came naturally, traversing the desert; let us come spiritually, leaving our sins.

These were guided by the sight of a star; let us be guided by faith in the divine Spirit, by the teaching of His word and all those blessed lights which the Lord uses to conduct men to Himself. Only let us come to Jesus.

DANIEL: DOING THINGS GOD'S WAY

But Daniel purposed in his heart that he would not defile
himself with the portion of the king's meat, nor with the
wine which he drank: therefore he requested of the prince
of the eunuchs that he might not defile himself.

Daniel 1:8 kjv

Some guys just seem to ask for trouble.

When the Jewish people were taken into captivity by the Babylonians, Daniel, as a young nobleman, had an opportunity to help himself. He was among the group selected to be taught the ways of the Babylonian court. It was to be an integration of the most comfortable sort. The young nobles would become as Babylonians and their captors could say, "Look how well we treat them!"

But Daniel, who could have settled for a life of luxury, chose to keep their integrity. At each step, he and his friends Hananiah, Mishael, and Azariah, were decried by enemies. Time and again they held to their faith, even when it seemed they would die because of it. But all four continued to prosper. Daniel himself became a powerful man and a positive influence on four different kings.

His captors—Nebuchadnezzar, Belshazzar, Darius, and Cyrus—were each in their time the most powerful men on earth. They weren't guys you wanted to annoy, but Daniel wasn't really looking for trouble. He was just more concerned for his soul than his life, which meant no one but God had any power over him. And God used that power to deliver him!

JOHN THE BAPTIST: WALK YOUR TALK

*"Prove by the way you live that you have
repented of your sins and turned to God."*

Matthew 3:8 nlt

Jewish leaders claimed to follow the Old Testament laws, but put special emphasis on oral traditions passed down for generations. John the Baptist criticized these leaders, calling them hypocrites for being too legalistic. He accused them of using religion to advance their political power. And John challenged these people to change their behavior, proving by their actions and the way they lived their lives that they had turned to God.

We've all heard these sayings: "Practice what you preach" and "Actions speak louder than words." We can say that we're Christians. We can read the Bible, go to church, even give tithes and offering. We might follow the rules of our denomination or faith tradition. But do we truly practice what we preach? Do we walk our Christian talk? Do others see Christ in our daily lives and activities?

God knows our true heart. He knows our intentions. He looks beyond our words and religious practices to our truest, deepest heart walk. Today, let's be sure to follow John the Baptist's direction, and prove by the way we live that we have turned to God.

JONAH: FEAR THE LORD

He said unto them, I am an Hebrew; and I fear the LORD, the God of heaven, which hath made the sea and the dry land. Then were the men exceedingly afraid, and said unto him. Why hast thou done this? For the men knew that he fled from the presence of the LORD.

JONAH 1:9–10 KJV

It's possible to say good things about God without really meaning them. Such is the case with Jonah's statement to the pagan sailors manning the ship he was on.

Jonah told the truth about his nationality, but he lied about fearing the Lord God, Creator of heaven and earth and seas. At that moment, Jonah was arrogantly, defiantly disobeying God by taking a ship in the opposite direction from the place he was called to.

Still, Jonah's acknowledgement of a "fear of the Lord" offers useful insights to our strength and success today. Recognizing God's awesome power, knowledge, and holiness should cause a certain amount of fear in us—the kind a mouse undoubtedly feels in the presence of a human being. But biblical fear is also a reverent respect, a desire to know, honor, and ultimately enjoy an eternal relationship with this awesome God, who is also love—demonstrated by the sacrificial death of His Son, Jesus Christ (Romans 5:8).

As sinful human beings, we're pulled in many directions by our own emotions, temptations, companions, and culture. But when we truly acknowledge and "fear" the Lord, He will happily guide and strengthen us in His will.

ABRAHAM: TAKING THE FIRST STEP

The LORD had said to Abram, "Go from your country, your
people and your father's household to the land I will show
you." . . . So Abram went, as the LORD had told him.

GENESIS 12:1, 4 NIV

◇━━━━━━━━◇

When God instructed Abraham (then called Abram) to leave Harran, the Lord made some amazing promises. Who wouldn't want the Creator of the universe Himself to promise greatness, blessings, protection, and an opportunity to bless every nation on earth?

But in Genesis 12:1–4, you'll notice that God didn't provide Abraham much in the way of details. The man wasn't even told where he would be going and what route he would take to get there (also see Hebrews 11:8). God simply told Abraham to pack up his family and "go from your country."

When God communicates a vision, most of us would like to see a travel plan, an itinerary, and a spreadsheet before we take that first step of obedience. It's human nature to prefer details.

But as we read biblical accounts of times God communicated with His people, we see that He doesn't always provide details ahead of time. Rather, He just says, "Get up and go!"

Don't worry if He hasn't given you the details of His plan. Just trust and follow Him, step by step. He'll never let you down or fail to keep a single promise.

CLASSICS: ANDREW MURRAY

HEZEKIAH: LEAVING A LEGACY

*And he did that which was right in the sight of the
LORD, according to all that David his father did.*

2 KINGS 18:3 KJV

Let us look at the testimony scripture gives of Hezekiah: "He did that which was right in the sight of the LORD, according to all that David his father did." Then follow the different elements of this life that was right in God's sight. "He trusted in the LORD God of Israel. He clave to the LORD. He departed not from following Him. He kept His commandments, which the LORD commanded Moses. And the LORD was with Him." His life was one of trust and love, of steadfastness and obedience. And the LORD was with him. He was one of the saints of whom we read, "By faith they obtained a good report." They had the witness that they were righteous, that they were pleasing to God.

THE HEALED LEPER: GIVING THANKS

One of them, when he saw he was healed, came back,
praising God in a loud voice. He threw himself at Jesus'
feet and thanked him—and he was a Samaritan.

LUKE 17:15–16 NIV

Before their encounter with Jesus, the band of ten lepers in Luke 17 had multiple strikes against them. First, as lepers they were obligated by Moses' Law to keep their distance from everyone else (Leviticus 13:46). And second, at least one of them was a Samaritan, and Samaritans were looked down on by Jews. For one thing, they were racially mixed. For another, Jews considered their religion deficient.

But Jesus never recoiled over physical or spiritual impurities. As the lepers saw Him coming, they cried out for mercy—and He responded, healing all ten. Only the man identified as a Samaritan returned to thank Jesus. While He expressed disappointment, going so far as to ask the Samaritan, "Where are the other nine?" (verse 17 NIV), Jesus' compassion hadn't been conditional. Nor was it dependent on how grateful the recipients would be in response to His granting their healing.

Sometimes, though, our own willingness to show compassion is conditional, based on our assumptions of their response to our kindness. What if we cared less about a needy person's response and more about his soul?

JOHN: FISHING FOR MEN

*[Jesus] saw two other brothers, James son of Zebedee and his
brother John. They were in a boat with their father Zebedee,
preparing their nets. Jesus called them, and immediately
they left the boat and their father and followed him.*

<small>MATTHEW 4:21–22 NIV</small>

◇━━━━━━━━◇

How often do we immediately do what we're told? That's what the
Bible says John and his brother James did.

It was probably just a regular day for John, not much different than
any other. He was a fisherman on the Sea of Galilee, like his father
and his brother, and they were in a boat near the shore preparing their
nets. Suddenly a man like no other called out. He said, "Follow Me!"

Jesus had been in Galilee preaching the kingdom of God. John
was probably already familiar with Him. But when Jesus made a
specific invitation, there was nothing for John to do but follow. He
immediately dropped what he was doing and went to Jesus. We don't
even have record of him saying goodbye to his father.

Jesus later said that anyone who would be His disciple must give
up everything he has (Luke 14:33). John did just that—and what a
gatherer of souls he became. He serves as an example to us even today.
What people or things do we hold dear? Would we give them up in
order to gain Jesus?

CLASSICS: MATTHEW HENRY

JACOB: HOLD YOUR TONGUE

And Jacob was wroth, and chode with Laban: and Jacob answered and said to Laban, What is my trespass? what is my sin, that thou hast so hotly pursued after me? Whereas thou hast searched all my stuff, what hast thou found of all thy household stuff? set it here before my brethren and thy brethren, that they may judge betwixt us both.

GENESIS 31:36–37 KJV

◇———————◇

Jacob's natural temper was mild and calm, and as grace had improved it he was a smooth man, and a plain man. And yet Laban's unreasonable carriage towards him put him into a heat that transported him into some vehemence. His chiding with Laban, though it may admit of some excuse, was not justifiable, nor is it written for our imitation. Grievous words stir up anger and commonly do but make bad worse.

It is a very great affront to one that bears an honest mind to be charged with dishonesty, and yet even this we must learn to bear with patience, committing our cause to God.

THE CENTURION: GREAT FAITH

The centurion sent friends to [Jesus], saying to Him, "Lord, do not trouble Yourself, for I am not worthy that You should enter under my roof. Therefore I did not even think myself worthy to come to You. But say the word, and my servant will be healed."

LUKE 7:6–7 NKJV

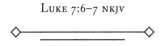

Although he was not Jewish, the centurion loved the Jewish people and even built them a synagogue. Jewish elders begged Jesus earnestly to come and heal the Gentile's servant, who was dear to him and gravely ill. Such regard for a foreigner was extraordinary.

Jesus proceeded at once. Not far from the centurion's home, He met some friends of the soldier, who passed along this message of today's scripture. The centurion added, "For I also am a man placed under authority, having soldiers under me. And I say to one, 'Go,' and he goes; and to another, 'Come,' and he comes; and to my servant, 'Do this,' and he does it" (Luke 7:8 NKJV).

Many people wanted Jesus to prove Himself. Not this man. The centurion simply said, "Just say the word." He knew enough about Jesus to believe that if Jesus spoke words of healing, even from afar, it would be done. Little wonder Jesus said, "I say to you, I have not found such great faith, not even in Israel!" (Luke 7:9 NKJV).

Faith is what pleases God (Hebrews 11:6). And He has given us plenty of reasons to believe, even though we can't see Him. From Bible stories like that of the centurion, to the many blessings of our own lives, we can have confidence that God has our best interests at heart. Simply trust Him and His plan.

JESUS: OUT OF THE LIMELIGHT

And seeing the multitudes, He went up on a mountain,
and when He was seated His disciples came to Him.
Then He opened His mouth and taught them.

Matthew 5:1–2 nkjv

There were plenty of times when Jesus was surrounded by crowds. Many of those times, He was speaking out publicly, sharing the Good News with whoever would listen.

But at other times He walked *away* from the crowd, headed to the hills, and found a quiet place to visit and share with His closest followers. This is a picture of intimate impartation to a handful of people—not a busy scene with stage lights, microphones, and multitudes.

Some men crave the spotlight, while others hate to be seen. But most all of us enjoy at least the occasional applause of our fellow man. There's nothing inherently wrong with a pat on the back, but we should always remember that Jesus Himself is our true audience. And He seeks faithfulness in the little things (Luke 16:10). If we have families, He expects us to prioritize feeding our own households and teaching our own children (Matthew 24:45; Ephesians 6:4; 1 Timothy 5:8).

Whether or not we're called to address the masses, let's be sure we make time for the smaller audiences who matter so much: Jesus Himself and the family He's given us.

CLASSICS: ANDREW MURRAY

PAUL: AN UNCEASING PRAYER LIFE

*For God is my witness, whom I serve with my spirit in the
gospel of his Son, that without ceasing I make mention of you
always in my prayers; making request, if by any means now at
length I might have a prosperous journey by the will of God to
come unto you. For I long to see you, that I may impart unto
you some spiritual gift, to the end ye may be established.*

ROMANS 1:9–11 KJV

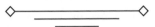

Paul was a minister who prayed much for his congregation. Let us
read his words prayerfully and calmly so that we may hear the voice
of the Spirit. "Without ceasing, I make mention of you always in my
prayers, making request. . .that I may impart unto you some spiritual
gift, to the end ye may be established."

What a study for the Inner Chamber, to teach us that unceasing
prayer formed a large part of Paul's service in the Gospel; we see the
high spiritual aim which he set before himself in his work on behalf
of believers; and the tender and self-sacrificing love with which he
ever continued to think of the church and its needs.

Let us ask God to bring each one of us, and all the ministers of
His Word, to a life of which such prayer is the healthy and natural
outflow.

JOSIAH: ACCEPTING GODLY GUIDANCE

Josiah was eight years old when he became king, and he reigned in Jerusalem thirty-one years. His mother's name was Jedidah daughter of Adaiah; she was from Bozkath.

2 KINGS 22:1 NIV

When you read this passage describing Judah's king as an eight-year-old boy, do you envision a toy truck in his hand? Or do you at least wonder how such a young child could understand concepts of patience, sacrifice, and humility, all of which are key character traits of a good ruler?

How could an eight-year-old boy lead a nation the way Josiah did? He became one of the best kings that God's people served under, bringing about godly reforms to the entire nation.

We know that Josiah's father, King Amon, was a wicked king who followed in his father Manasseh's idol-worshipping footsteps. Amon's officials hated him so much that they killed him. He certainly didn't provide Josiah with much spiritual guidance. We know far less about Josiah's mother, Jedidah, but it's quite possible that she was a godly woman who quietly guided her son in the ways of the Lord.

Scripture highlights many godly women, and we probably all know several personally. Let's always be willing to learn from their lives and example. That may have changed a nation in Josiah's time. What effect might it have in our lives and world?

CLASSICS: MATTHEW HENRY

GIDEON: LAUDABLE MODESTY

Then the men of Israel said unto Gideon, Rule thou over us, both thou, and thy son, and thy son's son also: for thou hast delivered us from the hand of Midian. And Gideon said unto them, I will not rule over you, neither shall my son rule over you: the LORD shall rule over you.

JUDGES 8:22–23 KJV

Here is Gideon's laudable modesty, after his great victory, in refusing the government which the people offered him. It was honest in them to offer it: "Rule thou over us, for thou hast delivered us." They thought it very reasonable that he who had gone through the toils and perils of their deliverance should enjoy the honor and power of commanding them ever afterward, and very desirable that he who in this great and critical juncture had had such manifest tokens of God's presence with him should ever afterward preside in their affairs. Let us apply it to the Lord Jesus: He hath delivered us out of the hands of our enemies, our spiritual enemies, the worst and most dangerous, and therefore it is fit He should rule over us, for how can we be better ruled than by one that appears to have so great an interest in heaven and so great a kindness for this earth? We are delivered that we may serve him without fear (Luke 1:74–75).

◇— *Day 24* —◇

DAVID: A PERSONAL STAKE

*And king David said to Ornan, Nay; but I will verily buy
it for the full price: for I will not take that which is thine
for the LORD, nor offer burnt offerings without cost.*

1 CHRONICLES 21:24 KJV

In 1 Chronicles 21, we find examples of David's willful sin and his careful response.

First the sin: In an apparent act of pride, David commanded Joab to count the number of Israelites. Joab tried to dissuade the king, but "the king's word prevailed" (verse 4 KJV). God was angered by David's decision, and offered him a choice of punishments: three years of famine in the land, three months of enemy oppression, or three days of pestilence sent by God. David chose the third option, trusting that God's mercy would limit the pain. Still, seventy thousand Israelites died. As David begged for mercy on his people, God sent a prophet to tell the king to set up an altar at the threshing floor of a farmer named Ornan.

Now, the response: When David requested Ornan's land for the altar, the farmer immediately offered to give it to David without cost—along with the materials for the sacrifice itself. But David wisely declined the offer, saying, "I will not take for the LORD what is yours, or sacrifice a burnt offering that costs me nothing" (verse 24 NIV).

The king paid Ornan and set up an altar, and God relented from His punishment. David realized that his own choice had created the problem, and he needed a personal stake in the solution. May we always do the same.

CLASSICS: ANDREW MURRAY

JOSEPH: MUCH LIKE JESUS

And Joseph was brought down to Egypt; and Potiphar, an officer of Pharaoh, captain of the guard, an Egyptian, bought him of the hands of the Ishmeelites, which had brought him down thither. And the LORD was with Joseph, and he was a prosperous man; and he was in the house of his master the Egyptian. And his master saw that the LORD was with him, and that the LORD made all that he did to prosper in his hand.

GENESIS 39:1–3 KJV

I want to call your attention to Joseph as a type of Christ. We sometimes speak in the Christian life, of entire surrender, and rightly, and here we have a beautiful illustration of what it is. First, Joseph was in Potiphar's house to serve him and to help him, and he did that, and Potiphar learned to trust him, so that he said, "All that I have I will give into his hands."

Now that is exactly what is to take place with a great many Christians. They know Christ, they trust Him, they love Him, but He is not Master; He is a sort of helper. When there is trouble they come to Him, when they sin they ask Him for pardon in His precious blood, when they are in darkness they cry to Him; but often and often they live according to their own will, and they seek help from themselves. But how blessed is the man who comes and, like Potiphar, says, "I will give up everything to Jesus!"

ELIJAH: GOD STILL PROVIDES

*Then the LORD said to Elijah, "Go to the east and hide
by Kerith Brook, near where it enters the Jordan River.
Drink from the brook and eat what the ravens bring
you, for I have commanded them to bring you food."*

1 KINGS 17:2–4 NLT

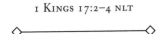

After a series of evil kings had ruled in Israel, God raised up Elijah
the prophet. A drought was on the way, and God told Elijah to shelter
near a brook that fed into the famed Jordan River. That would provide
the prophet's water. Meanwhile, the Lord was planning to provide
food for Elijah in the most unusual of ways—via ravens.

"If Providence calls us to solitude and retirement, it becomes
us to go," Matthew Henry wrote in his classic commentary. "When
we cannot be useful, we must be patient; and when we cannot work
for God, we must sit still quietly for him." This is what Elijah did,
submitting to God's plan for the ravens to bring his food. "Let those
who have but from hand to mouth, learn to live upon Providence,
and trust it for the bread of the day, in the day."

Sometimes we find ourselves in situations that make no human
sense. But if God calls us to stand on principle, give generously, love
our enemies, or any of a hundred other things that seem impossible,
know that He will provide for and in our obedience.

Don't hesitate to obey. As He did for Elijah, God still provides
for His people.

SAMUEL: DEPENDENCE ON GOD

Then the word of the LORD came to Samuel.
1 SAMUEL 15:10 NIV

Samuel's birth was an answer to a mother's prayer, and his life was dedicated to the service of God long before he ever took his first breath. As a young boy he served in the temple with Eli, a priest whose reputation was heavily tarnished.

Though it was rare for God to speak audibly in those days, He called to Samuel in the middle of the night. Once Samuel recognized it was the voice of God he listened to a prophecy against the aging priest. The next morning Samuel spoke to Eli, not as a child but as a prophet.

Samuel's résumé is impressive: He anointed kings, prophesied against rulers, was led by God to understand His Word, and spoke truth when it was unpopular. Samuel was manly, and his words had impact. Others may have disliked what he said, but the end result was often a message from God that none could argue against.

While never a king, Samuel was often sought out as if he were a ruler. He was sought out *by* kings, yet he always endeavored to serve the King of kings.

Samuel was truly unique. But any of us can serve the Lord like he did. Let's dedicate ourselves to dependence on God and doing His will. If we do, our lives will also have impact.

CLASSICS: D. L. MOODY

PETER: GREATER WORKS THAN JESUS

Then answered Peter, and said unto Jesus, Lord, it is good for us to be here: if thou wilt, let us make here three tabernacles; one for thee, and one for Moses, and one for Elias.

<small>MATTHEW 17:4 KJV</small>

Here, on the mount, was a man that was to be used perhaps more than any man that has ever lived in winning people to Christ; and that man was Peter. But there wasn't a man in the city of Jerusalem that thought he amounted to anything. He was an unlettered man; but he knew the Lord Jesus. He thought that if he could only get Elijah and Moses to go down to Jerusalem and hold some evangelistic meetings; if Moses would only go down and thunder out the law; if Elijah would go and tell the people how the prophecies had all been fulfilled in Christ, how it would stir the whole city!

Yet the man to do that mighty work was not Moses or Elijah; it was Peter himself. He did a greater work than Moses, a greater work than Elijah, a greater work in winning souls than even his Master, for Jesus said, "Greater works than these shall ye do."

ISAAC: QUIET FAITH

Now we, brethren, as Isaac was, are the children of promise.
GALATIANS 4:28 KJV

"Abraham, Isaac, and Jacob" are the three great patriarchs of the Old Testament. Abraham and Jacob take up most of the biblical storyline: Abraham is identified more than 300 times in the King James Version, and Jacob nearly 280, not to mention all the times his name is used as a synonym for the nation of Israel. Isaac, on the other hand, warrants only about 120 references.

We know that Abraham was the man specifically selected by God to be forefather of His chosen people. Jacob was the patriarch whose sons headed the "twelve tribes" of Israel. Both men had interactions with God and dramatic experiences following Him. And then there was Isaac, whose life seems pretty mild by comparison.

Apart from his near sacrifice at the hand of his father (a test for Abraham, ordered by God Himself), Isaac moves quietly through the pages of scripture. As with his father and son, Isaac made his mistakes. But this miraculously-conceived son of nonagenarian parents consistently followed God and fulfilled his role in the larger story of redemption. Without Isaac, there's no Jacob; without Jacob, there's no nation of Israel; without Israel, there's no Jesus.

If you ever think other guys have the plum assignments in the Christian life, don't worry. If God has called you to a quieter life, just live it out faithfully. In His own time and way, He'll use you for great things.

CLASSICS: ANDREW MURRAY

DAVID: AFTER GOD'S HEART

And when he had removed him, he raised up unto them
David to be their king; to whom also he gave their testimony,
and said, I have found David the son of Jesse, a man
after mine own heart, which shall fulfil all my will.

ACTS 13:22 KJV

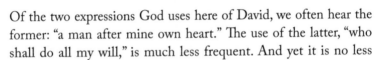

Of the two expressions God uses here of David, we often hear the former: "a man after mine own heart." The use of the latter, "who shall do all my will," is much less frequent. And yet it is no less important than the other.

"A man after Mine own heart": that speaks of the deep unseen mystery of the pleasure a man can give to God in heaven. "Who shall do all My will": that deals with the life down here on earth which can be seen and judged by men. Let us seek and get full hold of the truth that it is the man who does all God's will who is the man after His own heart.

Such men God seeks: when He finds them He rejoices over them with great joy: they are the very men He needs, men He can trust and use. His heart, with its hidden divine perfections, reveals itself in His will: he that seeks and loves *and does all His will* is a man altogether after His own heart: the man of absolute surrender to God's will.

OBADIAH: DANGEROUS SERVICE

"I'm not asking you to take them out of the world,
but to keep them safe from the evil one."

JOHN 17:15 NLT

The Obadiah of 1 Kings 18 is not the writer of the Old Testament book of that name. This man managed the palace of King Ahab and his wife, Jezebel. The royal household must have been a treacherous place to work. Ahab did more evil than any of the previous kings of Judah, and Jezebel was as evil as her husband and even more devious.

Though he lived in dark times, Obadiah was a devoted follower of the Lord. When Jezebel hunted down prophets of God, Obadiah managed to safely hide a hundred of them in caves, bringing them food and water.

During a severe famine, as Obadiah sought water and grazing land for Ahab's cattle, he met Elijah—a great prophet and very much a wanted man. Elijah instructed Obadiah to tell the king, "Elijah is here." Obadiah at first objected. If the Spirit carried Elijah away, then King Ahab would be furious and punish Obadiah. Despite his misgivings, however, he faithfully delivered the message, which led to Elijah's dramatic contest on Mount Carmel with the prophets of Baal.

Obadiah loved God more than he feared King Ahab. His example reassures us as Christians that we too can live in a dark, dangerous world, preserving righteousness in the face of evil.

ZACCHAEUS: LIVING IN JOY

*Now behold, there was a man named Zacchaeus
who was a chief tax collector, and he was rich.*

LUKE 19:2 NKJV

"Zacchaeus was a wee little man, a wee little man was he," many of us sang as children. As we grew, this wee man stayed in our hearts, the sign of a disadvantaged fellow who had plenty of money. Not only was Zacchaeus small—he also had a small life. He was ostracized by his fellow Jews, who resented his work for the occupying Romans. Who among us cannot relate to the underdog?

When Jesus came to town, little Zacchaeus determined to see Him, climbing a sycamore tree for a better view. But Jesus saw Zacchaeus, calling out to him and inviting Himself to the tax collector's home. No host could have been happier. Zacchaeus quickly repented of his sins and promised to pay back far more than the amount of money he'd cheated from people. Suddenly he was friends with Jesus. He had been saved.

We all began as Zacchaeus did, separated from God and out of touch with our fellow man. Called by Jesus, we leaped to believe and, perhaps more slowly than the tax collector, saw our lives change. We became friends with Jesus. Are you living in that joy today?

BARNABAS: ENCOURAGING OTHERS

*Joseph, a Levite from Cyprus, whom the apostles called Barnabas
(which means "son of encouragement"), sold a field he owned
and brought the money and put it at the apostles' feet.*

ACTS 4:36–37 NIV

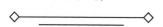

From the moment he appears in scripture, it's obvious that Barnabas is an admirable man. Scripture describes him as "a good man, full of the Holy Spirit and faith" (Acts 11:24 NIV).

First-century Christians didn't call this Church leader "Son of Encouragement" for nothing; look at his ministry, and you'll understand how he got his nickname.

Church leaders in Jerusalem sent Barnabas to Antioch to check out some fellow Cypriots who were preaching to the Greeks, unlike other Christian preachers at the time who were preaching only to the Jews.

Barnabas approved of what he found in Antioch, as many Greeks were being converted. Later, he brought Paul to Antioch. For a year the two taught new converts, leaving only briefly to take a relief collection to Jerusalem.

Barnabas was exactly what the early Church needed—a wise, patient leader. Wouldn't we like a handful of them in each of our own churches?

DAVID: WAITING ON GOD'S PROMISES

*So Samuel took the horn of oil and anointed him in
the presence of his brothers, and from that day on the
Spirit of the LORD came powerfully upon David.*

1 SAMUEL 16:13 NIV

In the story of Samuel anointing David to be king, we hear echoes of earlier readings: As with Samson, God's Spirit moved powerfully in this young man; as with Gideon, David was the youngest and the smallest of his family. Yet God specifically directed Samuel to anoint Jesse's youngest son (1 Samuel 16:1, 12).

There is one very important element of this story: David had to wait to become king. God's promise was slow in coming, though David had been anointed by God's own prophet.

The Lord's timeline is often far from our own. King Saul lived and reigned for a significant amount of time—and David even spent time in his service—before the younger man was eventually crowned king.

Are you waiting for God's promise to you to be fulfilled? Then you stand in a long line of biblical heroes, including Noah and Abraham. But make no mistake: God's timelines are intentional. Faithfulness and patience in the meantime will be rewarded.

CLASSICS: CHARLES SPURGEON

PAUL: VALUING TIME AND LIFE

But none of these things move me, neither count I my
life dear unto myself, so that I might finish my course
with joy, and the ministry, which I have received of the
Lord Jesus, to testify the gospel of the grace of God.

ACTS 20:24 KJV

Paul says that, in comparison with his great object of preaching the Gospel, he did not count even his life to be dear to himself; yet we are sure Paul highly valued life. He had the same love of life as other men, and he knew besides that his own life was of great consequence to the churches and to the cause of Christ.

In another place he said, "To abide in the flesh is more needful for you." He was not weary of life, nor was he a vain person who could treat life as though it were a thing to fling away in sport. He valued life, for he prized time, which is the stuff that life is made of, and he turned to practical account each day and hour, "redeeming the time because the days are evil."

Yet he soberly said to the elders of the church at Ephesus that he did not regard his life as a dear thing, in comparison with bearing testimony to the Gospel of the grace of God. . . . The life which he lived here below was only valued by him as a means to that end.

JESUS: DIFFERENT GOALS

"Blessed are…"

MATTHEW 5:3 NKJV

◇━━━━━━━━◇

Jesus begins the Sermon on the Mount with a list of proverbs that the Church calls the Beatitudes, a Latin word for "blessings." *Blessed* means "happy." This is eternal truth that Jesus proclaims, of a joy much fuller than the worldly blessings of health, wealth, pleasure, power, and the pursuit of happiness.

For those willing to follow Jesus up the mountain to be taught by Him, the Beatitudes are about life in pursuit of a different set of goals. Philippians 2:5–8 tells us to have the same attitude that Jesus had when He gave up heaven's haven to become a man. He humbled Himself, surrendered most of His rights as God, and became obedient to the Father in all things—even death on the cross.

Like Jesus, we must give up our own rights and submit to the Father. To be truly, deeply happy and blessed, we must become poor in spirit. We must mourn. We must be meek, merciful, and pure in heart. We must suffer for others in Jesus' name. We must even rejoice in the persecution that comes as we follow Christ.

The blessings of the Beatitudes aren't about houses, clothes, cars, or anything else on this planet. They're all about laying up treasures in heaven by living like Jesus on earth.

AQUILA: HONORING WOMEN

[Apollos] began to speak boldly in the synagogue. When Priscilla and Aquila heard him, they invited him to their home and explained to him the way of God more adequately.

ACTS 18:26 NIV

Aquila was an important teacher of the Gospel message mentioned several times in the New Testament. During his time, he had a radical approach to his ministry—and his marriage.

Aquila and his wife, Priscilla, traveled with the apostle Paul, established a church in their home in Ephesus (1 Corinthians 16:19), and taught and trained a Jewish teacher named Apollos, who went on to become a powerful preacher of the Gospel. This couple was an amazing example of hospitality, passion for Christ, sharing what they had learned of the Gospel message, and encouraging new believers in the faith.

What was so radical about Aquila's approach? It involved his wife, who appears to be an equal partner in all he did—and this at a time when the first-century Roman society didn't view women as equals to men.

It's probably no accident that when the couple is mentioned in the New Testament, Priscilla's name is usually mentioned first. Aquila lived out the truth that, in God's eyes, men and women are of equal value in building the kingdom and spreading the message of salvation.

CLASSICS: MATTHEW HENRY

EZRA: TRUSTWORTHY

*That thou mayest buy speedily with this money bullocks, rams,
lambs, with their meat offerings and their drink offerings,
and offer them upon the altar of the house of your God
which is in Jerusalem. And whatsoever shall seem good to
thee, and to thy brethren, to do with the rest of the silver
and the gold, that do after the will of your God.*

EZRA 7:17–18 KJV

We are here told that Ezra was entrusted, first, to receive this money
and to carry it to Jerusalem; for he was a man of known integrity,
whom they could confide in, that he would not convert to his own
use the least part of that which was given to the public. We find Paul
going to Jerusalem upon such an errand, to bring alms to his nation
and offerings (Acts 24:17).

Second, to lay out this money in the best manner, in sacrifices
to be offered upon the altar of God and in whatever else he or his
brethren thought fit, with this limitation only that it should be after
the will of their God, which they were better acquainted with than
the king was.

Let the will of our God be always our rule in our expenses, and
particularly in what we lay out for His service. God's work must always
be done according to His will.

JUDAH: FLAWED, BUT USED BY GOD

*The sons of Leah: Reuben the firstborn of Jacob,
Simeon, Levi, Judah, Issachar and Zebulun.*

GENESIS 35:23 NIV

As the fourth-born son of Jacob and Leah, Judah had little hope of inheriting what Reuben was entitled to as the firstborn. But when Reuben slept with his father's concubine (verse 22) and the next two brothers, Simeon and Levi, massacred the men of Shechem (Genesis 34), Judah ended up first in line for the blessing (Genesis 49:8–12).

But that didn't stop him from making a string of poor decisions. He married an ungodly Canaanite woman, Shua, and fathered three children with her: Er, Onan, and Shelah. He went on to choose a Canaanite wife for Er, a woman named Tamar.

Er was so wicked that God took his life. And after God took Onan's life as well, Judah visited a woman he believed to be a harlot—who turned out to be Tamar in disguise. After learning that Tamar was pregnant, Judah threatened to have her burned before he was forced to acknowledge the child was his (Genesis 38).

In spite of the messes Judah created, God used his family line to bring forth the Messiah (Matthew 1:3; Luke 3:33). While the Lord never promises to remove the ramifications of our sin, He is wise and powerful enough to redeem situations and people that we think beyond hope.

JOSHUA: FAITHFUL SUPPORTER

*The LORD said to Moses, "Come up to me on the mountain
and stay here, and I will give you the tablets of stone
with the law and commandments I have written for
their instruction." Then Moses set out with Joshua his
aide, and Moses went up on the mountain of God.*

EXODUS 24:12–13 NIV

You're captain-general of the Hebrews under Moses—the main
guy's right-hand man—when your leader tells you to accompany
him up the holy mountain of God. You will witness the Lord passing down the stone tablets containing His Law.

Scary? You bet. But just think what this invitation says about
Joshua's character.

One day, Joshua would become Moses' successor—but not yet. In
this moment, his duty was to support Moses as the leader of God's
people. The younger man had exhibited faithfulness in the past by
fighting and defeating the Amalekites, just as Moses had ordered
(Exodus 17:9). Now here he was—closer in proximity to God than
any man except Moses.

If you are second (or third, or fourth) in command at work, at
church, or in any other organization, don't stress over reaching the
top. Are you fully supportive of the person God has put in charge at
this time, always faithful to help carry out the vision God has given?
When you are, He will bless—your group, your leader, and you yourself.

CLASSICS: ANDREW MURRAY

NOAH: "PERFECT IN HIS GENERATIONS"

*These are the generations of Noah: Noah was a just man and
perfect in his generations, and Noah walked with God.*

GENESIS 6:9 KJV

We know how Noah fell. And yet the heart of Noah was perfect with
the Lord God.

To understand this, there is one thing we must remember. The
meaning of the word *perfect* must in each case be decided by that particular stage in God's education of His people in which it is used. What
a father or a teacher counts perfection in a child of ten is very different
from what he would call so in one of twenty. As to the disposition or
spirit, the perfection would be the same; in its contents, as the proofs
by which it was to be judged of, there would be a wide difference.

God looketh at the heart. A heart that is perfect with Him is an
object of complacency and approval. A wholehearted consecration to
His will and fellowship, a life that takes as its motto, *Wholly for God*,
has in all ages, even where the Spirit had not yet been given to dwell
in the heart, been accepted by Him as the mark of the perfect man.

ZECHARIAH:
SPEAKING GOD'S TRUTH

*At that time the prophets Haggai and Zechariah son of Iddo
prophesied to the Jews in Judah and Jerusalem. They prophesied
in the name of the God of Israel who was over them.*

Ezra 5:1 nlt

Zechariah wasn't the only prophet of his day. But he had a message
that affected the entire nation of Israel. Scattered and seemingly
weak, the people of Israel had been ruled by others for a long time.
Zechariah had big news—God was going to restore their fortunes,
but this wouldn't happen based on the people's strength. God made
it clear *He* was their strength. He had Zechariah write, "It is not by
force nor by strength, but by my Spirit, says the Lord of Heaven's
Armies" (Zechariah 4:6 nlt).

Knowing God would bless the people could lead to pride, so
there was a need for further instruction: "This is what the Lord of
Heaven's Armies says: Judge fairly, and show mercy and kindness to
one another. Do not oppress widows, orphans, foreigners, and the
poor. And do not scheme against each other" (Zechariah 7:9–10 nlt).

This prophet had a message and he shared that message. Zechariah's words brought the people together, and this gathering of the
people would ultimately introduce Jesus to the world. His is an example
that we as Christian men today can follow.

SHEPHERDS: OFFERING THE GIFT OF PRAISE

The shepherds went back to their flocks, glorifying
and praising God for all they had heard and seen.
It was just as the angel had told them.

LUKE 2:20 NLT

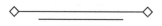

An angel appeared, carrying unprecedented news: God was sending His Son to our world as a baby. This eternity-altering communiqué came to a group of shepherds, among the lower strata of first-century society.

The radiance of the angel—reflecting the glory of God Himself—was terrifying. But he urged the shepherds to have courage, because "I bring you good news that will bring great joy to all people. The Savior—yes, the Messiah, the Lord—has been born today in Bethlehem, the city of David!" (Luke 2:10–11 NLT). And then that one angel was accompanied by a "vast host" of others (verse 13 NLT), filling the night sky with the sound of praise: "Glory to God in highest heaven, and peace on earth to those with whom God is pleased" (verse 14 NLT).

Told how to recognize this special baby, the shepherds quickly left for Bethlehem. Unlike the wise men, who visited later, the shepherds apparently carried no gifts. But they arrived, with wonder and worship, and returned to their fields "glorifying and praising God."

The shepherds were just average, workaday guys, but they were the first to meet the incarnated Jesus. Their example speaks volumes to us today: when we encounter Jesus, let worship be our gift.

NATHAN: HONEST CONFRONTATION

*The Lord sent Nathan the prophet to tell
David this story: "There were two men in a
certain town. One was rich, and one was poor."*

2 SAMUEL 12:1 NLT

Nathan the prophet had to tell hard truths to David, the popular king of Israel. When David decided to build a temple for the Lord, Nathan had to tell him his son Solomon would build it instead. As David's life drew to a close, Nathan had to give the king the sad news that one of his sons, Adonijah, intended to betray his father and usurp the throne. Nathan revealed the plot and convinced David to quickly appoint Solomon as king (1 Kings 1:5–20).

But Nathan's greatest challenge occurred when he exposed David's adultery with Bathsheba and the murder of her husband, Uriah, one of the king's faithful soldiers. To reveal this grievous sin, Nathan told a story of a rich man who believed his powerful position allowed him to steal a poor man's lamb. David was furious, telling Nathan, "This man deserves to die."

"You are that man!" Nathan replied. Devastated, David confessed, "I have sinned against the Lord."

Nathan was more than a wise, fearless counselor to David—he was a friend. May we commit ourselves to faithfully sharing God's truth with our friends. Or, hopefully in far less serious situations, to be ready to hear the counsel of our fellow Christians.

ASA: THE IMPORTANCE OF FINISHING STRONG

In the twentieth year of Jeroboam king of Israel, Asa became
king of Judah, and he reigned in Jerusalem forty-one
years. . . . Asa did what was right in the eyes of the LORD.

1 KINGS 15:9–11 NIV

◇ ═══════════════ ◇

One of the overarching themes in the Bible—especially in the New Testament—is the importance of finishing strong in the life of faith.

Asa, the third monarch of the kingdom of Judah, spent the first thirty-five years of his forty-one-year reign honoring God in every way he could. He led his nation in instituting reforms, including rooting out idolatry and restoring the worship of the one true God. After a battle with Egypt in the tenth year of Asa's reign, Judah enjoyed a quarter-century of peace.

Those things alone could have qualified Asa as one of the greatest Old Testament monarchs. Sadly, however, he stumbled late in his life. Rather than maintaining trust in God, Asa sought worldly means to solve his problems—including an alliance with King Ben-Hadad I of Damascus when the neighboring kingdom of Israel threatened Judah.

Scripture commemorates Asa as a good king, a leader who did many things well. But Asa didn't finish well, as 2 Chronicles 16:1–11 indicates. His life serves as a warning to all of us: careless choices can undo years (even decades) of faithful, God-honoring service. Pray today that God will enable you to finish strong.

CLASSICS: D. L. MOODY

MOSES: LINKED TO THE GOD OF HEAVEN

And when the Lord saw that he turned aside to see,
God called unto him out of the midst of the bush, and said,
Moses, Moses. And he said, Here am I. And he said,
Draw not nigh hither: put off thy shoes from off thy feet,
for the place whereon thou standest is holy ground.

Exodus 3:4–5 KJV

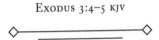

Look at Moses. He, too, was in communion with God. When Moses and Aaron stood before Pharaoh, the stubborn king did not see the third Person with them. If he had, he might have acted altogether differently. The idea of those two unarmed men going before the mighty monarch of Egypt and demanding that he should give three million slaves their liberty! The idea of these two men making such an extraordinary demand as that! But they were in communion with the God of heaven, and such men always succeed.

Moses was the mightiest man who lived in his day. Why? Because God walked with him, and he was linked to the God of heaven. Moses alone was nothing. He was a man like you and me; but he was the meekest of men, and "the meek shall inherit the earth" (Psalm 37:11 KJV; see also Matthew 5:5). He was famous because he walked with his God.

DAVID: A BIGGER FAITH

David said to Saul, "Let no one lose heart on account of this
Philistine; your servant will go and fight him." Saul replied, "You
are not able to go out against this Philistine and fight him; you are
only a young man, and he has been a warrior from his youth."

I SAMUEL 17:32–33 NIV

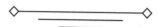

David was the baby of his family. He had been tending sheep until his father sent him to the battlefield with food for his brothers.

When David saw that Goliath the giant was taunting the army of God's people, he was furious. David insisted that he be allowed to battle the enemy himself.

What battle training did this young man have? He said he had killed a bear and a lion in defense of his sheep. He was handy with a slingshot. Are we supposed to believe that prepared him to face Goliath?

No. What prepared David for battle was his faith. In front of two armies, he declared there was a God in Israel and that He didn't need swords or spears to save. If David had had the slightest doubt, he would probably have died in that encounter. Instead he stepped forward in absolute trust and won the day.

Do any "giants" need to be brought down in your life? You don't need a bigger weapon or even to be a bigger man. . .you just need a bigger faith. Remember, Goliath the giant was tiny compared to God.

SIMON THE PHARISEE: UNDERSTANDING FORGIVENESS

One of the Pharisees asked Jesus to have dinner with him, so Jesus went to his home and sat down to eat.

LUKE 7:36 NLT

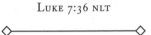

Pharisees like Simon found it difficult to like Jesus. He healed on the Sabbath, rubbed shoulders with the outcasts, and frankly, knew more than they did. Simon, however, was intrigued, and invited Jesus to his home to learn more about this unconventional teacher.

Immediately, the Pharisee found a reason to condemn Jesus. A prostitute entered the house, knelt before Jesus, and bathed His feet with her tears. Then she used her own hair as a washcloth, and anointed His feet with an expensive perfume. Simon wondered how Jesus didn't realize that this woman was a sinner.

But the Lord quickly helped Simon to understand that the woman's love was based on an understanding of the debt of sin she was being forgiven.

While it was customary for hosts to wash their guests' feet, it was also typical for guests to receive a kiss on the cheek and an anointing of olive oil. Simon had failed on both counts, but the sinful woman had done everything, at real personal cost.

We can always find reason to condemn the sin of others, but let's never forget that we are sinners too. Like the woman who anointed Jesus' feet, we have been forgiven much. May we in turn show much love to others.

PHILIP: TO THE ENDS OF THE EARTH

*"You will be my witnesses, telling people about me
everywhere—in Jerusalem, throughout Judea,
in Samaria, and to the ends of the earth."*

ACTS 1:8 NLT

After Philip's successes in Jerusalem and the well-populated province of Samaria, an angel of God sent him to the lonely Gaza road. Travelers in this isolated region, fearful of robbers, would be reluctant to stop and listen to him.

But when he saw a man in a chariot, Philip ran up to speak with the man. He was a eunuch serving as treasurer for the queen of Ethiopia. The government official was reading from the book of Isaiah, a passage that Philip knew referred to Jesus. When he asked the eunuch if he understood their meaning, he was invited into the chariot to explain. As they rode together, the Ethiopian was persuaded to become a Christian and asked to be baptized.

Ethiopia was on the fringe of the Roman Empire—the very edge of the known world. Before he met the Ethiopian, Philip must have wondered why the Holy Spirit had sent him to such a desolate place. Having ministered to Christians in Jerusalem, then preaching to crowds in Samaria, he now began to spread the Gospel message to "the ends of the earth."

Christian, be assured that where the Holy Spirit and the Word of God leads you is exactly where you should be.

CLASSICS: MATTHEW HENRY

MORDECAI: A GOOD SUBJECT

And when inquisition was made of the matter, it was found out; therefore they were both hanged on a tree: and it was written in the book of the chronicles before the king.

ESTHER 2:23 KJV

Mordecai got notice of their treason and, by Esther's means, discovered it to the king, hereby confirming her in the king's favor. How he came to the knowledge of it does not appear, but the thing was known to him. This ought to be a warning against all traitorous and seditious practices: though men presume upon secrecy, a bird of the air shall carry the voice.

Mordecai, as soon as he knew it, caused it to be made known to the king, which ought to be an instruction and example to all that would be found good subjects, not to conceal any bad design they know of against the prince or the public peace; for it is making a confederacy with public enemies. The traitors were hanged, but not till their treason was fully proved against them, and the whole matter was recorded in the king's journals, with a particular remark that Mordecai was the man who discovered the treason.

He was not rewarded presently, but a book of remembrance was written. Thus with respect to those who serve Christ, though their recompense is adjourned till the resurrection of the just, yet an account is kept of their work of faith and labor of love, which God is not unrighteous to forget (Hebrews 6:10).

ANDREW: LOOKING FOR SOMETHING MORE

*As Jesus walked beside the Sea of Galilee, he saw Simon and
his brother Andrew casting a net into the lake, for they were
fishermen. "Come, follow me," Jesus said, "and I will send you out
to fish for people." At once they left their nets and followed him.*

MARK 1:16–18 NIV

As you read of Jesus calling Andrew and his brother Simon (later
called Peter), notice how quickly and eagerly they dropped everything
to follow Him. Of course, the call was coming from God in the flesh,
so they were experiencing something truly unique.

But was there something else that prepared them to so readily
follow Jesus—something a little more "human"? Were they ready to
go because they longed for something more in their lives?

The Bible doesn't tell us much about the brothers' lives before they
followed Jesus. We know they were fisherman. They lived in a time
when Jewish people eagerly anticipated their Messiah's arrival. And
they had already met Jesus some time earlier along the Jordan River
(John 1:35–42). It's not hard to imagine Peter and Andrew talking
about Jesus, maybe even of the privilege of following Him. When the
call came, they responded immediately.

Has God put on your heart something greater, something of more
eternal significance, than what you're doing now? If you believe so, be
ready to drop everything and move out when He says, "Follow Me."

JAMES: TURNING THINGS AROUND

"It is my judgment, therefore, that we should not make it difficult for the Gentiles who are turning to God."

ACTS 15:19 NIV

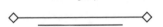

Try to imagine an older brother who never does anything wrong. He doesn't even run to tell Mom when you disobey—just helps you see the wisdom of getting back on the right path. He never complains about his chores. That's all tough enough to take. Hopefully, Mom never makes it worse by saying, "Why can't you be like Jesus?"

James, along with Joses, Simon, and Judas, were younger half brothers of Jesus. In spite of His perfect presence in their family, they decided Jesus wasn't the Messiah. At one point, the brothers even seemed to taunt Him, demanding that He show Himself in Jerusalem if He was really planning to save the world.

But after His crucifixion and resurrection, Jesus made a point of showing Himself to James, who became a true believer. When God had freed the apostle Peter from prison, he made a point of telling those who had prayed for his release to share the news with James.

As time went on, James became a respected leader of the church at Jerusalem—even a biblical author. It was quite a turnaround for a man who had missed the boat so badly earlier.

If you're ever disappointed or embarrassed by things in your own history, simply give them to Jesus. He specializes in turning things around.

Day 53

ISAIAH: QUICK TO VOLUNTEER

Also I heard the voice of the Lord, saying, Whom shall I send,
and who will go for us? Then said I, Here am I; send me.

ISAIAH 6:8 KJV

"Never volunteer for anything" is advice passed among military recruits. We can be thankful that Isaiah took a different attitude with God.

When the Lord gave Isaiah a soaring vision of heaven's throne room, the prophet-to-be immediately recognized his own unworthiness and sin: "Woe is me! for I am undone; because I am a man of unclean lips and I dwell in the midst of a people of unclean lips: for mine eyes have seen the King, the LORD of hosts" (Isaiah 6:5 KJV).

But God sent an angel to touch Isaiah's mouth with a live coal from heaven's altar, purging his sin and iniquity. So when the voice of the Lord was heard asking, "Whom shall I send, and who will go for us?" Isaiah was quick to volunteer.

The ministry may be just as demanding, in its own way, as military service, but you can be sure that God's rewards will be infinitely better. When He comes to you with an opportunity, resist the urge to hang back. Be like Isaiah, quick to volunteer and committed to faithfulness over the long haul. It won't be easy, but you'll have lasting impact on your world.

CLASSICS: ANDREW MURRAY

PAUL: READY TO DIE

And when he would not be persuaded, we ceased,
saying, The will of the Lord be done.

ACTS 21:14 KJV

Paul was at Caesarea, on his way to Jerusalem. Agabus, a prophet, had said by the Holy Spirit that Paul would there be bound and delivered into the hands of the Gentiles. Paul's friends besought him not to go up.

In his answer he spoke the noble words: "I am ready not to be bound only, but also to die at Jerusalem for the name of the Lord Jesus." When they heard this, they said: "The will of the Lord be done."

It was no longer a question of Jews or Gentiles, not even of the life or death of Paul; if it was to be, they would accept it as the will of God. The story teaches us the wisdom, the duty, the blessing of accepting disappointment or trial that cannot be averted as God's will, and so turning what naturally would cause sorrow or anger into an occasion of holy resignation and humble worship of God in His sovereign wisdom and power.

STEPHEN: NEXT MAN UP

*Stephen, a man full of God's grace and power, performed
amazing miracles and signs among the people.*

ACTS 6:8 NLT

Football coaches push the idea of the "next man up"—having a team full of backups ready to step in and perform if a starter goes down. Jesus had a football team's worth of starters, His original twelve disciples minus the traitor, Judas. After the crucifixion, resurrection, and ascension, Jesus sent His Holy Spirit at Pentecost to initiate the Christian Church, and there was need for more players on an expanding field. So Stephen and six others, "men who are well respected and are full of the Spirit and wisdom" (Acts 6:3 NLT), were chosen to carry forward the work that the apostles had begun.

Originally, these first deacons were to distribute food to widows in the church at Jerusalem. But Stephen went even further, performing miracles and debating the faith with Jews who saw Jesus as a threat to "the customs Moses handed down to us" (Acts 6:14 NLT).

Soon, Stephen's full-throated defense of the Christian faith got him killed—but not before he prayed publicly, "Lord, don't charge them with this sin!" (Acts 7:60 NLT).

A key player was down. . .who would be the next man up? In God's mysterious and wonderful ways, it would be a young man who had cheered on Stephen's death. Saul, later known as Paul, went from holding the coats of Stephen's killers, to persecuting other believers, to meeting Jesus on the road to Damascus, to giving his own life in Jesus' service.

Millions of men through history have been the "next man up" for God. Today, it may be you. Always be ready when the Lord calls.

MATTHEW: HUMILITY AND WITNESS

As Jesus went on from there, he saw a man named
Matthew sitting at the tax collector's booth. "Follow me,"
he told him, and Matthew got up and followed him.

MATTHEW 9:9 NIV

Today, Matthew is known and loved as one of the four Gospel writers who chronicled the life of Jesus. But before he met the Lord, Matthew wouldn't have felt much love. He was a Jew who collaborated with the occupying Romans. Worse, he even collected taxes for them. And tax collectors were known to become rich by overcharging their fellow citizens.

Then one day Jesus walked by. Seeing Matthew sitting at his tax collector's booth, the Lord issued a simple command: "Follow me." Matthew did, instantly, leaving his life of luxury for an unknown adventure.

Matthew quickly invited Jesus and His disciples back to his own house, where they dined with other tax collectors and "sinners." The supposedly respectable people—the Jewish religious leaders—scoffed at Jesus' willingness to eat with such a crowd. But He answered them by saying, "I have not come to call the righteous, but sinners" (Matthew 9:13 NIV).

By "righteous," Jesus meant "self-righteous"—those who proudly thought they were just fine with God. Matthew and his friends realized they needed the forgiveness that Jesus offered. We do too. So does everyone around us. May we follow Matthew's example of both humility and witness.

NATHANAEL: QUESTIONS TURNED TO FAITH

*Then Nathanael exclaimed, "Rabbi, you are
the Son of God—the King of Israel!"*

JOHN 1:49 NLT

How would you react if someone told you what you were doing and even thinking before they met you? When he first encountered Jesus, Nathanael went from asking, "Can anything good come from Nazareth?" to "You are the Son of God!" (John 1:46, 49 NLT). The sudden reversal occurred after Jesus told Nathanael he was "a genuine son of Israel—a man of complete integrity" (verse 47 NLT). Jesus then alluded to the story of Jacob's ladder in the book of Genesis.

While Nathanael had integrity, Jacob—later renamed Israel—didn't. He had taken his brother's birthright and his father's blessing by underhanded means. But he had also been blessed with a vision of angels on a ladder (or stairway), descending and ascending between heaven and earth. Might Jesus' reference to the story indicate it had recently been on Nathanael's mind?

That's simply speculation, but Nathanael certainly had a scriptural bent—because he quickly recognized Jesus as the One of whom Moses and the prophets wrote. He became a steadfast disciple, following Jesus to His crucifixion, resurrection, and beyond.

Nathanael doesn't occupy a large section of the Bible—he's mentioned only a half dozen times—but he sets an important example for men with questions. Our wondering doubts can be turned to faith by an honest, humble encounter with Jesus Himself.

SAUL: GOD EMPOWERS

Saul replied, "But I'm only from the tribe of Benjamin, the smallest tribe in Israel, and my family is the least important of all the families of that tribe! Why are you talking like this to me?"

1 SAMUEL 9:21 NLT

Saul's father, Kish, was a wealthy, influential man. And Saul was known for being the most handsome male in Israel (1 Samuel 9:1–2). But when he considered his tribe's heritage—they were the smallest tribe in Israel after being decimated in a civil war (Judges 20)—he couldn't understand why Samuel said Saul and his family were the focus of all Israel's hopes (1 Samuel 9:20).

We aren't told why Saul considered his family to be the least important in his small tribe. Maybe he was naturally humble. Maybe he was overwhelmed to think that his nation's hopes would fall on his shoulders. At this point, Saul didn't seem to understand that God was behind him—and that after Samuel anointed him as king, God would give Saul a new heart (1 Samuel 10:9).

The time may come when *you* are approached with an opportunity to serve. Will you respond like Saul, with a laundry list of reasons why you aren't able? Or will you consider the possibility that God is leading you into a new ministry? If the latter, be sure of this: God will empower you to perform the job.

SIMEON: GOD FULFILLS HIS PROMISES

Moved by the Spirit, he went into the temple courts. When the parents brought in the child Jesus to do for him what the custom of the Law required, Simeon took him in his arms and praised God.

LUKE 2:27–28 NIV

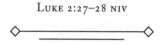

Mary and Joseph took their miracle Baby to the temple for purification. While they made their way through the crowds, the Holy Spirit urged an old man to enter the temple courts. Like other citizens in Jerusalem, Simeon had been waiting for the Messiah's arrival. Unlike anyone else, he had been promised that he wouldn't die until the Messiah arrived.

When Simeon found young Jesus, he held Him in his arms and prayed, "Sovereign Lord, as you have promised, you may now dismiss your servant in peace. For my eyes have seen your salvation" (Luke 2:29–30 NIV).

The Bible doesn't tell us when Simeon passed away. But he lived and died with the promise that he would see the Messiah. He goes down in history as one of the first people to recognize Jesus as the Savior of the world.

We don't know why God chose to make Simeon the recipient of such a blessed promise. But God has made blessed promises to every one of His children. As a son of God yourself, be sure to study His Word to know what those promises are. Then claim them in faith. He will fulfill every word He speaks.

ENOCH: COMMUNING WITH GOD

And Enoch lived sixty and five years, and begat Methuselah:
and Enoch walked with God after he begat Methuselah three
hundred years, and begat sons and daughters: and all the days
of Enoch were three hundred sixty and five years: and Enoch
walked with God: and he was not; for God took him.

Genesis 5:21–24 KJV

◇══════════◇

Enoch was one of the small number of men against whom nothing is recorded in the Bible. He lived in the midst of the world as Cain and his descendants had made it. In the midst of such a state of things, Enoch "walked with God"; and in the very same world we are also called to walk with God.

The record of his life is that he "had this testimony, that he pleased God" (Hebrews 11:5 KJV). Notice that this man accomplished nothing that men would call great, but what made him great was that he walked with God.

The faith of Enoch drew God down from heaven to walk with him. He maintained unbroken fellowship with God. A man in communion with God is one of heaven's greatest warriors. He can battle with and overcome the world, the flesh, and the devil.

PAUL: GLORY IN SUFFERING

Not only so, but we also glory in our sufferings, because we know that suffering produces perseverance; perseverance, character; and character, hope. And hope does not put us to shame, because God's love has been poured out into our hearts through the Holy Spirit, who has been given to us.

Romans 5:3–5 niv

It might be hard to imagine joy in suffering. But this is what the apostle Paul discovered.

He knew all about difficulties and opposition. In becoming a follower of Jesus, Paul betrayed the Jewish sect he'd been born into. And as he became an outspoken Christian leader, Paul put himself directly in the path of the persecution he had previously dealt out.

But following Jesus' footsteps, no matter the opposition, became Paul's mission. He knew that trouble would come, but also that he was serving the living God. Paul viewed persecution as an opportunity for growth, a chance to experience the love of Christ.

As with so many aspects of the Christian life, this mindset runs counter to our human expectations. Glory in suffering? Yes, it is possible. And, even more than possible, it is a promise to faithful believers. As Paul wrote, "we also glory in our sufferings, because we know that suffering produces perseverance; perseverance, character; and character, hope. And hope does not put us to shame, because God's love has been poured out into our hearts through the Holy Spirit, who has been given to us."

Hard times are certain. But so is God's ability to use them for your good.

JOSEPH: FLEE TEMPTATION

She caught him by his cloak and said, "Come to bed with me!"
But he left his cloak in her hand and ran out of the house.

GENESIS 39:12 NIV

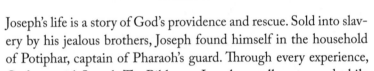

Joseph's life is a story of God's providence and rescue. Sold into slavery by his jealous brothers, Joseph found himself in the household of Potiphar, captain of Pharaoh's guard. Through every experience, God was with Joseph. The Bible says Joseph actually prospered while he was a slave. God blessed Joseph, as well as Potiphar's household because of Joseph.

However, there was danger in Potiphar's house—the man's wife. Genesis 39:6–7 describes Joseph as well-built and handsome, drawing the attention of Potiphar's wife. Day after day, she tried to seduce Joseph, but he resisted. One time, she caught him by his cloak and tried to draw him into her bed—but Joseph wiggled out of his coat and ran.

First Corinthians 6:18 (NIV) explicitly tells us to "flee from sexual immorality." Other verses instruct us to do the same with other temptations: 1 Corinthians 10:14 tells us to flee from idolatry, and 1 Timothy 6:11 says to flee from ungodliness. Clearly, one of the best ways to resist temptation is to avoid it entirely. When temptation comes to you, do like Joseph did—flee!

CLASSICS: MATTHEW HENRY

THE LEVITES: HELPING OTHERS SERVE

*And afterward they made ready for themselves, and for the priests:
because the priests the sons of Aaron were busied in offering of
burnt offerings and the fat until night; therefore the Levites
prepared for themselves, and for the priests the sons of Aaron.*

2 CHRONICLES 35:14 KJV

The priests and Levites took care to honor God by eating of the Passover themselves. Let not ministers think that the care they take for the souls of others will excuse their neglect of their own, or that being employed so much in public worship will supersede the religious exercises of their closets and families.

The Levites here made ready for themselves and for the priests, because the priests were wholly taken up all day in the service of the altar; therefore, that they might not have their lamb to dress when they should eat it, the Levites got it ready for them against supper time.

Let ministers learn hence to help one another and to forward one another's work, as brethren, and fellow servants of the same Master.

THE PARALYTIC'S FRIENDS: FIND YOUR TEAM

And they came, bringing to him a paralytic carried by four men.
And when they could not get near him because of the crowd,
they removed the roof above him, and when they had made an
opening, they let down the bed on which the paralytic lay.

MARK 2:3–4 ESV

News of Jesus' ability to heal the sick had spread widely. When He returned to Peter's house after a trip through Galilee, where He had recently healed a leper, many people gathered outside, hoping for their own encounter with Jesus.

By the time these four men and their paralyzed friend arrived, they couldn't get near the door. So the healthy ones got creative: they removed a portion of the roof and lowered their friend down to Jesus' presence. And He responded in a remarkable way: "When Jesus saw their faith, he said to the paralytic, 'Son, your sins are forgiven'" (Mark 2:5 ESV). By referencing "their faith," Jesus saw the four men and their friend as a collective unit, a spiritual superteam who exercised faith in His ability to forgive and ultimately heal.

There is a supernatural power that this world cannot understand wherever two or three gather in Jesus' name. He comes in strength to His own. Do you have a group of spiritual brothers who share your faith? Are you willing to "tear off the roof" for each another?

NEHEMIAH: DEALING WITH MOCKERY

"Hear us, our God, for we are being mocked. May their scoffing fall back on their own heads, and may they themselves become captives in a foreign land! Do not ignore their guilt. Do not blot out their sins, for they have provoked you to anger here in front of the builders."

NEHEMIAH 4:4–5 NLT

Sanballat, an enemy of the Jews, was upset when he learned that they were rebuilding Jerusalem's walls. He mocked them openly, saying: "What does this bunch of poor, feeble Jews think they're doing? Do they think they can build the wall in a single day by just offering a few sacrifices? Do they actually think they can make something of stones from a rubbish heap—and charred ones at that?" (Nehemiah 4:2 NLT).

Nehemiah didn't hurl insults back at Sanballat. He prayed, and then went back to work. Shortly afterward, the wall was finished to half its height, all the way around the city.

As Christians, we'll all face some form of opposition. But we don't have to respond in kind. Like Nehemiah, we can express our frustrations to God Himself, and leave the "vengeance" to Him (Romans 12:19). Then get back to work.

We should expect the world to mock us. When they do, it really means they see us living differently than everybody else. "Live such good lives among the pagans," the apostle Peter wrote, "that, though they accuse you of doing wrong, they may see your good deeds and glorify God on the day he visits us" (1 Peter 2:12 NIV).

CLASSICS: CHARLES SPURGEON

DAVID: LISTEN TO GOD, NOT PEOPLE

*Thy servant slew both the lion and the bear: and this uncircumcised
Philistine shall be as one of them, seeing he hath defied the
armies of the living God. David said moreover, The LORD that
delivered me out of the paw of the lion, and out of the paw of
the bear, he will deliver me out of the hand of this Philistine.
And Saul said unto David, Go, and the LORD be with thee.*

1 SAMUEL 17:36–37 KJV

We have all thought a great deal of the courage of David in meeting
giant Goliath, but probably we have not given him credit for his
conduct in a previous contest. We have not sufficiently noticed that
immediately before the encounter with the Philistine he fought a
battle which cost him far more thought, prudence and patience.

The word-battle in which he had to engage with his brothers and
with king Saul was a more trying ordeal to him than going forth in the
strength of the Lord to smite the uncircumcised boaster. Many a man
meets with more trouble from his friends than from his enemies; and
when he has learned to overcome the depressing influence of prudent
friends, he makes short work of the opposition of avowed adversaries.

THE LAME BEGGAR: PRAISING GOD

*And a certain man lame from his mother's womb was carried,
whom they laid daily at the gate of the temple which is called
Beautiful, to ask alms of them that entered into the temple.*

ACTS 3:2 KJV

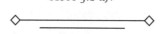

Imagine this life: You aren't known by your name, but rather, for your lifelong physical disability. There are no hospitals, long-term care facilities, or disability benefits, so your life consists of begging for money near the temple gate. But you can't even get there by yourself—as a man over forty (Acts 4:22), you rely on your friends to pick you up every morning and carry you to your spot.

You live in a perpetual survival mode, never even daring to hope for better things. Then one day, Peter and John walk by, headed for the temple at the hour of prayer. They hear your cry for money, but Peter offers something else: healing in the name of Jesus. And that healing is instantaneous. How could you do anything but enter the temple with them, "walking, and leaping, and praising God" (Acts 3:8 KJV)?

Even if we're physically strong, we're all spiritually disabled. We're not all that different from this first-century beggar. Apart from Jesus Christ, we survive on the crumbs of this world, with no hope of better things. But when He offers us healing, we are suddenly new, free, and filled with hope. May we too be ready to walk and leap and praise the Lord.

BEZALEL: EQUIPPED BY GOD

"See, the LORD has chosen Bezalel son of Uri, the son of Hur, of the tribe of Judah, and he has filled him with the Spirit of God, with wisdom, with understanding, with knowledge and with all kinds of skills."

EXODUS 35:30–31 NIV

When we think of God's calling, it's easy to lean toward vocations such as preaching, teaching, or evangelism. But an Old Testament character named Bezalel exemplifies two important biblical truths: (1) God uses all sorts of human skill to further His kingdom, and (2) He is the source of all the talents we need to do His work.

Bezalel was an artisan, chosen by God to lead the development of the tabernacle, its furniture, and its decorations. He worked very skillfully, creating beautiful items with metal, wood, and stone.

Skills like Bezalel's are often the result of years of training and experience, but we know that every aspect of our lives is empowered by God. And today's scripture shows that God, at times, specially anoints people to accomplish the work He calls them to do.

Perhaps your skill set or employment doesn't feel like a divine calling. But know that God has equipped you to do whatever work He has for you. Do your work faithfully, humbly, and joyfully—and see how He'll use it for His glory.

LAZARUS: JESUS GIVES LIFE

*Now a man named Lazarus was sick. He was from Bethany,
the village of Mary and her sister Martha. . . . So the sisters
sent word to Jesus, "Lord, the one you love is sick."*

JOHN 11:1, 3 NIV

◇═══════════◇

As he lay on his sickbed, hoping Jesus would show up in time to heal him, Lazarus's sisters, Mary and Martha, were doing everything they could to help him—including sending word to Jesus about their brother's condition. But the Lord didn't appear for several days. By the time He did, Lazarus was in the tomb.

Four days dead, Lazarus was suddenly awakened. A familiar voice was calling, "Lazarus, come out!" (John 11:43). Resurrection power surged through his body. His eyes blinked open, only to discover that he was wrapped in grave clothes and lying in a tomb. But Lazarus obeyed His friend's command, making his way out of the cave to find a stunned crowd watching. Jesus told people to remove Lazarus's grave wrappings, and suddenly he was healthy and free again. He'd been dead, but now he was alive.

Jesus performs a similar miracle every time a person who is dead in sin repents, turning toward Him. He calls us forth from spiritual death and eternal separation to everlasting life in a heavenly mansion. As Colossians 2:13 says, "When you were dead in your sins and in the uncircumcision of your flesh, God made you alive with Christ" (NIV).

Praise the Lord!

CLASSICS: CHARLES SPURGEON

PERSECUTED CHRISTIANS: INSTRUMENTS OF GOD'S MERCY

*And the hand of the Lord was with them: and a great
number believed, and turned unto the Lord.*

ACTS 11:21 KJV

The brethren who had dwelt together in church fellowship at Jerusalem were scattered abroad by persecution which arose about Stephen. Their Master had told them that when they were persecuted in one city they were to flee to another. They obeyed His command, and in the course of escape from persecution they took very long journeys—very long journeys indeed for that age of the world when locomotion was exceedingly difficult: but wherever they found themselves they began at once to preach Jesus Christ, so that the scattering of the disciples was also a scattering of good seed in broader fields.

The malice of Satan was made the instrument of the mercy of God. Learn from this, dear brethren, every one of you, that wherever you are called to go you should persevere in making known the name and Gospel of Jesus. Look upon this as your calling and occupation.

SAMSON: SET APART, IN REALITY

When her son was born, she named him Samson.
And the LORD blessed him as he grew up.

JUDGES 13:24 NLT

Almost everything about Samson was unusual. To begin with, God chose an angel to personally announced Samson's birth to his previously infertile parents: "You will soon become pregnant and give birth to a son" (Judges 13:3 NLT). Samson would become the most famous Nazirite of the Old Testament, visibly different from his peers.

To be a Nazirite meant to be set apart. They had restrictions on what they could eat and drink. They followed laws that forbade them to cut their hair. In time, his incredible physical strength was just as apparent as his long locks. But just because Samson's body was "set apart" doesn't mean was fortified with internal virtue and character.

When it came time for Samson to marry, he saw a woman of the enemy Philistines who "looked good" to him (Judges 14:3). Reluctantly, his parents arranged the marriage—and before he ever met the infamous Delilah, this impulsive strongman experienced the sting of a woman's betrayal.

Christians are called to be set apart (or "holy"), but this must include more than just how we *look* to others. When our hearts are truly set apart to God, the internal change will produce far greater results than merely following outward rules.

NICODEMUS: PROGRESSION OF BELIEF

"Rabbi," he said, "we all know that God has sent you to teach us. Your miraculous signs are evidence that God is with you."

John 3:2 NLT

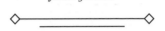

Nicodemus was a religious leader. A Pharisee and member of the ruling Jewish Sanhedrin, he appears three times in the Gospel of John. Each event shows his growing awareness that Jesus was the Son of God.

In his first appearance, Nicodemus came to Jesus at night—probably so no one would see or recognize him talking with the upstart Rabbi. Jesus told him that he needed to be born of water and the Spirit. Nicodemus's question of how to be "born again" elicited the most quoted verse of the New Testament: John 3:16.

When Nicodemus is next mentioned, he advised the Sanhedrin to avoid rash action against Jesus. "Is it legal to convict a man before he is given a hearing?" (John 7:51 NLT). Finally, after the crucifixion of Jesus, Nicodemus supplied myrrh and aloes to anoint the body of Jesus. Then he helped Joseph of Arimathea put the body in an unused, empty tomb (John 19:39, 41).

Every person needs the Savior. Some people become suddenly aware of that fact. Others, like Nicodemus, follow a progression—they begin with a questioning mind, a general acceptance, and finally a full belief of that most quoted verse: "For God so loved the world, that he gave his only begotten Son, that whosoever believeth in him should not perish, but have everlasting life" (John 3:16 KJV).

How did you come to your faith? How can you help someone else reach the same decision?

NEHEMIAH: PRAYER REQUIRED

*The king asked, "Well, how can I help you?" With a prayer
to the God of heaven, I replied, "If it please the king, and
if you are pleased with me, your servant, send me to Judah
to rebuild the city where my ancestors are buried."*

NEHEMIAH 2:4–5 NLT

While working in the court of Artaxerxes, king of Persia, Nehemiah learned that the walls of Jerusalem were still in disrepair. Artaxerxes released his Jewish cupbearer to put the city in order.

Nehemiah's success is often used as a pattern for effective leadership: it begins with a passion for the job. He inspected the walls thoroughly, formulated a plan, and inspired others to join and accomplish the work. Nehemiah developed a team of workers, guards, and watchmen, and gave each family a certain section of the wall to rebuild. When viewed only in this way, though, the story lacks spiritual context.

The book of Nehemiah is really about prayer and a trusting relationship with God. Nehemiah prayed about the problem while he was still in Persia, while performing the work in Jerusalem, and at the end of the successful effort. And he didn't stop there. The nation of Israel had been shattered by foes without and sins within. So he also helped rebuild the faith of his people. After finishing the walls, he joined Ezra in shoring up the spiritual strength of his people.

Nehemiah's successful leadership was built on prayer. And prayer is something any man can do.

CLASSICS: ANDREW MURRAY

ABRAHAM: AS THE LORD HAD SPOKEN

So Abram departed, as the Lord had spoken unto him.

GENESIS 12:4 KJV

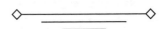

How well the Old Testament saints understood this connection between God's words and ours, and how really prayer with them was the loving response to what they had heard God speak! If the word were a promise, they counted on God to do as He had spoken. "Do as Thou hast said"; "For Thou, Lord, hast spoken it"; "According to Thy promise"; "According to Thy word": in such expressions they showed that what God spoke in promise was the root and the life of what they spoke in prayer. If the word was a command, they simply did as the Lord had spoken: "So Abram departed as the Lord had spoken."

Their life was fellowship with God, the interchange of word and thought. What God spoke they heard and did; what they spoke God heard and did. In each word He speaks to us, the whole Christ gives Himself to fulfill it for us. For each word He asks no less that we give the whole man to keep that word and to receive its fulfillment.

DANIEL: GOD EXALTS THE HUMBLE

*At Belshazzar's command, Daniel was clothed in purple,
a gold chain was placed around his neck, and he was
proclaimed the third highest ruler in the kingdom.*

DANIEL 5:29 NIV

During a lengthy absence of King Nabonidus, his eldest son, Belshazzar, served as coregent over the Babylonian empire. At his command, Daniel was made "the third highest ruler in the kingdom" the very night the capital fell, without a battle, to Darius the Mede.

Belshazzar was killed, and one could have reasonably expected the same fate for Daniel, who had originally worked for Babylon's King Nebuchadnezzar. Instead, "It pleased Darius to appoint 120 satraps to rule throughout the kingdom, with three administrators over them, one of whom was Daniel" (Daniel 6:1–2 NIV). This means that—for nearly seventy years—Daniel directly served the most powerful conquerors the world had ever known. What was his secret?

First, Daniel never compromised his faith in the one true Lord, the maker of heaven and earth, whose power dwarfs the entire universe. In comparison, who is man?

Second, Daniel never traded his humility for pride, despite every human temptation to do so. He and his three friends had it all, including good looks and sharp minds (Daniel 1:4). Nebuchadnezzar had judged them ten times better than anyone else who served him (Daniel 1:18–20).

Humble faith makes us strong. When we know we serve the almighty God—and know that we are not Him!—there's no limit to what He can do through us.

Think about it: people are *still* talking about Daniel.

CALEB: POSITIVE. . .IN GOD

Then Caleb silenced the people before Moses and said, "We should go up and take possession of the land, for we can certainly do it." But the men who had gone up with him said, "We can't attack those people; they are stronger than we are."

NUMBERS 13:30–31 NIV

Twelve men, the leaders of large family groups within the nation of Israel, were given the task of investigating the land that God had promised to Abraham. Compared to the sands of Egypt and the barren wilderness of the Arabian Peninsula, Canaan was a place of true beauty and productivity. They called it a land "flowing with milk and honey" (Numbers 13:27 NIV).

Sadly, ten of the twelve spies argued against entering the land. The people there were too strong, they said. "We seemed like grasshopper in our own eyes," they reported, "and we looked the same to them" (Numbers 13:33 NIV).

Caleb disagreed with his fellow spies. A man of great faith, he took God at His word. Caleb remembered God's protection in Egypt. He remembered God's deliverance from slavery. He remembered crossing the Red Sea on dry ground. And he knew that God had promised this land to His people.

"Positive thinking" doesn't automatically change things. But thinking positively of God's promises enhances our faith and hope in His ultimate blessing. Be positive in God, and you'll enjoy the emotional and spiritual strength of Caleb.

APOLLOS: HUMILITY BRINGS GROWTH

*Meanwhile a Jew named Apollos, a native of
Alexandria, came to Ephesus. He was a learned man,
with a thorough knowledge of the Scriptures.*

ACTS 18:24 NIV

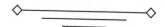

This might be generalizing a bit, but the best educated among us aren't always the humblest or most teachable. After all, they're the ones with the specialized training, presumably with the ability to impart that knowledge to others.

Apollos, a teacher who would become a friend of the apostle Paul, was a well-educated man who knew his Bible. He traveled from Alexandria, a major center of learning in Egypt, to Ephesus, where he began teaching with great passion in the synagogue.

But the Bible tells us that this man's knowledge of the Gospel message was incomplete. When he met a married couple named Priscilla and Aquila, they took Apollos into their home and became what we would call his mentors.

After humbly and eagerly soaking up Priscilla and Aquila's teaching, Apollos was soon ready to preach and defend the message of salvation through Jesus more completely and effectively (Acts 18:27–28).

Someone once said, "I don't know everything, but I know a lot more than nothing. And I am willing to learn what God wants me to learn." That is a humble attitude we should share with Apollos.

CLASSICS: CHARLES SPURGEON

JOHN THE BAPTIST: "I MUST DECREASE"

He must increase, but I must decrease.

JOHN 3:30 KJV

John sought no honor among men. It was his delight to say concerning our Lord Jesus, "He must increase, but I must decrease."

Yet, though John sought no honor of men, he had honor; for it is written, "Herod feared John." Herod was a great monarch; John was but a poor preacher whose garment and diet were of the coarsest kind; but "Herod feared John."

John was more royal than royal Herod. His character made him the true king, and the nominal king trembled before him. A man is not to be estimated according to his rank, but according to his character. The peerage which God recognizes is arranged according to a man's justice and holiness. He is first before God and holy angels who is first in obedience; and he reigns and is made a king and a priest whom God hath sanctified and clothed with the fair white linen of a holy life.

Be not covetous of worldly honors, for you will have honor enough even from wicked men if your lives are "holiness unto the Lord."

THE RICH YOUNG RULER: CHECKLISTS DON'T WORK

Jesus answered, "If you want to be perfect, go, sell your possessions and give to the poor, and you will have treasure in heaven. Then come, follow me."

MATTHEW 19:21 NIV

On the religious scale of goodness, the rich young ruler seemed to be off the charts. He must have had a "good guy" checklist, and he was committed to marking off each accomplishment. When he heard about Jesus, he may have believed this teacher might have a few more merit badges he could acquire, thinking they might bring perfection and right standing before God. Plus, others would be impressed.

When he heard Jesus' response, though, he left saddened. Maybe he thought following Jesus was just too high a price to pay. He had proven he could juggle a lot of outward religious deeds, but taking that next step was something he ultimately wouldn't do. He loved his riches—and the luxuries and comforts they afforded—too much.

By placing possessions over relationship the rich young ruler left heavyhearted. Did he realize that what he owned had become the objects of worship for him? Did he understand that all the outward signs he was quick to demonstrate came up short? Was the commitment to follow too much?

When confronted with truth, we all have a choice to make. When Jesus says, "Come, follow me," may we see the value in that relationship and wholeheartedly follow.

EZEKIEL: FAITHFUL IN THE IMPOSSIBLE

"The people to whom I am sending you are obstinate and stubborn. Say to them, 'This is what the Sovereign LORD says.' And whether they listen or fail to listen—for they are a rebellious people—they will know that a prophet has been among them."

EZEKIEL 2:4–5 NIV

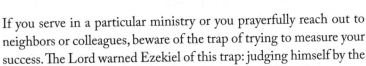

If you serve in a particular ministry or you prayerfully reach out to neighbors or colleagues, beware of the trap of trying to measure your success. The Lord warned Ezekiel of this trap: judging himself by the response of others. Ezekiel's calling was simply to share the message that God had entrusted to him. Whether or not the obstinate and stubborn people responded was well beyond Ezekiel's control.

The prophet's responsibility was to listen carefully and hear correctly what God had to say, then communicated it to the people. He played the role of a prophet. If people wouldn't listen, he might understandably question his own performance. But in this case he had already received God's surprising message that his mission was doomed to failure.

Few of us will face the demanding challenges of Ezekiel. But like him, we cannot control the thoughts, words, and actions of the people to whom we minister. Let us prayerfully consider how God is directing us to live and speak, then act accordingly. Sometimes our own faithfulness is the only measure of "success" that matters.

DAVID: A PRACTICAL FAITH

"The LORD who rescued me from the paw of the lion and the paw of the bear will rescue me from the hand of this Philistine."

1 SAMUEL 17:37 NIV

When we read of David's anointing, we can just imagine what his older brothers were thinking: *This scrawny kid, God's anointed?* Yet we have no indication that David inspired the hatred that an earlier upstart, Joseph, provoked in his older brothers (Genesis 37:5, 12–32).

David's father sent him to the front lines of Israel's battle with the Philistines to resupply his brothers. There, David heard about Goliath's arrogance in the face of God's people. His oldest brother, Eliab, was irritated when David questioned why Goliath was getting away with his insults. But David volunteered himself for battle, and King Saul ultimately gave him his blessing.

As the boy approached Goliath, God's Spirit encouraged David's own. Eager to prove God's power in the face of his enemies, David relied wholeheartedly on his Lord. He trusted God to engage his enemy—and to win.

This practical faith is a hallmark of the man of God. David approached Goliath with what he had, using his God-given talent with the sling to fell the giant. What's the sling in your hand, and the stones in your pouch? If you allow Him, God will use what He's given you to accomplish His purposes.

CLEOPAS: CONFUSED BUT STILL FAITHFUL

*And it came to pass, as he sat at meat with them, he took bread,
and blessed it, and brake, and gave to them. And their eyes were
opened, and they knew him; and he vanished out of their sight.*

LUKE 24:30–31 KJV

Following the crucifixion of Jesus, Cleopas and an unnamed friend
appear briefly in scripture. They were leaving Jerusalem, perhaps in an
attempt to avoid persecution. They had heard rumors of Jesus rising
from the dead, but weren't sure what to think.

Then a stranger joined them on the pathway, asking why they
seemed troubled. Cleopas answered with a recap of recent events,
which the resurrected Jesus Himself explained from the ancient
Hebrew scriptures. Jesus would not reveal His identity to Cleopas and
his friend until they sat down to dinner in the next village. But after
they realized who they were speaking with—and He "vanished out of
their sight"—the two men quickly returned to Jerusalem to share the
happy news with Jesus' other followers. The confusion Cleopas had
felt was replaced by confidence once he'd personally experienced Jesus.

Confusion isn't an unusual thing for Christians. Many of God's
ways are far beyond our own wisdom and understanding. But if we
respond like Cleopas—holding on to our faith in Christ no matter
what comes—we'll ultimately have our trust confirmed in the most
wonderful ways. That's the point of faith. And it's what pleased God
most (Hebrews 11:6).

CLASSICS: CHARLES SPURGEON

PAUL: THE CROSS WAS HIS THEME

And when they had appointed him a day, there came many to him into his lodging; to whom he expounded and testified the kingdom of God, persuading them concerning Jesus, both out of the law of Moses, and out of the prophets, from morning till evening.

ACTS 28:23 KJV

Wherever Paul is, he has but one errand; and whenever Paul preaches, he has but one subject.

Once at Athens, when he addressed the Areopagus, he seemed to wander a little from his main point, and no special good followed, but this experience bound him all the faster to the cross; for he afterwards said to the Corinthians, "I determined not to know anything among you, save Jesus Christ, and him crucified." The cross of Christ was his one theme. He henceforth hammered on the head of this one nail. Whatever faculty, ability and power he had, he turned its whole current into this one channel and cried, "God forbid that I should glory, save in the cross of our Lord Jesus Christ, by whom the world is crucified unto me, and I unto the world."

Brethren, we have not strength enough for a dozen things; we have not even strength enough for two. What little vigor we have, let us use it all in one direction; let us say, "For me to live is Christ."

NOAH: FINISH THE ASSIGNMENT

So God said to Noah, "I am going to put an end to all people, for the earth is filled with violence because of them. I am surely going to destroy both them and the earth. So make yourself an ark of cypress wood; make rooms in it and coat it with pitch inside and out."

GENESIS 6:13–14 NIV

◇──────◇

Put yourself in the place of Noah. Apparently, you and your family are the only God-honoring individuals currently alive. You have been given a task which will be quite public and will eventually occupy forty-three thousand days of your life. Nobody else will believe in you or your work. What do you do?

Noah, along with his three sons, rose to the challenge. They found strength in the fact that God Himself had given them this assignment. They understood that their ability to survive the coming flood was dependent on getting the job done.

Our tasks would seem to be trivial compared to what the Lord asked of Noah. But God would disagree with that assessment. The apostle Paul wrote to those who work, "Serve wholeheartedly, as if you were serving the Lord, not people, because you know that the Lord will reward each one for whatever good they do, whether they are slave or free" (Ephesians 6:7–8 NIV).

It may seem counterintuitive, but hard work begets strength. Do what God has said, in the power He gives, and you'll ultimately succeed. God will make sure you not only survive, but thrive.

JOSEPH: REFUSING TO SIN

When his master [Potiphar] heard the story his wife told him, saying, "This is how your slave treated me," he burned with anger. Joseph's master took him and put him in prison, the place where the king's prisoners were confined.

GENESIS 39:19–20 NIV

Potiphar's wife accused Joseph of trying to seduce her, when it was actually the other way around. "She caught him by his cloak and said, 'Come to bed with me!' But he left his cloak in her hand and ran out of the house" (Genesis 39:12 NIV). When scripture says that Potiphar "burned with anger," many assume he was angry at Joseph. But Genesis simply says Potiphar was mad. If he was furious at Joseph—just a foreign slave—he probably would have killed him.

But Potiphar didn't. It's very possible that he knew his wife was lying—and maybe not for the first time. This Egyptian official had already benefited greatly from Joseph's work, and recognized that God was behind his servant's effectiveness. But Potiphar couldn't side with a slave against his wife. So he treated Joseph about as well as he could, sending him to a prison for high-class offenders. Even at that, it was no picnic for the young Hebrew.

Joseph was almost invisible for two years, before God orchestrated his rise from the ashes to second in command of Egypt. And it all started when God saw Joseph doing one vitally important thing: refusing to sin.

That is our duty as well. When we choose to deny ourselves and honor God, who knows where He'll take us?

MOSES: PREPARED FOR THE TASK

But Moses protested to God, "Who am I to appear before Pharaoh? Who am I to lead the people of Israel out of Egypt?"

EXODUS 3:11 NLT

After being raised in Pharaoh's palace, Moses fled from Egypt. Why? Because he had killed an Egyptian who was beating a Hebrew slave.

Escaping to Midian, Moses stopped by a well. There, he saw seven sisters who had come to water their flock. When other shepherds drove them away, Moses came to their rescue. Later, he married one of the girls and became a shepherd himself.

The skills Moses had gained in Pharaoh's household were probably not those he needed to be a shepherd. Now he busied himself with leading, protecting, feeding, watering, shearing, and delivering sheep, as well as finding those that had wandered away. Moving his charges from one grazing area to another required him to set a pace that the weakest, slowest member of the flock could manage.

Moses was tending sheep when he saw the burning bush and received his commission to tell Pharaoh to let the Hebrew slaves go. His experience in the forty years of tending sheep may not have prepared him to confront Pharaoh, but it certainly prepared him for leading the people in the wilderness for the next forty years.

As Christians, our lives may move straight forward to the goal God has set for us. But more often there are fits and starts, twists and turns—and only in hindsight do we realize that, like Moses, God has been preparing us to accomplish a specific task.

CLASSICS: CHARLES SPURGEON

JACOB: PREVAILING IN PRAYER

*I am not worthy of the least of all the mercies, and of all the truth,
which thou hast shewed unto thy servant; for with my staff I
passed over this Jordan; and now I am become two bands.*

GENESIS 32:10 KJV

Say what you will of Jacob, he was a master of the art of prayer, and
he that can pray well is a princely man. He that can prevail with God
will certainly prevail with men.

It seems to me that when once a man is taught of the Lord to
pray, he is equal to every emergency that can possibly arise. Depend
upon it, it will go hard with any man who fights against a man of
prayer. All other weapons may be dashed aside; but the weapon of
All-prayer, invisible though it may be and despised of the worldling,
hath in it a might and majesty which will secure the victory.

The sword of prayer hath such an edge that it will cut through coats
of mail. Jacob was a prevailing prince when he came upon his knees.

TITUS: BE WORTHY OF RESPECT

Teach the older men to exercise self-control, to be
worthy of respect, and to live wisely. They must have
sound faith and be filled with love and patience.

TITUS 2:2 NLT

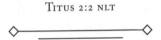

Although Paul told Titus to teach the truth of today's scripture to "older men," the apostle also urges young men to "live wisely" in verse 6. So nobody gets a free pass as it relates to that key phrase, "be worthy of respect."

It's interesting that Paul didn't command Titus and Christian men to "be respected." That is the decision of other people; "to be worthy of respect" is a pursuit that each of us can choose for ourselves. In other words, whether or not you receive the esteem of others, live in a manner that's worthy of it.

How do we do that? The key phrase is flanked by two critical commands that will lead to worthiness of respect: if you "exercise self-control" and "live wisely," you'll achieve the goal—to be worthy of respect.

If our focus is on ourselves—to earn the attention we think we deserve or gain a following—we risk becoming our own idols. But when we choose to make the Lord famous above ourselves, we become worthy of respect. And that leaves plenty of room for God to do His work in and around us.

CAIN: ACCEPTING GOD'S WILL

Then the LORD said to Cain, "Why are you angry? Why is your face downcast? If you do what is right, will you not be accepted? But if you do not do what is right, sin is crouching at your door; it desires to have you, but you must rule over it."

GENESIS 4:6–7 NIV

Very early in the Bible, we encounter the disappointing story of Cain and Abel. The two oldest sons of Adam and Eve are presenting offerings to the Lord, but Cain, the firstborn, brings a sacrifice that does not follow God's standard. When Abel presents an acceptable offering, Cain responds in sinful anger.

Cain wanted God's acceptance even though his offering did not warrant it. The obvious solution is that Cain should have used his God-given abilities to obtain and make an appropriate offering. His decision to murder his younger brother, who gave the acceptable offering, is one of the greatest failures in human history.

Jealousy is just one of many challenges that we as men face. It easily leads to anger which easily leads to sin. How much better is it to simply do the right thing in the first place, to approach all of life with simple obedience to the Word of God. As the prophet Samuel said to the erring King Saul, "Does the LORD delight in burnt offerings and sacrifices as much as in obeying the LORD? To obey is better than sacrifice" (1 Samuel 15:22 NIV).

When God's direction is clear, let us be obedient.

SERGIUS PAULUS: HEARING GOD'S MESSAGE

When the governor saw what had happened, he became a
believer, for he was astonished at the teaching about the Lord.

ACTS 13:12 NLT

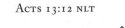

On his first missionary journey, the apostle Paul arrived on the island
of Cyprus where he met a sorcerer and false prophet known by two
names, Bar-Jesus and Elymas. If it sounds like Paul discovered a
spiritual circus on Cyprus, it did bear a remarkable resemblance.

Under the proverbial big top was the governor, Sergius Paulus,
who is described as an intelligent man. In spite of the sorcerer's
protests, the governor was interested in hearing Paul speak. Elymas
did all he could to corrupt the content of the message for Sergius Paulus. But Paul delivered a message for the false prophet—
blindness, for "perverting the true ways of the Lord" (Acts 13:10
NLT). God used this miracle to bring the governor to faith in Jesus.

We live in a world full of false prophets, the Elymas types who
do everything in their power to interfere with God's message. But
the word of God is "alive and powerful" (Hebrews 4:12 NLT), and
capable of getting through the noisiest environments to the neediest
recipients. If you know a Sergius Paulus, pray for him to hear God's
voice. And pray for yourself, that you will be an apostle like Paul. God
Himself will take care of everything else.

CLASSICS: CHARLES SPURGEON

ABRAHAM: FAITH IN EVERYTHING

*And he believed in the LORD; and he counted
it to him for righteousness.*

GENESIS 15:6 KJV

◇─────────────◇

Faith, restricted merely to religious exercise is not Christian faith; it must show itself in everything. A merely religious faith may be the choice of men whose heads are softer than their hearts, fitter for cloisters than markets; but the manly faith which God would have us cultivate is a grand practical principle adapted for every day in the week, helping us to rule our household in the fear of God and to enter upon life's rough conflicts in the warehouse, the farm or the exchange.

This is the faith which came of Abram's calling, so also does it shine in his justification and is, indeed, that which God counted unto him for righteousness.

DEVOUT MEN: RISKING ALL FOR CHRIST

*And devout men carried Stephen to his burial,
and made great lamentation over him.*

ACTS 8:2 NKJV

After Pentecost, as the Word of God spread in Jerusalem, the number of disciples began to increase, and even a "great many of the priests were obedient to the faith" (Acts 6:7 NKJV). But not all of the religious leaders were happy about that. When Stephen, one of the early Church's original seven deacons, was questioned by the high priest, he held nothing back—calling the leaders stiff-necked and uncircumcised in their hearts and ears, as well as resisters of the Holy Spirit (Acts 7:51).

Speaking the truth cost Stephen his life. The religious leaders stoned him to death, leading to a great persecution against the Jerusalem church, forcing many believers to be scattered throughout Judea and Samaria (Acts 8:1).

The next verse says "devout men carried Stephen to his burial." Commentators vary regarding the identity of these men. At least one believes these men may have been unconverted Jews who didn't like what had taken place. Others believe these were members of the Jerusalem church. Either way, nobody can doubt their courage after seeing what had happened to a man who crossed the authorities. But honoring a man destroyed by injustice meant more to them than any personal repercussions.

As our world becomes increasingly antagonistic to Jesus and His message, we may find ourselves in the shoes of these "devout men" of the first century. Why not pray now that God will strengthen you for perilous times to come?

JEREMIAH: PROMISED GOD'S PRESENCE

"This is what the LORD says, he who made the earth, the LORD who formed it and established it—the LORD is his name: 'Call to me and I will answer you and tell you great and unsearchable things you do not know.'"

JEREMIAH 33:2–3 NIV

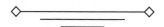

If you aren't in a season of uncertainty, you'll soon experience one. It may reveal itself gradually or come rushing in unexpectedly. When life begins to spin out of control or you find yourself at a fork in the road, it's natural to worry about the future.

At a time when the prophet Jeremiah confronted the uncertainty and terror of the invasion of a foreign army, the Lord assured him that when he called out in prayer, he could expect an answer. Of course, the Lord didn't guarantee that Jeremiah would *like* the answer he received. But Jeremiah was assured of God's deep, often mysterious wisdom. Really, that's far better than the clear-cut human answers we set up for ourselves and then hope God will approve.

The answers to our true, honest prayers may defy our comprehension. They could take years—even a lifetime—to fully unfold. And even when we think we understand God's ways, we'll find that there were layers of complexity underneath our prayers that had escaped our attention.

No matter what, this passage in Jeremiah teaches that God is present even in the most uncertain of times.

CLASSICS: D. L. MOODY

ELIJAH: WALKING WITH GOD

And it came to pass, when Ahab saw Elijah, that Ahab said unto him, Art thou he that troubleth Israel? And he answered, I have not troubled Israel; but thou, and thy father's house, in that ye have forsaken the commandments of the LORD, and thou hast followed Baalim. Now therefore send, and gather to me all Israel unto mount Carmel, and the prophets of Baal four hundred and fifty, and the prophets of the groves four hundred, which eat at Jezebel's table.

1 KINGS 18:17–19 KJV

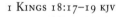

When Elijah stood on Mount Carmel, Ahab did not see who was with him. Little did he know the prophet's God; little did he think that, when Elijah walked up Mount Carmel, God walked with him.

Talk of an Alexander making the world tremble at the tread of his armies! Of the marches and victories of a Caesar, or a Napoleon! The man who is walking with God is greater than all the Caesars and Napoleons and Alexanders who ever lived.

Little did Ahab and the false prophets of Baal know that Elijah was walking with the same God with whom Enoch walked before the flood. Elijah was nothing when out of communion with God; but when walking in the power of God, he stood on Mount Carmel like a king.

PAUL: UNASHAMED

For I am not ashamed of the gospel, because it is the power of God that brings salvation to everyone who believes: first to the Jew, then to the Gentile.

ROMANS 1:16 NIV

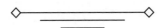

If you have a favorite pizza place, you tell your friends. You don't hesitate to tell someone about a great experience you had at a vacation resort, a concert venue, or a sporting event. So why do many Christians keep quiet about Jesus? You know the Savior of the universe. You know the greatest man who ever lived. Don't be shy about sharing the Good News. Don't feel embarrassed to embrace your Christian faith and share it with others.

The apostle Paul was not ashamed to preach the Gospel. He withstood strong opposition and even went to prison for his beliefs—but he boldly and consistently found ways to preach the Word of the Lord.

If the people closest to you don't know you are a Christian, you aren't doing your job. You have the best news anyone should ever want to hear. Jesus changes lives and saves souls. So tell them. Give them an opportunity to hear how the Lord has worked wonders in your life. They may be ready to hear it and accept Him, if only you speak up.

KING CYRUS: AN EXAMPLE OF OBEDIENCE

Thus saith Cyrus king of Persia, The LORD God of heaven hath given me all the kingdoms of the earth; and he hath charged me to build him an house at Jerusalem, which is in Judah.

EZRA 1:2 KJV

Did King Cyrus know God? Not really, but he had at least a passing acquaintance. However, God knew King Cyrus. . .and used him in a powerful way.

The Lord's chosen people had severely tried His patience—so He sent the Babylonians to remind them how much they needed Him. Jews were taken from their homes, their temple was destroyed, and their nation only existed in memory and in exile.

But though God had used the Babylonians for His purpose, He wasn't happy with them either. So He allowed Cyrus the Great of Persia to sweep down from the northeast and conquer the Babylonian empire. Cyrus quickly declared a general amnesty, telling captive peoples—including the Jews—that they could go home again. He even provided money for rebuilding Jerusalem and let the Jews take back sacred objects that had been looted from the temple.

Why would he do that? Surely a king could use all the slaves he could get. But God informed Cyrus of a different plan, and Cyrus obeyed.

As Christians, we do know God, through His Son, Jesus Christ. We entertain His Holy Spirit in our deepest being. We have every reason to obey everything God tells us. If King Cyrus could be obedient, surely we can!

CLASSICS: MATTHEW HENRY

JOTHAM: IMPERFECT BUT PIOUS

In the second year of Pekah the son of Remaliah king of Israel began Jotham the son of Uzziah king of Judah to reign. . . . And he did that which was right in the sight of the LORD: he did according to all that his father Uzziah had done. Howbeit the high places were not removed: the people sacrificed and burned incense still in the high places. He built the higher gate of the house of the LORD.

2 KINGS 15:32, 34–35 KJV

We have here a short account of the reign of Jotham king of Judah, of whom we are told that he reigned very well, did that which was right in the sight of the LORD. Josephus gives him a very high character, stating that he was pious toward God, just toward men, and laid out himself for the public good—that, whatever was amiss, he took care to have it rectified—and, in short, wanted no virtue that became a good prince.

Though the high places were not taken away, yet to draw people from them and keep them close to God's holy place, he showed great respect to the temple and built the higher gate which he went through to the temple. If magistrates cannot do all they would for the suppressing of vice and profaneness, let them do so much the more for the support and advancement of piety and virtue and the bringing of them into reputation. If they cannot pull down the high places of sin, yet let them build and beautify the high gate of God's house.

JESUS: BLESSING, NOT CURSING

"Love your enemies, bless those who curse you,
do good to those who hate you, and pray for
those who spitefully use you and persecute you."

MATTHEW 5:44 NKJV

Matthew 5:44 is more than a love potion for our enemies—it's a remarkable summary of the application of love in all relationships: to bless, pray, and do good. We bless with our lips. We pray from our hearts. We do good with our hands. Let's consider that "bless" commandment.

In the context, Jesus is addressing someone who has "cursed" you, intentionally said bad and hurtful things about you. They're mad at you or don't like you, maybe even hate you—so they express ill will toward you vocally. They're not physically harming you, but they're speaking evil, maybe behind your back, maybe to your face. When cursed like this, Jesus says, "Bless!" When others say bad things about us, we say good things to and about them in return. Of course, many of us would rather blast than bless. Some of us even pride ourselves on how quickly we can come back with a sarcastic one-liner. But scripture says, "Don't repay evil for evil. Don't retaliate with insults when people insult you. Instead, pay them back with a blessing. That is what God has called you to do, and he will grant you his blessing" (1 Peter 3:9 NLT).

Jesus, our perfect example, flipped the script on our verbal exchanges. Honor Him with obedience, and you might just shock your antagonist into better behavior!

ABRAHAM'S SERVANT: SELFLESS PRAYER

Then he prayed, "LORD, God of my master Abraham, make me successful today, and show kindness to my master Abraham."

GENESIS 24:12 NIV

Are you comfortable asking God for success? Or does the thought of praying for your own accomplishment make you feel a little too self-serving?

Well, there is nothing wrong with praying for success. In fact, the Bible encourages us to pray that we be successful in all we do. The key is in what motivates our prayers.

There are two major schools of thought today, the first being rooted in the idea that God wants His people to be successful in everything, especially their finances. The second school, which is more rooted in the written Word of God, holds that when we pray for success, it should be with an eye firmly focused on the purposes of God, His kingdom, and other people.

The latter is how Abraham's servant prayed.

The beginning of this man's prayer demonstrates the kind of selflessness—the kind of others-centeredness—God wants to see in all those who serve Him. Yes, he prayed for success, but the kind of success that would benefit someone else. That makes this one of the Bible's model prayers.

So go ahead and selflessly pray with Abraham's servant, "Lord God, make me successful today, and show kindness to family, friends, and even my enemies."

CLASSICS: CHARLES SPURGEON

NOAH: CHEERFUL VOLUNTEER

*And the Lord said unto Noah, Come thou and all
thy house into the ark; for thee have I seen righteous
before me in this generation. . . . And Noah went in,
and his sons, and his wife, and his sons' wives with him,
into the ark, because of the waters of the flood.*

<small>Genesis 7:1, 7 kjv</small>

God in infinite grace had entered into covenant with Noah that He would preserve him and his family alive. The tenor of that covenant you will find in the eighteenth verse of the sixth chapter. "With thee will I establish my covenant; and thou shalt come into the ark, thou, and thy sons, and thy wife, and thy sons' wives with thee."

There was a positive foretelling of Noah's coming into the ark and finding safety. The thing was fixed, and ordained so to be, and yet, when the time came, Noah was not carried into the ark by force, nor lifted into it against his will by a benevolent violence. He was bidden to come into the ark in the most natural manner possible; and he entered it voluntarily and cheerfully.

He and his family left their houses to find a home in the ark, and so they were saved. The covenant promise and purpose were fulfilled.

DAVID: GOD IS FAITHFUL

*David said to the Philistine, "You come against me with sword
and spear and javelin, but I come against you in the name of the
LORD Almighty, the God of the armies of Israel, whom you have
defied. This day the LORD will deliver you into my hands."*

1 SAMUEL 17:45–46 NIV

You've probably heard and read—countless times—the story of David
slaying Goliath, the ten-foot-tall giant. You know that David accomplished that feat with a sling and five smooth stones. In fact, he killed
the enemy with his first shot. But have you ever considered where
David's confidence came from?

He didn't even wear armor in the battle. But that wasn't a
chest-beating display of his own manliness. David just wanted to
stand up for Israel and its soldiers (1 Samuel 17:26). He had confidence in the Lord, based on his previous experience.

As a shepherd, David had told King Saul, he had gone after
lions and bears that attacked his flock, striking them and rescuing
sheep from their mouths. At times, he even killed the predators. "This
uncircumcised Philistine will be like one of them," David declared,
"because he has defied the armies of the living God. The LORD who
rescued me from the paw of the lion and the paw of the bear will
rescue me from the hand of this Philistine" (verses 36–37 NIV).

When you are about to face your own Goliath, what story of
God's faithfulness can you tell yourself? Take some time today to
recall victories that He has given you—and you'll be armed with His
confidence for the future.

AN UNNAMED BOY: GIVING ALL, EVEN WHEN IT'S NOT MUCH

Another of his disciples, Andrew, Simon Peter's brother, spoke up, "Here is a boy with five small barley loaves and two small fish, but how far will they go among so many?"

JOHN 6:8–9 NIV

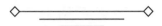

Do you ever wake up in the morning thinking, *Today God is going to use me to do something miraculous?*

It's hard to imagine the unnamed boy—mentioned in the story of Jesus feeding the five thousand—thinking anything beyond his own physical needs as he began his day. He was toting a small sack lunch of two small fish and what was not much more than five small biscuits.

As it was, he probably had barely enough food to nourish a growing boy for the day. But he gave Jesus what he had—and the Lord made it multiply. . .over and over and over, until it became more than enough to feed five thousand men and who-knows-how-many women and children besides.

What we have may seem insignificant in comparison with what others can give. But when we give God what little we have, in faith, He has a way of doing miracles with it. He can multiply our gifts far beyond our imagination.

Even if your gift is as insignificant as a kind word, a small favor, or a quick reminder that "God loves you, and so do I," God can make it something incredible. In fact, He specializes in using such gifts.

CLASSICS: CHARLES SPURGEON

JOB: PREACHING AT HOME

And his sons went and feasted in their houses, every one his day; and sent and called for their three sisters to eat and to drink with them. And it was so, when the days of their feasting were gone about, that Job sent and sanctified them, and rose up early in the morning, and offered burnt offerings according to the number of them all: for Job said, It may be that my sons have sinned, and cursed God in their hearts. Thus did Job continually.

Job 1:4–5 KJV

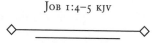

Job was a godly man, and so godly, that unlike Eli he brought up his household in the fear of God and was not only quick to observe any known sin, but was exceedingly jealous over his children, lest secretly and inadvertently in their hearts, while they were at their loaded tables, they might have said or thought anything which might be termed blaspheming God.

He therefore as soon as the feasting was over, called them all together and then, as a preacher, told them of the danger to which they were exposed, and as a priest (for every patriarch before the law was a priest) he offered burnt sacrifices, lest any sin should by any possibility remain upon his sons and daughters.

May God grant that our parents, or we, if we be parents, may be as Job, and when the feasting shall be over, may there come the sacrifice and the prayer, lest we should have sinned and blasphemed God in our hearts!

SOLOMON: DECIDE DAILY TO FOLLOW GOD

At Gibeon the LORD appeared to Solomon during the night in a dream, and God said, "Ask for whatever you want me to give you."

1 KINGS 3:5 NIV

King Solomon boldly asked God for wisdom. That gift meant Israel's king made decisions that brought unprecedented peace and prosperity to Israel. That wisdom was sought by dignitaries from throughout the world.

Solomon was used by God to pen Ecclesiastes, Song of Solomon, and most of Proverbs. He judged the people with a wisdom that astounded. It seemed that Solomon understood people, culture, and law, and because he'd requested wisdom, God also gave him health, prosperity, and honor. However, the wisdom Solomon used in leading the people of Israel was not always reflected in his personal life choices.

He married hundreds of women, and many of them came from nations God had warned the people of Israel against marrying. In the latter years of Solomon's life, "his wives turned his heart after other gods, and his heart was not fully devoted to the LORD his God" (1 Kings 11:4 NIV). Solomon's actions were evil, and God became angry with him. Solomon's writing in Ecclesiastes demonstrates a sense of depression and disillusionment.

A good start never guarantees a great ending. Solomon was one of many biblical characters who started well, but ended badly. Following God is a daily decision that resists complacency while trusting that there is purpose in each step forward.

DIONYSIUS: BREAK FROM THE PACK

Some of the people became followers of Paul and believed.
Among them was Dionysius, a member of the Areopagus,
also a woman named Damaris, and a number of others.

ACTS 17:34 NIV

It seems the people of Athens were very keen on hearing about and discussing the latest ideas. In that kind of setting, ideas very rarely get turned into realities because there is always a new notion waiting to take the place of the previous one. Talking tends to be all that gets done.

Paul was brought before the Areopagus (also known as Mars Hill) to explain this strange new faith he was so keen on spreading. The Areopagus was the equivalent of a high court or a religious senate. Those in attendance would have been very important men in Athenian society.

Most of them would have been curious, but too busy to take this wandering Christian seriously. He may have been an interesting distraction, but they had their own set ideas. Of course, Paul went nowhere under his own will. He wasn't there to entertain bored wealthy men. God knew there was at least one there who was tired of philosophies and wanted truth. That man was Dionysius.

In a crowd of intellectual, big-talking, self-satisfied men, Dionysius stepped out on his own to follow Jesus. May we do the same in our culture, today and every day. Who knows what impact Dionysius had on his own community. . .or what we might have on ours?

CLASSICS: ANDREW MURRAY

JESUS: ALONE WITH THE FATHER

And he said unto them, Come ye yourselves apart into a desert place, and rest a while: for there were many coming and going, and they had no leisure so much as to eat.

MARK 6:31 KJV

In His life of secret prayer, my Savior is my example. He could not maintain the heavenly life in His soul without continually separating Himself from man and communing with His Father.

With the heavenly life in me it is not otherwise: it has the same need of entire separation from man, the need not only of single moments, but of time enough for intercourse with the Fountain of Life, the Father in heaven. If thou and I would be like Jesus, we must especially contemplate Jesus praying alone in the wilderness. There is the secret of His wonderful life.

What He did and spoke to man was first spoken and lived through with the Father. Even though it cost the sacrifice of night rest, of business, of intercourse with friends, the time must be found to be alone with the Father.

ELI: NEVER LET YOUR GUARD DOWN

In that day I will perform against Eli all things which I have
spoken concerning his house: when I begin, I will also make an end.

1 SAMUEL 3:12 KJV

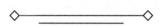

Before the coming of kings, Judges led Israel. But though Eli the high priest served God for forty years, he wasn't named as a judge. He acted nobly at first, then turned a blind eye to injustices as he grew older.

Most of these injustices had to do with his own sons. They were abusing the women of the temple and helping themselves to the offering. When Eli discovered what was happening, he rebuked them—sort of—but he spared the rod and spoiled his whole bloodline. As punishment, God made sure the line of Eli would disappear.

He was not a total failure, though. Though a poor father to his own sons, Eli was a good foster father to Samuel, the miracle boy given as an offering to Yahweh. He raised Hannah's son in an atmosphere of faith, and Samuel went on to become the last of the judges and the first major prophet since Moses.

Every individual, even many of the Bible's heroes, is a strange conglomeration of good and bad. As Christians, enjoying the presence of God's Holy Spirit in our lives, we must always pursue the best. When we let our guard down, as Eli did, bad things can happen. But when we consciously pursue God and His ways, He will make sure we succeed. After all, He is the one perfect Father.

AGABUS: SPEAKING THE TRUTH

*Coming over to us, he took Paul's belt, tied his own hands
and feet with it and said, "The Holy Spirit says, 'In this
way the Jewish leaders in Jerusalem will bind the owner
of this belt and will hand him over to the Gentiles.'"*

ACTS 21:11 NIV

Agabus was an early New Testament believer who was a picture of
courage. He appears for the second time in Acts 21, when he performs a strange act of prophetic theater. Then he announces that
the Jewish religious leadership would arrest the apostle Paul in Jerusalem and hand him over to the Romans.

That couldn't have been an easy message to speak, and Agabus
must have known it wouldn't be well received among those who
loved and worked with Paul. But while he could have "soft sold" the
message God had given him—or possibly spoken to Paul privately
so as to protect his friends' feelings—Agabus instead courageously
and openly spoke the truth God had given him.

Our opportunities to show Christian courage will differ from
Agabus's. But we can still follow his example, speaking the truth
and the whole truth—lovingly and gently—to the people God has
placed in our lives.

CLASSICS: ANDREW MURRAY

THE SICK MAN: JESUS RESTORES

*Whether is easier, to say, Thy sins be forgiven
thee; or to say, Rise up and walk?*
LUKE 5:23 KJV

I might mention many marks of spiritual health. Our text leads us to take one—walking. Jesus said to the sick man, "Rise and walk," and with that restored him to his place among men in full health and vigor, able to take his part in all the work of life. It is a wonderfully suggestive picture of the restoration of spiritual health.

To the healthy, walking is a pleasure; to the sick, a burden, if not an impossibility. How many Christians there are to whom, like the maimed and the halt and the lame and the impotent, movement and progress in God's way is indeed an effort and a weariness. Christ comes to say, and with the word He gives the power, "Rise and walk."

Just think of this walk to which He restores and empowers us. It is a life like that of Enoch and Noah, who "walked with God." A life like that of Abraham, to whom God said, "Walk before Me," and who himself spake, "The LORD before whom I walk."

THE ETHIOPIAN EUNUCH: ASK FOR HELP

The Spirit told Philip, "Go to that chariot and stay near it."
Then Philip ran up to the chariot and heard the man reading
Isaiah the prophet. "Do you understand what you are reading?"
Philip asked. "How can I," he said, "unless someone explains it
to me?" So he invited Philip to come up and sit with him.

ACTS 8:29–31 NIV

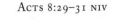

When an Ethiopian treasury official read the words of the prophet Isaiah, he was stumped. Philip, a deacon in the church at Jerusalem, was led by the Spirit to get close to the man's chariot. Hearing the Ethiopian official reading aloud, Philip asked a simple question: "Do you understand what you are reading?"

The man in the chariot was an important person. As such, he could have dismissed Philip's inquiry. Instead, he wisely replied with humility. The Ethiopian official received both an explanation of Isaiah's prophecy and eternal life when he surrendered his heart to Jesus.

The key through many (if not most) of our trials isn't trying harder—it's seeking wisdom from good, mature, wise believers who may have just the help we need. Often times, those around us have had similar experiences, and they can help us with firsthand information.

In Proverbs 18:15 we read, "The heart of the discerning acquires knowledge, for the ears of the wise seek it out" (NIV). No matter what challenge we face, we can ask our heavenly Father and our faithful brothers in Christ to help us get through it.

EPHRAIM: FIRST THOUGH SECOND

*And he blessed them that day, saying, In thee shall
Israel bless, saying, God make thee as Ephraim and as
Manasseh: and he set Ephraim before Manasseh.*

Genesis 48:20 KJV

We know Ephraim for his childhood and his descendants. Between those two extremes precious little is told of his life, but because he was given precedence over his older brother when both were small and unproven, we can only surmise that God picked him out for a reason.

Ephraim's father, Joseph, was well situated in Egypt. He made homes there for his brothers and his father. But the "pilgrimage" of Jacob, Joseph's father, was coming to an end. He asked to see his grandsons before he died, so Joseph brought Ephraim and Manasseh to him. The boys were small enough to stand between their father's knees. When Jacob blessed Ephraim before Manasseh, Joseph told him he had made a mistake. The first blessing should go to the older child, Manasseh. Jacob, who was almost blind but knew what God wanted, told his son there had been no mistake.

We can assume Ephraim became a worthy man and lived a faithful life. What of his descendants? Well, how about Joshua, son of Nun of the tribe of Ephraim, successor to Moses and possibly Israel's greatest leader in war? It seems God and Jacob knew what they were doing when they made Ephraim first even though he was second—kind of like Jesus taught, "Many that are first shall be last; and the last shall be first" (Matthew 19:30 KJV).

BOAZ: A MODEL OF KINDNESS

So Boaz said to Ruth, "My daughter, listen to me. Don't go and glean in another field and don't go away from here. Stay here with the women who work for me."

RUTH 2:8 NIV

◇————————◇

It would be hard to read the book of Ruth and not see Boaz, one of its key characters, as a role model for other men.

Boaz's very first words recorded in the book—a hearty and kindly "The LORD be with you!" (Ruth 2:4 NIV) to the harvesters working in his field—tell us exactly where Boaz was coming from. His employees' warm response tells us that they believed he genuinely cared about them.

Then Boaz demonstrated amazing kindness and generosity to Ruth, the woman who would one day become his wife, when he protected and provided for her as she gleaned leftover grain from his field. It might not seem like chivalry toward a woman in whom he had a personal interest is all that noteworthy, but Boaz clearly was the kind of man who made godly kindness a way of life.

Every one of us has opportunities in life to engage in acts of kindness and generosity. But when those acts are motivated out of a true love for God and for others, we'll find ourselves helping those who have little or nothing to offer us in return.

Isn't that just like Jesus, who came to earth to save a race that had chosen to reject God?

CLASSICS: D. L. MOODY

JOHN THE BAPTIST: SIMPLE OBEDIENCE

*Then cometh Jesus from Galilee to Jordan
unto John, to be baptized of him.*

MATTHEW 3:13 KJV

John stops. The people wonder what it means. The eye of the Baptist is fixed; and the crowd gives way before a Man of no very extraordinary mien, who approaches the Jordan and, addressing John, asks to be baptized.

"Baptize You?" he remonstrates. It was the first man whom he had hesitated to baptize. The people are asking, "What does this mean?"

John says, "I have need to be baptized of Thee, and comest Thou to me? I am not worthy to baptize Thee."

The Master said, "Suffer it to be so now, for thus it becometh us to fulfill all righteousness;" and they both went down into the Jordan, and Jesus was baptized by John.

The Master commanded, and John obeyed. It was simple obedience on his part.

PETER: WHO HE BECAME

Then Simon Peter drew a sword and slashed off the
right ear of Malchus, the high priest's slave.

JOHN 18:10 NLT

Peter had great faith. But he sometimes got ahead of that faith, such as when he stepped out of the boat to walk on storm-tossed water to Jesus. On another occasion, when Peter was at the transfiguration of Jesus and saw Moses and Elijah talking with the Lord, Peter bumbled. Not knowing what to say, he suggested building three shelters to honor the men—but God then put things in proper focus, saying, "This is my Son, my Chosen One. Listen to him" (Luke 9:35 NLT).

On the night of Jesus' arrest, Peter also acted by reflex. After the Last Supper, the Lord and His apostles walked to Gethsemane. The betrayer, Judas, arrived with a large crowd to arrest Jesus. Peter was carrying a sword and used it, severing Malchus's right ear. Jesus restored Malchus physically. Peter would need to be restored spiritually, after denying Jesus three times.

Peter eventually matured, grown into a pillar of the early Church by God's Holy Spirit. He may have remembered his own failure in the garden when he included self-control in his list of Christian character qualities, along with faith, goodness, knowledge, patience, godliness, and love (2 Peter 1:5–7).

If (more likely, *when*) you bumble, take encouragement from Peter. Yes, he failed, sometimes in big ways. But never forget who he ultimately became by God's grace.

PAUL: PERSISTENCE OF VISION

*And I am convinced that nothing can
ever separate us from God's love.*
ROMANS 8:38 NLT

Paul's early life was filled with Jewish law and tradition. Though hailing from Tarsus, then called Saul, he'd been brought up and educated in Jerusalem under Gamaliel, a well-known Jewish scholar. Whatever he had intended after this education, his life changed suddenly when Jesus spoke to him on the road to Damascus. He began a remarkable new journey.

During his second missionary tour of the Mediterranean region, Paul received a message from God: a vision of a man calling him to Macedonia. After evangelizing Greece and Asia Minor, he wanted to visit Rome, chief city of the Gentile world. By the end of his third missionary journey, however, he still had not done so.

Paul returned to Jerusalem where a series of events—an arrest, three trials, and a shipwreck—ended with the "apostle to the Gentiles" in Rome. Though kept under guard, Paul had his own rented home, where no one stopped him from receiving visitors, writing, and preaching.

How many times—facing hunger, robbers, beatings, and the opposition of men who only claimed to be Christians—could Paul have quit? But he didn't. His persistence of vision carried him safely through to heaven, and resulted in the missionary outreach and biblical record that have contributed to your own salvation. Never quit! Your persistence today might mean everything to someone you know now, or even a person of the far future you'll never meet on this earth.

CLASSICS: MATTHEW HENRY

ASA: A STEADY CONSTANT

And Asa did that which was right in the eyes of the LORD, as did David his father. . . . But the high places were not removed: nevertheless Asa's heart was perfect with the LORD all his days.

1 KINGS 15:11, 14 KJV

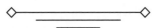

The general good character of it: *Asa did that which was right in the eyes of the LORD,* and that is right indeed which is so in God's eyes; those are approved whom He commends. He did *as did David his father,* kept close to God and to His instituted worship, was hearty and zealous for that, which gave him this honorable character, that he was like David, though he was not a prophet or psalmist, as David was. If we come up to the graces of those that have gone before us it will be our praise with God, though we come short of their gifts. Asa was like David, though he was neither such a conqueror nor such an author; for *his heart was perfect with the LORD all his days,* that is, he was both cordial and constant in his religion. What he did for God he was sincere in, steady and uniform, and did it from a good principle, with a single eye to the glory of God.

MARK: IN FRIGHTENING MOMENTS

A young man, wearing nothing but a linen garment, was following Jesus. When they seized him, he fled naked, leaving his garment behind.

MARK 14:51–52 NIV

The place: Gethsemane. The situation: Jesus is being arrested. Mark records a character unmentioned by the other Gospel writers: a naked man.

Imagine the setting: Judas has given his infamous kiss. Soldiers stand with representatives of the high priest. Peter whips out a sword and cuts off someone's ear. Jesus is seized, taken away for judgment and execution.

The moment of Jesus' arrest must have filled His disciples with terror. The center of their universe, the strongest man among them, had just showed weakness. He could have said a word to stop the whole thing, but He didn't. Now He was being led away by soldiers.

When a young follower of Christ followed a little too closely, soldiers seized him too. He only got away by shrugging out of his clothes, more willing to face the shame of public nudity than to share Jesus' fate. After all, if Jesus was too weak for the soldiers, what chance did any of the disciples have?

But Jesus wasn't being weak. He was applying His awesome strength to one of hardest things for anyone: self-sacrifice. The naked man in the garden—believed by many to be the Gospel writer Mark—sacrificed his clothes to save his life. Jesus would sacrifice His life to save the world from sin.

We are not called to save the world, but we are expected to stand for and with Jesus. Unlike the disciples of Gethsemane, we who follow Jesus today have the strength of the Holy Spirit in our lives. He will help us through every frightening experience.

TIMOTHY: STRENGTH IN ANXIETY

*For God has not given us a spirit of fear and timidity,
but of power, love, and self-discipline.*

2 TIMOTHY 1:7 NLT

◇══════════◇

Does it help you to realize that some key Bible characters dealt with anxiety and fear?

Notice how the apostle Paul speaks to Timothy in today's verse. This follows Paul describing Timothy as "my dear son" (1:2), a phrase he would repeat in 2:1, and noting Timothy's tears when he and the apostle had last parted (1:4). We get the impression that Timothy was a gentle and loving man, which is a positive thing. But because of his tenderness, Timothy might have struggled with the demands of leading the church in Ephesus.

So Paul encouraged the younger man with the words of 2 Timothy 1:7. When we are feeling the effects of anxiety in on our lives, this verse is a wonderful reminder of God's provision. Fear, anxiety, and depression are not things that the Lord gives us. He may allow us to experience them for our growth, but if He does, there's a good reason.

In those moments, return to this scripture. Know for sure that God has given you a spirit of power, of love, and of self-discipline. Use this reminder to give yourself strength.

CLASSICS: MATTHEW HENRY

THE ELDERS OF THE JEWS: COURAGE IN OPPOSITION

But the eye of their God was upon the elders of the Jews, that they could not cause them to cease, till the matter came to Darius: and then they returned answer by letter concerning this matter.

EZRA 5:5 KJV

The care which the divine Providence took of this good work: *The eye of their God was upon the elders of the Jews,* who were active in the work, so that their enemies could not cause them to cease, as they would have done, till the matter came to Darius. They desired they would only cease till they had instructions from the king about it. But they would not so much as yield them that, for *the eye of God was upon them,* even their God. And that baffled their enemies, infatuated and enfeebled them, and protected the builders from their malicious designs. While we are employed in God's work we are taken under His special protection; His eye is upon us for good.

That quickened them. The elders of the Jews saw *the eye of God upon them,* to observe what they did and own them in what they did well, and then they had courage enough to face their enemies and to go on vigorously with their work, notwithstanding all the opposition they met with. Our eye upon God, observing His eye upon us, will keep us to our duty and encourage us in it when the difficulties are ever so discouraging.

HABAKKUK: FINDING JOY IN THE LORD

Even though the fig trees have no blossoms, and there are no grapes on the vines; even though the olive crop fails, and the fields lie empty and barren; even though the flocks die in the fields, and the cattle barns are empty, yet I will rejoice in the LORD!

HABAKKUK 3:17–18 NLT

The prophet Habakkuk foresaw a day of trouble coming, and he took to prayer. How much better is it to be in prayer before trouble begins, thus preparing your heart and resolving to endure it joyfully, than to be surprised by it and grumble?

Habakkuk saw a time of drought in which the trees, vines, and crops would fail and most of the livestock would die. (This was likely the drought described in Jeremiah 14:1–6.) Yet Habakkuk said he would rejoice in the Lord. In a preemptive strike against his own soul, he filled himself up with faith in God so that bitterness couldn't creep into his heart when everything fell apart.

Have you ever prayed a prayer like this? If the economy takes a downturn and you're laid off, are you prepared to find joy in the Lord anyway? He is well able to place you in a new position. But will you praise Him during the time of uncertainty?

CLASSICS: CHARLES SPURGEON

LUKE: GOD USES YOUR NATURAL ABILITIES

*And it came to pass on a certain day, as he was teaching, that
there were Pharisees and doctors of the law sitting by, which
were come out of every town of Galilee, and Judaea, and
Jerusalem: and the power of the Lord was present to heal them.*

LUKE 5:17 KJV

Luke, the writer of this Gospel, was a physician, and therefore had
a quick eye for cases of disease and instances of cure; you can trace
throughout the whole of his Gospel the hand of one who was skilled in
surgery and medicine. From which I gather that whatever may be our
calling, or in whatever art or science we may have attained proficiency,
we should take care to use our knowledge for Christ; and that if we be
called being physicians we may understand the work of the Lord Jesus
all the better by what we see in our own work, and we may also do
much for our Lord in real substantial usefulness among our patients.

Let no man despise his calling; whatever instrument of usefulness
God hath put into thine hand, consider that the Great Captain knew
what weapon it were best for thee to wield. See what it is that thou
canst do where thou art, and use such things as thou hast in glorifying
thy Lord and Master.

LEVI: FROM VIOLENCE TO PRIESTHOOD

Three days later, while all of them were still in pain, two of Jacob's sons, Simeon and Levi, Dinah's brothers, took their swords and attacked the unsuspecting city, killing every male.

GENESIS 34:25 NIV

Jacob's sons were furious that their sister, Dinah, had been raped by Shechem, the son of Hamor the Hivite. When Hamor approached their father to ask for Dinah's hand in marriage for the offender, the brothers stepped in and gave Shechem a condition—every male must be circumcised so that the Shechemites would be like Dinah's family.

They agreed. But as the Shechemites were healing, Levi, the eleventh-born son of Jacob, and his brother Simeon killed every male in the city, taking all of their wealth as well as their women and children (verse 29). In so doing, Jacob feared that Simeon and Levi had brought trouble and possible retribution to his household.

Levi reacted to the news of his sister's rape out of emotion rather than righteousness. Later, as Jacob lay on his deathbed, he cursed Simeon and Levi's uncontrolled anger (Genesis 49:5). Yet God later appointed the tribe of Levi as His priests (Numbers 1:50)—to be set apart for His ministry.

No violence or wrongdoing is beyond the redeeming hand of God. If you're hesitant to believe that someone with a troublesome past can receive divine mercy—even if that someone is you—consider the tribe of Levi. God is in the business of making all things new.

BARTIMAEUS: A LESSON IN PERSISTENCE

Many rebuked him and told him to be quiet, but he shouted all the more, "Son of David, have mercy on me!"

MARK 10:48 NIV

The account of blind Bartimaeus, recorded in Mark 10:46–52, has two important messages—one for Jesus' followers and one for those who actively seek Him.

Bartimaeus made a bit of a scene that day in Jericho as he loudly and persistently called out to Jesus. That day, Jesus' followers—being imperfect people following their perfect Lord—had no patience for Bartimaeus. To them, he was simply a blind beggar, a societal throw-away to be ignored. Not so with Jesus. Jesus saw not just the man's circumstances but a heart that believed the Savior had something he needed and craved.

Those around the blind man made it abundantly clear that they didn't want him bothering their Lord, but Bartimaeus wasn't about to be shamed into holding his tongue. And because of his persistence, he received both his sight and a new purpose in life: following Jesus.

The story of blind Bartimaeus stands as an example of transformation through Jesus Christ—and an example of why we should never let others discourage us from calling out to Him. But let's not miss another important lesson in this story: we should always make certain that our words, attitudes, and actions welcome people to call out to Jesus, not prevent them from doing so.

CLASSICS: CHARLES SPURGEON

JESUS: THE HEART OF THE MATTER

And he said, That which cometh out of the man, that defileth the man. For from within, out of the heart of men, proceed evil thoughts, adulteries, fornications, murders, thefts, covetousness, wickedness, deceit, lasciviousness, an evil eye, blasphemy, pride, foolishness: all these evil things come from within, and defile the man.

MARK 7:20–23 KJV

The Savior makes short work of human traditions and authorities. Your meats and your drinks, your fasting thrice in the week, your paying of the tithe of mint, anise and cummin, your broad phylacteries and fringes; He waves them all away with one motion of His hand, and He comes straight to the real point at issue. He deals with the heart and with the sins which come out of it.

He draws up a diagnosis of the disease with fearless truthfulness and declares that meats do not defile men, that true religion is not a matter of observation or non-observation of washings and outward rites; but that the whole matter is spiritual and has to do with man's inmost self, with the understanding, the will, the emotions, the conscience, and all else which makes up the heart of man. He tells us that defilement is caused by that which cometh out of the man, not by that which goeth into him.

Defilement is of the heart, and not of the hands.

SIMON OF CYRENE: HOW JESUS CHANGES OUR LIVES

*A passerby named Simon, who was from Cyrene,
was coming in from the countryside just then, and
the soldiers forced him to carry Jesus' cross.*

MARK 15:21 NLT

It was the time of Passover. Jerusalem was much busier than usual. Simon, a man of Cyrene, had just arrived with his two sons, Alexander and Rufus. The streets were full of people intent on viewing a very specific event: a man being led to a hill just outside town where He would be crucified. The crowd divided for this man, Jesus, as He carried His own cross, severely wounded and struggling under its weight.

An impatient soldier grabbed Simon and forced him to carry the cross for the condemned man. We don't know what words Simon might have exchanged with Jesus or how this forced labor affected Simon's sons. However, it's widely believed that his son Rufus became a leader in the early Church (Romans 16:13).

All who came in contact with Jesus were given the opportunity to change their life direction—from the woman at the well to Nicodemus, the Pharisee. So we can only guess how shouldering the weight of the cross used to kill the Son of God would have changed Simon.

Such reflection should make us think of our own first connection with a risen Savior and how that encounter has changed the course of our lives.

PAUL: PURSUING GODLY AMBITIONS

*My ambition has always been to preach the Good News
where the name of Christ has never been heard, rather than
where a church has already been started by someone else.*

ROMANS 15:20 NLT

You probably have several ambitions. Professionally, you have your
eyes set on a prize—maybe a promotion or ownership of your own
business. Personally, you're striving to become a better leader in your
home and take better care of yourself. But what about your spiritual
ambitions? Where do your spiritual passions lie?

After his conversion, the apostle Paul had set his sights on preaching the Gospel in places where the name of Jesus had never been heard,
and he spent the rest of his life doing so. He wasn't disrespecting the
work done in churches started by others. He just left that work to
someone else who had a godly zeal for it.

Do you have such clarity of thought? Maybe your ambition is
outside of the box—like starting an online Christian news site in
your city, or giving away everything you own to the poor, or starting
a ministry to mentally ill men who have fallen through the cracks
of society.

You don't need a "calling" to pursue most godly ambitions. You
simply need to acknowledge that one exists deep inside your heart
and then prayerfully seek ways to live it out.

Whatever your ambition is, jump into it!

CLASSICS: ANDREW MURRAY

ABRAHAM: WALKING BEFORE GOD

*And when Abram was ninety years old and nine, the
LORD appeared to Abram, and said unto him, I am the
Almighty God; walk before me, and be thou perfect.*

GENESIS 17:1 KJV

Walk before Me, and be thou perfect. It is in the life fellowship with
God, in His realized presence and favor, that it becomes possible to
be perfect with Him. Walk before Me: Abraham had been doing this;
God's Word calls him to a clearer and more conscious apprehension
of this as his life calling.

It is easy for us to study what scripture says of perfection, to form
our ideas of it and argue for them. But let us remember that it is only
as we are walking closely with God, seeking and in some measure
attaining, uninterrupted communion with Him, that the divine command will come to us in its divine power and unfold to us its divine
meaning. Walk before Me, *and* be thou perfect.

God's realized presence is the school, is the secret, of perfection.
It is only he who studies what perfection is in the full light of God's
presence to whom its hidden glory will be opened up.

ANANIAS: SUMMONING COURAGE

*The Lord told him, "Go to the house of Judas on Straight
Street and ask for a man from Tarsus named Saul, for he
is praying. In a vision he has seen a man named Ananias
come and place his hands on him to restore his sight."*

ACTS 9:11–12 NIV

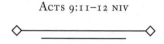

The message Ananias received made no sense at all: Go and find
Saul, the man who almost singlehandedly chased the church from
Jerusalem, and tell that violent persecutor about Jesus? This sounded
less like God's direction and more like a trap. But when Jesus told
Ananias a second time, he trusted the Lord and went.

Such obedience is easier said than done. Ananias was originally
fearful, responding to Jesus' request by saying, "Lord, I have heard
many reports about this man and all the harm he has done to your
holy people in Jerusalem. And he has come here with authority from
the chief priests to arrest all who call on your name" (verses 13–14).

But Jesus reminded Ananias (as He reminds all of us) that God's
plans are good. Saul was His "chosen instrument to proclaim my
name to the Gentiles" (verse 15). With this truth in mind, Ananias
summoned his courage and did his job—confirming a conversion
that would literally change the world.

There will be times when doing the right thing seems frightening, when you want to say, "Are You sure, Lord?" But remember His
faithfulness in the past. Study His promises in scripture. And then
just step out in obedience. He'll take care of you the way He took
care of Ananias.

JAMES: SETBACKS HELP US GROW

Consider it pure joy, my brothers and sisters, whenever
you face trials of many kinds, because you know that
the testing of your faith produces perseverance.
JAMES 1:2–3 NIV

◇————————————◇

Everyone wants to experience "pure joy," but not many would think of a trial or test of faith as an opportunity to experience it. What was James thinking?

For starters, James was looking at the big picture for Christians. He saw the whole of life stretched before him and even into eternity, where God will reward those who have remained faithful. Each believer will face difficulties in the future as well, so trusting God in today's trial will prepare us to remain faithful in future challenges.

James didn't see faith as something that you either have or don't have. Faith must be developed and grown over time. We can say that we "have" faith, but our faith becomes stronger the more we use it. Those who see trials and difficulties as opportunities to draw near to God and grow their faith will find greater joy in the most unlikely places.

More than anything else, James was eager for his readers, including us, to see that their relationship with Jesus Christ is more valuable than their comfort. It is like a pearl of such great value that a man sells everything he has to purchase it. If we remain close to Christ, then each apparent setback will help our faith leap forward.

CLASSICS: MATTHEW HENRY

THE NOBLES: SETTING
A PUBLIC EXAMPLE

*They clave to their brethren, their nobles, and entered into a curse,
and into an oath, to walk in God's law, which was given by Moses
the servant of God, and to observe and do all the commandments
of the LORD our Lord, and his judgments and his statutes.*

NEHEMIAH 10:29 KJV

Observe how the concurrence of the people is expressed. They clave
to their brethren one and all. Here those whom the court blessed,
the country blessed too! The commonalty agreed with their nobles
in this good work.

Great men never look so great as when they encourage religion
and are examples of it, and they would by that, as much as anything,
secure an interest in the most valuable of their inferiors. Let but the
nobles cordially espouse religious causes, and perhaps they will find
people cleave to them therein closer than they can imagine.

Their nobles are called their *brethren*, for, in the things of God,
rich and poor, high and low, meet together. They entered into a curse
and an oath. As the nobles confirmed the covenant with their hands
and seals, so the people with a curse and an oath, solemnly appealing
to God concerning their sincerity and imprecating His just revenge if
they dealt deceitfully. Every oath has in it a conditional curse upon the
soul, which makes it a strong bond upon the soul for our own tongues,
if false and lying tongues, will fall, and fall heavily, upon ourselves.

DAVID: ASSURED OF GOD'S PRESENCE

David left Gath and escaped to the cave of Adullam.

1 SAMUEL 22:1 NIV

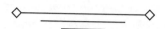

The title of Psalm 142 reads: "When he was in the cave. A prayer." David and his men had moved to Adullam when the winter rains began, when life out in the open became miserable. For a couple months, they hunkered down in the damp cavern near the city. In Israel, it often rains heavily for three days nonstop, and to David it felt like a prison (Psalm 142:7).

He had been a much-loved hero of Israel. Now he was vilified, and King Saul and his army were hunting David, seeking to kill him. David had been forced to flee, leaving his wife Michal behind. It was in this context that he poured out his complaint to God, all the while proclaiming, "You are my refuge, my portion in the land of the living" (Psalm 142:5 NIV). David was deeply discouraged, yet he prayed, "When my spirit grows faint within me, it is you who watch over my way" (Psalm 142:3 NIV). God was all David had left. So he looked to Him for help.

You too can be assured that God is with you (Hebrews 13:5).

Are you going through a similar experience? Do you feel hemmed in and abandoned by God? Look to Him for help. In your darkest moments, He will be right by your side.

TERAH: SETTING CHANGE IN MOTION

Terah took his son Abram, his grandson Lot son of Haran,
and his daughter-in-law Sarai, the wife of his son Abram,
and together they set out from Ur of the Chaldeans to go to
Canaan. But when they came to Harran, they settled there.

GENESIS 11:31 NIV

Terah's ancestry can be traced to Shem, Noah's son. His family had settled in Ur of the Chaldeans, but as an older man, Terah gathered those who were willing to follow—his son (Abram), daughter-in-law (Sarai), and grandson (Lot)—and left town.

Why Terah felt he should leave—and why he didn't complete the trip to Canaan—isn't revealed, but we do know that his son Abram (later Abraham) was called by God to be the father of nations.

Other passages of scripture confirm the importance of his leaving Ur (Genesis 15:7; Nehemiah 9:7). Perhaps God was preparing Terah's son for the final leg of his trip and the challenges he would face. Or maybe Terah understood that his son would be better off leaving the cultural influences of his childhood home behind. Regardless of the reason, Abram couldn't stay.

Harran became their temporary home until Terah died. Then Abram, Sarai, and Lot completed their journey to Canaan—thus changing history forever.

Are you being led by God into a new venture or phase of life? What definite steps are you taking to make the vision a reality?

CLASSICS: CHARLES SPURGEON

SAMSON: HINTING AT JESUS TO COME

And after a time he returned to take her, and he turned aside to see the carcase of the lion: and, behold, there was a swarm of bees and honey in the carcase of the lion. And he took thereof in his hands, and went on eating, and came to his father and mother, and he gave them, and they did eat: but he told not them that he had taken the honey out of the carcase of the lion.

JUDGES 14:8–9 KJV

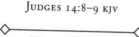

It seems to me that the Israelitish hero with a slain lion in the background, standing out in the open road with his hands laden with masses of honeycomb and dripping with honey, which he holds out to his parents, makes a fine picture, worthy of the greatest artist. And what a type we have here of our divine Lord and Master: Jesus, the conqueror of death and hell.

He has destroyed the lion that roared upon us and upon Him. He has shouted "victory" over all our foes. "It is finished" was His note of triumph; and now He stands in the midst of His church with His hands full of sweetness and consolation. To each one of us who believe in Him He gives the luscious food which He has prepared for us by the overthrow of our foes; He bids us come and eat that we may have our lives sweetened and our hearts filled with joy.

To me the comparison seems wonderfully apt and suggestive: I see our triumphant Lord laden with sweetness, holding it forth to all His brethren and inviting them to share in His joy.

PAUL: WATCHFUL PROTECTION

I urge you, brothers and sisters, to watch out for those who cause
divisions and put obstacles in your way that are contrary to the
teaching you have learned. Keep away from them. For such people
are not serving our Lord Christ, but their own appetites. By
smooth talk and flattery they deceive the minds of naive people.

ROMANS 16:17–18 NIV

Paul was always watchful of his flock. He poured out his life to build
the Church of Christ on a solid foundation. But he knew others would
come who worked only for their own interests as slaves of "their own
appetites." You can tell who they are, he warned, because they create
arguments where there shouldn't be any. They stand out because they
teach what is contrary to the truth found in Christ.

Jesus described these same people: "Watch out for false prophets.
They come to you in sheep's clothing, but inwardly they are ferocious
wolves. By their fruit you will recognize them" (Matthew 7:15–16
NIV). What kinds of "fruits"? For one, their "smooth and flattering
speech," which never has a place in the body of Christ. Flattery always
comes from an ulterior motive, to manipulate the listener. It always
serves the flesh.

To heed Paul's warning about such people, we need to be sure
we are not one of the "naive"—those who have never made the effort
to mature in Christ. "Anyone who lives on milk, being still an infant,
is not acquainted with the teaching about righteousness." (Hebrews
5:13 NIV). Growing in our understanding of Christ is the only way
to guard against deception.

ZACCHAEUS: A MODEL OF REPENTANCE

But Zacchaeus stood up and said to the Lord, "Look, Lord! Here and now I give half of my possessions to the poor, and if I have cheated anybody out of anything, I will pay back four times the amount."

LUKE 19:8 NIV

◇════════◇

We often hear pastors and teachers say that repentance means turning around and changing course. However, we may struggle to imagine what this could look like in our own lives. The story of Zacchaeus provides one of the most powerful pictures of true repentance in action.

Zacchaeus didn't just commit to follow Jesus. He recognized that following Jesus meant completely changing his life according to Jesus' priorities and standards. He saw Jesus' invitation as an opportunity to pursue a new course in life.

At his moment of conversion, Zacchaeus didn't just stop cheating people. He vowed to right the wrongs he had committed. He also pledged to give generously to the poor from his wealth. Zacchaeus knew he had acquired much of his wealth dishonestly, and he rightly recognized that following Jesus required justice, both for those he'd wronged and for the poor in his community.

He signaled his newfound trust in Jesus and his allegiance to the kingdom of God by removing the wealth and dishonest tactics that he had relied on for so long. Zacchaeus repented by not only changing his future but by repairing his past.

EPAPHRAS: A WILLING PRISONER

Epaphras, who is one of you and a servant of Christ Jesus,
sends greetings. He is always wrestling in prayer for you,
that you may stand firm in all the will of God, mature
and fully assured. I vouch for him that he is working hard
for you and for those at Laodicea and Hierapolis.

COLOSSIANS 4:12–13 NIV

We don't know if Epaphras was jailed with Paul, but both men seem to have thought of themselves as prisoners of Christ. What does that mean? Surely Jesus doesn't lock people up!

What Jesus does is show us unimaginable love and the incredible wonders of the kingdom of heaven. Both are so far beyond our expectations that once we begin to understand them, we cannot force ourselves to walk away. Having known Jesus, we become captivated by Him and refuse to leave His work to do our own thing.

Epaphras might have been a literal prisoner for his faith, but he is also a fine example of how our circumstances should never determine our beliefs. Being locked up didn't mean he wasn't still working for the kingdom. Paul tells us that Epaphras was constantly in prayer for the new churches, and we know what wonders are often wrought by prayer.

Whatever situation Epaphras was in, he was where he wanted to be—with Jesus! And, in jail or otherwise, he was always doing God's work.

Day 137

MOSES: PRAYER VS. ACTION

And the LORD said unto Moses, Wherefore criest thou unto me? speak unto the children of Israel, that they go forward.

EXODUS 14:15 KJV

Spiritual men, in their distresses, turn at once to prayer, even as the stag when hunted takes to flight. Prayer is a never-failing resort; it is sure to bring a blessing with it. The very exercise of prayer is healthy to the man engaged in it. Far be it from me ever to say a word in disparagement of the holy, happy, heavenly exercise of prayer. But, beloved, there are times when prayer is not enough—when prayer itself is out of season.

Moses prayed that God would deliver His people; but the Lord said to him, "Wherefore criest thou unto me?" As much as to say this is not the time for prayer; it is the time for action.

When we have prayed over a matter to a certain degree, it then becomes sinful to tarry any longer; our plain duty is to carry our desires into action, and having asked God's guidance, and having received divine power from on high, to go at once to our duty without any longer deliberation or delay.

HEZEKIAH: DEATH ISN'T THE END

"Go back and tell Hezekiah, the ruler of my people, 'This is what the LORD, the God of your father David, says: I have heard your prayer and seen your tears; I will heal you.'"

2 KINGS 20:5 NIV

King Hezekiah's terminal illness seemed to come out of the blue. When the Lord told the faithful king to put his house in order because he wasn't going to recover, Hezekiah did what any of us would do: he prayed. Oddly, though, he didn't pray directly for healing.

"Remember, LORD," he said, "how I have walked before you faithfully and with wholehearted devotion and have done what is good in your eyes" (2 Kings 20:3 NIV). In other words, Hezekiah "reminded" God that he had lived in a way that seemed worthy of a *longer* life. He'd been as faithful to God as a man could be. The Lord graciously heard Hezekiah's prayer and granted him an additional fifteen years.

Hezekiah was facing what we will all face someday—mortality. Most of us don't really want to think about our own deaths, but when we follow Jesus, our mortality should hold no terror. No matter how long we live, we are destined to die, and for believers, the Lord alone is our goal (Psalm 16:5). Do not fear. Death isn't the end for us—it's simply the beginning of a perfect, sinless, everlasting life.

JESUS: ON SOLITUDE AND TAKING RISKS

At daybreak, Jesus went out to a solitary place. The people were looking for him and when they came to where he was, they tried to keep him from leaving them. But he said, "I must proclaim the good news of the kingdom of God to the other towns also, because that is why I was sent."

LUKE 4:42–43 NIV

Jesus had just preached a powerful sermon in Nazareth and healed many in the village of Capernaum. His popularity was at an all-time high in the village where He had started to make His home, and the people begged Him to stick around. Why shouldn't He consolidate His position and continue to perform miracles among His friends and neighbors?

But Jesus had very different plans. He had a clear mission that called Him beyond the familiarity of His hometown. Despite the attractiveness of staying comfortable and popular, Jesus saw that His ministry required Him to pursue solitude and venture beyond His village into many others.

While God may call some to stay put, this story reminds us that God's calling often flies in the face of conventional wisdom. In fact, Jesus' pursuit of solitude and His commitment to His mission were undoubtedly linked. The power and clarity He drew from solitude certainly prepared Him to make the difficult decision to leave what was familiar and to pursue God's calling for His life.

CLASSICS: CHARLES SPURGEON

AHIJAH: IMMORTAL TILL HIS WORK IS DONE

Ahijah could not see; for his eyes were set by reason of his age. And the LORD said unto Ahijah, Behold, the wife of Jeroboam cometh to ask a thing of thee for her son; for he is sick: thus and thus shalt thou say unto her: for it shall be, when she cometh in, that she shall feign herself to be another woman. And it was so.

1 KINGS 14:4–6 KJV

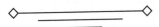

Mark well this venerable prophet. . .is it not time for him to die? Has he not outlived his usefulness when he is made entirely dependent upon his fellow creatures and a burden to himself? There he sits without any apparent perception of the scenes transpiring around him; surely, surely it is time for the Master to call him away! But, no, He does not. Ahijah must not die; he has another message to deliver, and he is immortal till his work is done.

Brethren and sisters, you and I have no right to want to go to heaven till our work is done. There is a desire to be with Christ which is not only natural but spiritual; there is a sighing to behold His face, which if a man be without I shall question if he be a Christian at all; but to wish to be away from the battle before we win the victory, and to desire to leave the field before the day is over, were but lazy and listless; therefore let us pray God to save us from it.

ELISHA: WATCHING, LEARNING, FOLLOWING

Elisha then picked up Elijah's cloak that had fallen from him and went back and stood on the bank of the Jordan. He took the cloak. . .and struck the water with it. "Where now is the LORD, the God of Elijah?" he asked. When he struck the water, it divided to the right and to the left, and he crossed over.

2 KINGS 2:13–14 NIV

Elisha was plowing his field when Elijah called. Knowing this was God's will, Elisha didn't hesitate. Well. . .he did a little. He hesitated long enough to kiss his parents, break apart his plow, cook his oxen, and give the meat to the people. He definitely wasn't going back to the farming life!

We don't hear anything more about Elisha for several years, implying that he kept his head down, watched, learned, and served. He was a dedicated servant of the prophet of God. Even when he heard the Lord was about to take his master, Elisha refused to leave him.

He was rewarded with a double portion of Elijah's spirit, becoming his recognized successor and performing twice as many miracles.

Spiritual teachers like Elijah are scarce. But if you find one who is a true man of God, then do what Elisha did: Watch, learn, and follow.

JOSEPH: UNSHAKABLE FAITH

Joseph's master took him and put him in prison, the place where the king's prisoners were confined. But while Joseph was there in the prison, the Lord was with him; he showed him kindness and granted him favor in the eyes of the prison warden.

GENESIS 39:20–21 NIV

Working for the Egyptian official Potiphar, Joseph always did the right thing. He respected Potiphar's business dealings, his possessions, and his family. However, when Joseph rejected the advances of Potiphar's wife, she falsely accused him of assault—and Joseph found himself in prison.

Joseph could have responded to this downturn in circumstances by complaining, crying, or casting off his trust in God. But his faith was not shaken. Joseph quickly began serving the prison warden, earning his trust as he had Potiphar's. Since God had faithfully met his needs in the past, Joseph knew God would provide in this situation also. As he would later tell his brothers, who had initially sold him into slavery, "God sent me ahead of you to preserve for you a remnant on earth and to save your lives by a great deliverance" (Genesis 45:7 NIV).

We will all face downturns in life, some minor and others overwhelming. But we mustn't forget to view present-day events from God's perspective, watching for His work even in our most difficult times.

Remember, there is a God in heaven who desires your best. Keep your focus on Him and wait for His deliverance.

CLASSICS: ANDREW MURRAY

NOAH: FAITH, FEAR, AND DILIGENCE

*And Noah did according unto all
that the LORD commanded him.*

GENESIS 7:5 KJV

By faith Noah prepared an ark. Faith wrought fear, and fear wrought diligence, and faith guided heart and hand for the work of deliverance.

No one had ever heard of a coming flood and the destruction of a world by water. No one could ever have thought, if the world were drowned, of an ark escaping alone. But faith lives in fellowship with God; it knows His secrets of judgment and of salvation; it so possesses a man that he gives up his life to act it out.

In the face of the mockery of men, and the long delay of the day, and all the difficulties of the work, Noah held fast to God's word. Simply to listen to what God says and in the obedience of faith to give up our whole heart and life to carry it out: this is faith.

DAVID: FEAR GOD, NOT MAN

*Once again David inquired of the LORD, and the
LORD answered him, "Go down to Keilah, for I am
going to give the Philistines into your hand."*

1 SAMUEL 23:4 NIV

◇————————◇

After learning that enemy soldiers were looting the threshing
floor in Keilah—a city in southern Judah near the border with the
Philistines—David had one question for the Lord: "Shall I go and
attack these Philistines?" (1 Samuel 23:2 NIV).

Even though the Lord said yes, David's men weren't ready for
battle. They admitted that they were afraid even while in Judah. Perhaps they feared retaliation from King Saul for aligning themselves
with David. Maybe they even wondered if some among their number
were loyal to Saul. So David inquired of the Lord again, and the Lord
gave the same answer. David and his men went to battle and inflicted
heavy losses on the Philistines.

We as Christians are like David's men. We will certainly face
opposition for standing with Jesus—from friends, coworkers, and
maybe even our families. When the Lord sent out His twelve disciples,
He promised opposition would come (Matthew 10:23; Luke 21:12;
John 15:20). But He also told them, "Do not be afraid of those who
kill the body but cannot kill the soul. Rather, be afraid of the One
who can destroy both soul and body in hell" (Matthew 10:28 NIV).

In other words, have more reverence for God than fear of man.
God is stronger, wiser, and more loving than we can even imagine.
Just as He took care of David, He'll take care of you.

JONATHAN: COMPLETE SURRENDER

*Jonathan said to David, "Whatever you
want me to do, I'll do for you."*

1 SAMUEL 20:4 NIV

As a prince—the oldest son of Saul, King of Israel—Jonathan had proven himself in battle multiple times. He was next in line to the throne—that is, until a young man named David came along.

First, the prophet Samuel anointed David as the future king of Israel. Next, David killed the Philistine Goliath and then gained fame through many successful battles. Jonathan had plenty of reasons to be jealous of David, but he wasn't. In fact, 1 Samuel 18:1 (NIV) says, "Jonathan became one in spirit with David, and he loved him as himself."

What devotion to a man who would take Jonathan's birthright! Jonathan's love and faithfulness to David remained steadfast even as his father Saul turned against David. Even as Saul tried to kill David, Jonathan pledged his fidelity to him.

Eventually, Jesus was born from the line of David and became King of kings—ruler over all creation. This King demands your all, but it is the sweetest of demands. When you're faced with this King, what is your response? Will you rebel out of a sense of pride? Or will you respond like Jonathan and say, "Whatever you want me to do, I'll do for you"?

CLASSICS: ANDREW MURRAY

JESUS: CONSTANT RENEWAL

And it came to pass in those days, that he went out into a mountain to pray, and continued all night in prayer to God. And when it was day, he called unto him his disciples: and of them he chose twelve, whom also he named apostles.

LUKE 6:12–13 KJV

The work of the day and evening had exhausted Him. In His healing of the sick and casting out devils, power had gone out of Him. While others still slept, He went away to pray and to renew His strength in communion with His Father. He had need of this; otherwise He would not have been ready for the new day. The holy work of delivering souls demands constant renewal through fellowship with God. Think again of the calling of the apostles.

Is it not clear that if anyone wishes to do God's work, he must take time for fellowship with Him, to receive His wisdom and power? The dependence and helplessness of which this is an evidence open the way and give God the opportunity of revealing His power. How great was the importance of the choosing of the apostles for Christ's own work, for the early church and for all time! It had God's blessing and seal; the stamp of prayer was on it.

AARON: DON'T JUST GET ALONG

*Moses saw that the people were running wild and that
Aaron had let them get out of control and so become
a laughingstock to their enemies. So he stood at the
entrance to the camp and said, "Whoever is for the LORD,
come to me." And all the Levites rallied to him.*

EXODUS 32:25–26 NIV

Where would the people of Israel have been without Moses' brother
Aaron? He acted as Moses' mouthpiece to Pharaoh in Egypt. He
was an instrument in the hand of God, performing the miracles that
convinced Pharaoh to free the Hebrews from slavery. Later, Aaron
had the amazing privilege and responsibility of starting Israel's formal
priesthood. Yet Aaron had his moments of weakness—the most
grievous being the part he played in Israel's fall into idolatry.

Moses had ascended Mount Sinai and stayed there longer than
the people had expected, so they pressured Aaron to fashion a golden
calf to worship. Aaron had an opportunity to stand strong for God,
but he instead chose to "go along to get along." The results were
tragic. Not only were the people of God involved in pagan revelry,
but thousands of them died as a penalty for their sin.

Aaron's failure teaches us an important lesson: everything we say,
do, and tolerate has consequences.

Do you stand strong for God, even when it means running
against the crowd? Or do you "keep the peace" by tolerating things
that dishonor Him and bring reproach on His Church?

CLASSICS: CHARLES SPURGEON

BOAZ: CHEERING AND STRENGTHENING

*The LORD recompense thy work, and a full
reward be given thee of the LORD God of Israel,
under whose wings thou art come to trust.*

RUTH 2:12 KJV

This was the language of Boaz, a man of substance and of note in Bethlehem, to a poor stranger of whom he had heard that she had left her kindred and the idols of her nation, that she might become a worshipper of the living and true God. He acted a noble part when he cheered her and bade her be of good courage, now that she was casting in her lot with Naomi and the chosen nation.

Observe that he saluted her with words of tender encouragement; for this is precisely what I want all the elder Christians among you to do to those who are the counterparts of Ruth. You who have long been believers in the Lord Jesus, who have grown rich in experience, who know the love and faithfulness of our covenant God, and who are strong in the Lord and in the power of His might; I want you to make a point of looking out for the young converts and speaking to them goodly words and comfortable words, whereby they may be cheered and strengthened.

PHILIP: WELCOMING THE OUTSIDER

Brothers, select seven men who are well respected and are
full of the Spirit and wisdom. . . . Everyone liked this idea,
and they chose the following: Stephen (a man full of
faith and the Holy Spirit), Philip, Procorus, Nicanor,
Timon, Parmenas, and Nicolas of Antioch.

ACTS 6:3, 5 NLT

This Philip, known as Philip the Evangelist to distinguish him from Philip the Apostle, experienced firsthand how much the early Church could grow. When poor foreign Jews in Jerusalem were being overlooked in the charitable distribution, Philip along with six others were selected to address their concerns. They successfully did so, and the Church remained strong.

Shortly afterward, persecution scattered the believers, and Philip traveled to the province of Samaria. Traditional Jews had a centuries-old feud with Samaritans, counting them as heretics even though the Samaritans worshipped God too, after a fashion. But when Philip carried the Gospel to these despised people, many Samaritan men and women were baptized. The apostles Peter and John came to Samaria and accepted the Samaritans as fellow Christians.

Philip and the Church faced two decisive moments, one in Jerusalem and another in Samaria. In both cases, Philip chose to take down barriers and assure the outcasts that Jesus loved them.

When faced with the decision to love or shun those who make you uncomfortable, what will you choose?

JESUS: DOING HARD THINGS

"Now my soul is troubled, and what shall I say? 'Father, save me from this hour'? No, it was for this very reason I came to this hour. Father, glorify your name!" Then a voice came from heaven, "I have glorified it, and will glorify it again."

JOHN 12:27–28 NIV

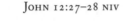

There's always that one task. We cross off the other items on our to-do list, but when we get to that one thing, we hesitate. Or maybe it isn't an item on a to-do list, but a tough conversation with a loved one. Perhaps it's admitting we need help to quit an addiction. It could be switching jobs or breaking off an unhealthy relationship or any of countless other challenges. Something about the situation ahead is troubling your soul.

Jesus has been there. And He has given us the example to follow.

With His public ministry ending and the crucifixion ahead, Jesus was troubled. He recognized the troublesome task. He reaffirmed His mission. Then He requested that God be glorified.

We can do the same thing. Recognize, reaffirm, and request. When we seek to glorify God's name with our weakness, He will give us the strength for the task ahead. God's name has already been glorified because we recognize our need for Him, but He will glorify it again when we complete the task with His strength.

Whatever that one task is, God wants us to succeed. He will provide the encouragement and strength we need to glorify His name.

NIMROD: LASTING GREATNESS

*Cush was the father of Nimrod, who became
a mighty warrior on earth.*

1 CHRONICLES 1:10 NIV

Nimrod was a great-grandson of Noah. For a time, he was admired: "People would say, 'This man is like Nimrod, the greatest hunter in the world'" (Genesis 10:9 NLT). Then, when he built a kingdom in Babylonia and several cities including Nineveh, he became a formidable ruler (Genesis 10:10–11). Finally, he became intensely despised: Joel describes the countries of Israel's enemies as the "gates of Nimrod."

Where did Nimrod go wrong? Chapter 10 of Genesis says the descendants of Noah were spread over various lands. Chapter 11 tells why they scattered. On the plains of Shinar, they began building a city with a tower to reach the heavens. They constructed the tower not to glorify their Creator but to make a name for themselves. So before the tower was completed, God confused their speech and scattered them. The place where they started the tower became known as Babylon—from *Babel*, meaning "confusion."

Unlike his great-grandfather who built the ark to save himself and his family—and then an altar to sacrifice to God—Nimrod built cities to make a name for himself. He had a great impact during his time, but the Bible mentions his name only four times. Lasting greatness comes from honoring God and serving others.

CLASSICS: ANDREW MURRAY

PETER: CARING FOR THE LAMBS

*So when they had dined, Jesus saith to Simon Peter,
Simon, son of Jonas, lovest thou me more than these?
He saith unto him, Yea, Lord; thou knowest that I
love thee. He saith unto him, Feed my lambs.*

JOHN 21:15 KJV

Peter was a fisherman. After the first miraculous draught of fishes, the Lord had said, "Follow Me, and I will make you fishers of men." Peter's work on earth was made the symbol of his heavenly calling.

After the second miraculous draught of fishes, in the days preceding the ascension, our Lord no longer calls Peter a fisherman, but a shepherd. There is a deep meaning in the change. One great point of difference between the fisherman and the shepherd is, that while the former catches what he has neither reared nor fed, and only seeks what is full-grown, casting away all the little fish out of his net back into the sea, the shepherd directs his special attention to the young and the feeble; on his care for the lambs all his hope depends.

THE PHILIPPIAN JAILER: BETTER THAN PHYSICAL SAFETY

*[He] brought them out, and said, Sirs, what must I do to be
saved? And they said, Believe on the Lord Jesus Christ, and
thou shalt be saved, and thy house. And they spake unto him
the word of the Lord, and to all that were in his house. . . . And
when he had brought them into his house, he set meat before
them, and rejoiced, believing in God with all his house.*

ACTS 16:30–34 KJV

The jailer at Philippi was sleeping soundly while Paul and Silas sang
praises to God at midnight. But God caused an earthquake that left
him wide awake and terrified. All the locked prison doors swung
open and all the prisoners' constraints fell off. Since his own blood
would be shed if they escaped, the jailer probably saw his life flash
before his eyes.

When the jailer pleaded with Paul and Silas to tell him how to
be saved, they told him what Jesus had done. Whether he first wanted
to be saved from the wrath of God or of Rome is unknown. But after
they explained the Gospel, he believed in the saving power of the
crucified and risen Messiah.

Often, it takes a disaster to awaken us to our own need for a Savior.
And when we cry out to Jesus in that moment of desperation, we receive
something far better than physical safety—we receive eternal life.

CALEB: A PATIENT FOLLOWER

"But I wholly followed the LORD my God."
JOSHUA 14:8 NKJV

Imagine having to wait forty years for the realization of your dream. That's how long it took for Caleb, Joshua's comrade-in-arms, to obtain Mount Hebron in the land of Canaan. Quite likely, Caleb first discovered his heart's desire while spying out the land of Canaan with Joshua and the ten others whom Moses dispatched for that purpose. He was then forty-five years old.

But when Caleb and Joshua's fellow spies issued a disheartening report about the land, Israel tragically and disgracefully succumbed to their fear. Caleb proclaimed that he (along with Joshua) had followed the Lord wholeheartedly. Together, the two faithful men delivered a favorable, determined report—one that nearly got them stoned, were it not for the intervention of God Himself (Numbers 14). So began a miserable wandering in the desert for forty long years: one year for each day the spies spent in the land of Canaan. Everyone Joshua and Caleb knew fell in that desert wasteland.

At last, Canaan was finally apportioned among the twelve tribes of Israel. While Judah was receiving its portion, Caleb boldly stepped forward and told Joshua, "You know the word which the LORD said to Moses the man of God concerning you and me in Kadesh Barnea. . . . Now therefore, give me this mountain" (Joshua 14:6, 12 NKJV). Caleb hadn't given up on his dream, and he was prepared to fight for it if he had to.

God has a dream in mind for each of us, just as He did for Caleb. It might not require us to wait forty years for its fulfillment; it does require that we follow the Lord our God wholeheartedly.

CLASSICS: MATTHEW HENRY

JEROBOAM: INDUSTRY VS. UPRIGHTNESS

And Jeroboam the son of Nebat. . .was a mighty man of valour:
and Solomon seeing the young man that he was industrious,
he made him ruler over all the charge of the house of Joseph.

1 KINGS 11:26–28 KJV

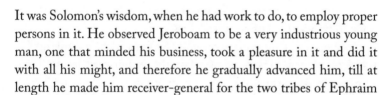

It was Solomon's wisdom, when he had work to do, to employ proper persons in it. He observed Jeroboam to be a very industrious young man, one that minded his business, took a pleasure in it and did it with all his might, and therefore he gradually advanced him, till at length he made him receiver-general for the two tribes of Ephraim and Manasseh.

Industry is the way to preferment. Seest thou a man diligent in his business, that will take care and pains and go through with it? He shall stand before kings and not always be on the level with mean men. Observe a difference between David, and both his predecessor and his successor: when Saul saw a valiant man he took him to himself (1 Samuel 14:52); when Solomon saw an industrious man he preferred him; but David's eyes were upon the faithful in the land, that they might dwell with him: if he saw a godly man, he preferred him, for he was a man after God's own heart, whose countenance beholds the upright.

PAUL: AN APPEAL FOR UNITY

I appeal to you, dear brothers and sisters, by the authority
of our Lord Jesus Christ, to live in harmony with each
other. Let there be no divisions in the church. Rather,
be of one mind, united in thought and purpose.

1 CORINTHIANS 1:10 NLT

There is no shortage of issues that Christians are divided over, and unity often seems hopeless. So how in the world can Christians ever hope to find it? Paul offers a few clues.

For starters, Paul's appeal for unity isn't just wishful thinking. He wants his readers to respond based on the authority of Jesus Christ. However, that authority isn't a top-down decree. Rather, Christ's authority comes from His Spirit dwelling within believers, uniting us together as His body.

Also, unity doesn't necessarily mean uniformity, as there will certainly be times when Christians either misbehave or deviate from the truth. Paul admits as much elsewhere. Rather than demanding uniformity, he compels his readers to unite in their thoughts and purpose.

All Christians should aim to reach the same goals of knowing God and sharing His compassion with others. You should desire to think of God's love and salvation. In your worship and actions you can find a unity that reaches far beyond a doctrinal statement.

◇—— *Day 157* ——◇

THOMAS: A CHANGE OF HEART

*Then Thomas (also known as Didymus) said to the rest of
the disciples, "Let us also go, that we may die with him."*
JOHN 11:16 NIV

◇——————◇

Thomas was a "glass half empty" disciple with a side order of trust
issues. Maybe, like Thomas, you refuse to believe anything unless you
see it with your own eyes.

We have only four total references to things Thomas said—three
of which exemplify his gloomy spirit. The first is when Jesus told
His disciples He was going to see Lazarus, who had recently died.
Thomas assumed the likely outcome would be death for all of them.
The second incident was when Jesus said the disciples should know
where He was going (heaven), but Thomas basically responded, "Nope,
don't have a clue."

The third incident is the most notable. After Jesus rose from the
dead, the disciples told Thomas they had seen Him. Thomas said,
"Unless I see the nail marks in his hands and put my finger where
the nails were, and put my hand into his side, I will not believe"
(John 20:25 NIV).

However, Thomas' final recorded statement indicates a profound
change of heart. When he finally saw Jesus following the Resurrection, Jesus granted his request. Convinced and overwhelmed, Thomas
exclaimed, "My Lord and my God!" (verse 28).

Jesus has always had the power to overcome tough trust issues—
for Thomas and for you.

CLASSICS: CHARLES SPURGEON

JESUS: PREACHING ANYTIME

Jesus saith unto him, Rise, take up thy bed, and walk.
JOHN 5:8 KJV

It was the Sabbath day! Where would Jesus spend that day, and how? He would not spend it, we are quite sure, in any unhallowed manner or in any trifling sort. What would He do? He would do good, for it is lawful to do good on the Sabbath day. Where would He do good? He knew that there was one sight in Jerusalem which was particularly painful—the sight of a number of poor persons, blind, and lame, and halt, who were lying round a pool of water, waiting for a boon which seldom came. He thought He would go and do good there, for there good was most wanted.

Would to God that all Christ's servants felt that the most urgent necessity has the greatest claim upon them—that where there is the most need they ought to exercise the most kindness, and that no way of spending the Sabbath could be better than that of bearing the Gospel of salvation to those who are most in need of it.

MOSES, AARON, AND HUR: A TEAM EFFORT

*So Joshua fought the Amalekites as Moses had ordered, and Moses,
Aaron and Hur went to the top of the hill. As long as Moses
held up his hands, the Israelites were winning, but whenever he
lowered his hands, the Amalekites were winning. When Moses'
hands grew tired, they took a stone and put it under him and he
sat on it. Aaron and Hur held his hands up—one on one side,
one on the other—so that his hands remained steady till sunset.
So Joshua overcame the Amalekite army with the sword.*

EXODUS 17:10–13 NIV

Joshua could not complete his task without the work of Moses. Moses
could not support Joshua in his task without the work of Aaron and
Hur. The work was a full day, and in the end, the task was accomplished. Many times, we find strength for the challenge by relying
on the help of others.

This was not the first time these men had worked together. They
knew each other's strengths and weaknesses and were ready to assist
when the moment called.

When we encourage our family, coworkers, or fellow citizens,
we more effectively complete tasks and accomplish goals. And the
receiving of strength from these same individuals can help us get past
our challenges.

Who is on your team? Or who should be? Reach out to them,
offering and receiving encouragement in Jesus' name.

THE THIEF ON THE CROSS: PARADISE GAINED

*Then he said, "Jesus, remember me when
you come into your kingdom."*

LUKE 23:42 NIV

At Golgotha—also known as "the place of the skull"—three men were crucified one Friday afternoon. Jesus had endured the derision and verbal abuse of Jewish leaders and a gathering crowd of spectators, and He faced it once more from a criminal who ridiculed Him from his own cross.

A second thief hung nearby, but he recognized Jesus was different. He rebuked the other criminal for the words he'd spoken then said, "This man has done nothing wrong" (Luke 23:41 NIV).

Perhaps a criminal's endorsement meant little to the crowd, but it came from the heart. This thief admitted blame, recognized Jesus' innocence, and asked the Creator of all to "remember" him when He entered His kingdom.

Where one thief expressed sarcasm and ridicule, the other expressed remorse and faith. Hanging from the cross, the thief could do nothing to earn God's attention. His past left nothing good for God to consider. He simply trusted in the most profound example of grace. Jesus' words opened eternity to him: "Truly I tell you, today you will be with me in paradise" (Luke 23:43 NIV).

Salvation is easily obtained because the price Jesus paid was beyond comprehension. We are left to offer belief or ridicule. One saves—one separates. Which one do you choose?

CLASSICS: MATTHEW HENRY

THE RETURNING JEWS: WELL BEGUN IS HALF ENDED

*Now in the second year of their coming unto the house of
God at Jerusalem, in the second month, began Zerubbabel
the son of Shealtiel, and Jeshua the son of Jozadak, and the
remnant of their brethren the priests and the Levites, and all
they that were come out of the captivity unto Jerusalem; and
appointed the Levites, from twenty years old and upward,
to set forward the work of the house of the Lord.*

Ezra 3:8 kjv

There was no dispute among the returned Jews whether they should build the temple or no. That was immediately resolved on and that it should be done with all speed. What comfort could they take in their own land if they had not that token of God's presence with them and the record of His name among them? We have here therefore an account of the beginning of that good work.

Observe when it was begun—in the second month of the second year, as soon as ever the season of the year would permit, and when they had ended the solemnities of the Passover. They took little more than half a year for making preparation of the ground and materials so much were their hearts upon it. When any good work is to be done it will be our wisdom to set about it quickly, and not to lose time, yea, though we foresee difficulty and opposition in it. Thus we engage ourselves to it and engage God for us. Well begun (we say) is half ended.

DAVID: BEING THE BETTER MAN

He said to his men, "The LORD forbid that I should do
such a thing to my master, the LORD's anointed, or lay
my hand on him; for he is the anointed of the LORD."

1 SAMUEL 24:6 NIV

David was a faithful servant to an undeserving king. Why? Because he believed Saul had God's backing, and David's first loyalty was to God. If the king threw spears at him, David would just have to duck: there must be a reason God hadn't explained yet. David didn't approve of Saul's behavior, but he wouldn't go against his rightful king even to save his own life.

Was he a fool? By worldly standards, yes. He could have claimed the crown and probably done his people a favor. He would have seemed perfectly justified. But he would have had to compromise his own standards to do it. David refused to become a worse man in order to give his nation a better king.

Instead, he suffered the taunts and threats and waited for God's plan to play out. Eventually, Saul died and the Lord gave Judah a king with impeccable standards, one who wouldn't let himself or God down—for a while anyway.

As children of the King of kings, we should always seek to live up to His standards, no matter what the world thinks.

THE LUNATIC'S FATHER: "HELP MY UNBELIEF!"

*Immediately the father of the child cried out and said
with tears, "Lord, I believe; help my unbelief!"*

MARK 9:24 NKJV

How many of us have spoken these words? Because of our fallenness, each of us is tied to this world. We are accustomed to harsh realities that so often seem overwhelming. They challenge our faith and make it difficult at times to believe God can help us.

This caring father was at his wit's end in seeking relief for his son, whom he watched being terribly afflicted by a demon. Imagine what it was like for him to repeatedly pull his child out of flames and water. His own sanity no doubt hung by a slender thread.

Then Jesus appeared on the scene, telling the father that all things are possible if he could believe. The father, beside himself with desperation, screamed, "I believe; help my unbelief!" For all his misfortune, here was an honest man. Jesus didn't take him to task for his lack of faith. Instead, He met the father and his son at their point of need and healed the boy right then and there.

Cry out to Jesus, even when your doubts seem insurmountable. He will listen.

◇— *Day 164* —◇

CLASSICS: ANDREW MURRAY

MOSES: THE EFFECTS OF BEING WITH GOD

And when Aaron and all the children of Israel saw Moses,
behold, the skin of his face shone; and they were afraid to come
nigh him. And Moses called unto them; and Aaron and all
the rulers of the congregation returned unto him: and Moses
talked with them. And afterward all the children of Israel
came nigh: and he gave them in commandment all that the
LORD had spoken with him in mount Sinai. And till Moses
had done speaking with them, he put a vail on his face.

EXODUS 34:30–33 KJV

The lessons which the story of Moses with the veil on his face teach are very suggestive. Close and continued fellowship with God will in due time leave its mark and make itself manifest before men.

Moses knew not that his face shone: the light of God shining from us will be unconscious; it will but deepen the sense of our being an earthen vessel. The sense of God's presence in a man may often cause others to fear, or at least to feel ill at ease in, his company. When others observe what is to be seen in him, the true believer will know what it is to veil his face and prove by humility and love that he is indeed a man of like passions with those around him. And yet, through all, there will be the proof, too, that he is a man of God, who lives in, and has dealings with, an unseen world.

ISHMAEL: NEVER GIVE UP

And God heard the voice of the lad; and the angel of God called to Hagar out of heaven, and said unto her, What aileth thee, Hagar? Fear not; for God hath heard the voice of the lad where he is.

GENESIS 21:17 KJV

Nobody gets to choose anything about his birth, but we all can choose what to do with the life we've been given.

After Ishmael's birth was arranged by Abram's wife, Sarai, God told his Egyptian mother, Hagar, that Ishmael would live without the support of human society and produce twelve sons who would become leaders. God also said Ishmael would live to the east of his brothers, remaining at odds with everyone.

When Ishmael was a young teenager, he and Hagar were sent packing when Sarai caught him mocking his little brother. They soon ran out of water; however, as Hagar waited for death, God showed her a nearby well and promised that Ishmael would be the father of a great nation.

Later, Ishmael went on to become an archer—an art which someone must have taught him, given the complexities of the craft at the time. And if he lived by his archery, he must have learned to hunt.

All this implies that, even though he had become an outcast, Ishmael never gave up on life. Why? Because "God was with the lad" (Genesis 21:20 KJV), just as He is with all of us.

ISAIAH: HOPE IN GOD

"Darkness as black as night covers all the nations of the earth,
but the glory of the LORD rises and appears over you. All nations
will come to your light; mighty kings will come to see your radiance."
ISAIAH 60:2–3 NLT

◇—————————◇

Where do you find your hope today? Many look to politics in order to change our world. However, there is an even greater power—one that Isaiah said remains at work in God's people but will one day become visible to all.

You can begin to offer hope to a world struggling in darkness by first asking God to show His radiance in you. How might you surrender to God's plans today so that His radiance overshadows the darkness of this world? Relying on your own light only brings frustration and discouragement.

Isaiah assures us that God's radiant light in His people will be undeniable. There's no mistaking God's redemption in this world when lives are restored and made whole. In the face of darkness, your first step is to present yourself to the Lord so that you can more fully reflect Him to others.

JESUS: OUR ETERNAL BREAD

"Do not work for food that spoils, but for food that endures to eternal life, which the Son of Man will give you. For on him God the Father has placed his seal of approval."

JOHN 6:27 NIV

When Jesus taught His disciples how to pray, He told them to ask God for the provision of their daily bread—a food that, in Jesus' day, couldn't be stored up for the long term. He didn't instruct them to pray for storehouses of grain or even reserves of coins that would give them the ability to manage any crisis. They were welcome to ask God for provision, but only daily provision.

How often are we tempted to pray for a long-term solution to our problems and needs? It's almost maddening to think that a God with limitless resources would instruct us to ask for so small a provision, but perhaps Jesus knew something of human ambition and our tendency to rely on our resources rather than God. Ironically, even our best "long-term" solutions are actually quite limited and fleeting.

The presence of Christ in our lives and a long-term faith in Him will never let us down, but our strength, finances, and even relationships may well let us down when we need them the most. The only sure "long-term" bet is the eternal bread of Jesus Himself, who nourishes us and provides for our needs day by day.

CLASSICS: CHARLES SPURGEON

JOSEPH OF ARIMATHEA: THE MAN FOR THE HOUR

Joseph of Arimathaea, an honourable counsellor, which also waited for the kingdom of God, came, and went in boldly unto Pilate, and craved the body of Jesus. And Pilate marvelled if he were already dead: and calling unto him the centurion, he asked him whether he had been any while dead. And when he knew it of the centurion, he gave the body to Joseph. And he bought fine linen, and took him down, and wrapped him in the linen, and laid him in a sepulchre which was hewn out of a rock, and rolled a stone unto the door of the sepulchre.

MARK 15:43–46 KJV

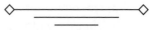

God hath today somewhere, I know not where, in yon obscure cottage of an English village, or in a log-hut far away in the backwoods of America, or in the slums of our back streets, or in our palaces, a man who in maturer life shall deliver Israel, fighting the battles of the Lord. The Lord hath His servant making ready, and when the time shall come, when the hour shall want the man, the man shall be found for the hour. The Lord's will shall be done, let infidels and doubters think what they please.

I see in this advent of Joseph of Arimathea exactly at the needed time, a well of consolation for all who have the cause of God laid upon their hearts. We need not worry our heads about who is to succeed the pastors and evangelists of today: the apostolical succession we may safely leave with our God.

ELIJAH: BE A MENTOR

Elijah and Elisha were on their way from Gilgal.

2 KINGS 2:1 NIV

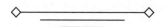

Elisha's relationship to his mentor, Elijah, was essential. He could not fulfill God's call for his life without Elijah. From what the scripture says about their last day together, we discover five essential qualities of a spiritual mentor (2 King 2:1–18).

First, Elijah and Elisha were close. Elisha knew that the time had come for them to part, and he put off the final goodbye as long as he could. Three times Elijah tells Elisha to stay behind. Three times Elisha refused.

Second, Elijah was selfless, willing to give of himself to Elisha even at the last moment. "Tell me, what can I do for you before I am taken from you?" (2 Kings 2:9 NIV).

Third, Elijah continued to teach his mentee, demonstrating practices—such as parting the Jordan waters by striking it with his rolled-up mantle (2 Kings 2:8, 14)—that Elisha needed to complete his journey.

Fourth, Elijah invested in Elisha. He spent time with Elisha and taught him after Elisha obeyed the call to be his successor (2 Kings 19:19–21).

Fifth, Elijah had what Elisha wanted—the mantle, which represented the power and presence of God. Spiritual mentors must have their own vital spiritual life; mentors cannot give another person what they don't possess. Though the mantle had no power of its own, Elijah's faith helped Elisha know, experience, and operate in the power of God until it was time for Elisha to own it for himself.

Mentors can't do for us what we won't do for ourselves, but as Elisha's story illustrates, they can be a fundamental catalyst for spiritual growth.

MICAH: FILLED WITH POWER

But as for me, I am filled with power, with the Spirit
of the Lord, and with justice and might, to declare
to Jacob his transgression, to Israel his sin.

MICAH 3:8 NIV

Micah urged his readers to pay attention to the Lord's warnings of pending judgment. Like his contemporary Isaiah and several other prophets who would come later, Micah repeatedly told God's people to listen. Why? Because their sins were many and their judgment sure.

Like Isaiah, Micah didn't hesitate to denounce the godless rulers, corrupt priests, false prophets, and degenerate people who filled the kingdoms of Israel and Judah (chapters 1–3). Like Isaiah, Micah spoke of days far into the future (chapters 4–5). Like Isaiah, Micah pictured the Lord putting His people on trial (chapter 6). And like Isaiah, Micah contrasted the godlessness of his day with the glorious future ahead (chapter 7).

What inspired Micah to speak out so boldly against the sins of his people? The verse above makes it clear that the Spirit of the Lord gave him the strength.

If God's Spirit lives in us, we too will have the power to speak boldly against injustice and sin—and we'll have the power to deny those sins first in our own lives. We'll be "filled with power" to do whatever it is that God calls us to do.

The key is the indwelling Spirit, which every true Christian possesses, and our conscious, minute-by-minute decision to allow Him to control our lives.

CLASSICS: D. L. MOODY

PAUL: GOD WORKS THROUGH THE WEAK

But God hath chosen the foolish things of the world to confound the wise; and God hath chosen the weak things of the world to confound the things which are mighty; and base things of the world, and things which are despised, hath God chosen, yea, and things which are not, to bring to nought things that are: that no flesh should glory in his presence.

1 CORINTHIANS 1:27–29 KJV

How it ought to encourage us all to believe we may each have a part in building up the walls of the heavenly Zion. In all ages God has delighted to use the weak things.

In his letter to the Corinthians Paul speaks of five things God uses: foolish things, weak things, base things, despised things, and things which are not. What for? "That no flesh should glory in His presence." When we are weak then we are strong.

People often think they have not strength enough; the fact is we have too much strength. It is when we feel that we have no strength of our own, that we are willing God should use us and work through us. If we are leaning on God's strength, we have more than all the strength of the world.

This world is not going to be reached by mere human intellectual power. When we realize we have no strength, then all the fulness of God will flow in upon us. Then we shall have power with God and with man.

PETER: FORWARD IN FAITH

When he had finished speaking, he said to Simon, "Now go out
where it is deeper, and let down your nets to catch some fish."
"Master," Simon replied, "we worked hard all last night and didn't
catch a thing. But if you say so, I'll let the nets down again."
LUKE 5:4–5 NLT

◇━━━━━◇

Simon, also known as Peter, wasn't a rabbi—he was a fisherman. He didn't tell Jesus how to teach or heal, and he didn't expect Jesus to tell him how to fish. But when Jesus gave him an order, Peter knew enough to listen.

He was about to be schooled.

After following Jesus' instructions, the fish that evaded Peter the night before were now lured miraculously into his nets. Soon, Peter and his brother Andrew had to signal another boat to help them with the catch, lest the haul of fish sink their boat. The Gospel writer Luke reports, "When Simon Peter realized what had happened, he fell to his knees before Jesus and said, 'Oh, Lord, please leave me—I'm such a sinful man' " (Luke 5:8 NLT).

Peter learned the limits of his own expertise and the faith required to follow the One who called him to fish for men.

When we rely on our own expertise—whether we're fishermen, plumbers, businessmen, or evangelists—we aren't depending on God to provide what we truly need. Like Peter, let's admit our own sinfulness and move forward in faith alone.

JOB: BELIEVING FOR OURSELVES. . . AND OUR LOVED ONES

His wife said to him, "Are you still maintaining your integrity? Curse God and die!"

JOB 2:9 NIV

There will be times when we must live our lives as if there were only two people in the entire world: ourselves and Jesus Christ.

Remember that Job was blameless and upright. The calamities that hammered him were not in any way God's judgment for moral or spiritual failure—they were purely the result of Satan's malevolence. Job 1 describes Satan asking God's permission to take the man's possessions. Job 2 shows Satan demanding Job's health. God allowed the devil to harm Job physically, though not to kill him. "He still maintains his integrity," God said of Job, "though you incited me against him to ruin him without any reason" (verse 3). Soon, Job's wife was recognizing Job's integrity too, but urging him to drop it. "Curse God and die!" she said.

Sometimes the people closest to us will say and do terrible things that are not easily undone. Words like "curse God and die" are a clear indication that a situation has pushed another person beyond their capacity to act and speak in a godly manner. In situations like this, we must be like Job, holding tightly to Christ alone, believing for ourselves *and our loved ones* that God is still good. When we do, we have the prophet Isaiah's promise: "You will keep him in perfect peace, whose mind is stayed on You, because he trusts in You" (Isaiah 26:3 NKJV).

JUDAS: UNDER THE RADAR

When they arrived, they went upstairs to the room where they were staying. Those present were Peter, John, James and Andrew; Philip and Thomas, Bartholomew and Matthew; James of Alphaeus and Simon the Zealot, and Judas son of James.

ACTS 1:13 NIV

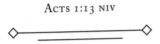

Ever wished you had a different name? Imagine how the apostle Judas (whom scripture also refers to as Lebbaeus, Thaddaeus, and Judas son of James) must have felt after Judas Iscariot betrayed Jesus for thirty pieces of silver.

Even now, as we read the Bible and come across the name of Judas, we automatically think of Iscariot. The Gospel of John (14:22) refers to the apostle as "Judas" and immediately adds the words "not Iscariot" for the sake of clarity.

While we don't know a lot about this particular Judas, one commentator says he "held but a low place among the apostles." But even so, he was among those who traveled back to the upper room after the ascension of Jesus, where they were of one accord in devoting themselves to prayer (Acts 1:14), knowing that Christ had commissioned them to take the Gospel to the ends of the earth. Tradition holds that Judas went on to preach the Gospel far and wide, all the while appearing to be content to live in the shadows of the other apostles.

Often, we do our best work for God under the radar, without public recognition. Are you willing to follow in this Judas's footsteps?

CLASSICS: CHARLES SPURGEON

JESUS: SHARING THE GOSPEL BOLDLY

*In the last day, that great day of the feast, Jesus stood and cried,
saying, If any man thirst, let him come unto me, and drink.*

JOHN 7:37 KJV

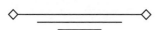

The officers were after our Lord, and He knew it. He could spy them out in the crowd, but He was not therefore in the least afraid, or disconcerted. He reminds me of that minister who, when he was about to preach, was stopped by a soldier, who held a pistol at his head and threatened that if he spake he would kill him. "Soldier," said he, "do your duty; I shall do mine"; and he went on with his preaching.

The Savior, without saying as much in words, said so by His actions. If they were sent to take Him, let them take Him; as for Himself, the time was come to speak boldly, and therefore He stood and cried, saying, "If any man thirst, let him come unto me, and drink."

You have long heard the Gospel, and although you have never given it due attention, still does the good Savior strive with you and press you to be considerate of your own best interests. Jesus urges you to live, persuades you to be saved.

JEPHTHAH: JUST BE OBEDIENT

*Then Jephthah went over to fight the Ammonites, and the
LORD gave them into his hands. He devastated twenty
towns from Aroer to the vicinity of Minnith, as far as
Abel Keramim. Thus Israel subdued Ammon.*

JUDGES 11:32–33 NIV

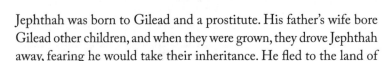

Jephthah was born to Gilead and a prostitute. His father's wife bore
Gilead other children, and when they were grown, they drove Jephthah
away, fearing he would take their inheritance. He fled to the land of
Tob, where a gang of scoundrels badgered him.

But when war with the Ammonites broke out, the elders of Gilead
went to Jephthah—who was known as a warrior—promising to make
him commander if he would fight with them. After Jephthah agreed
to join Israel, the Spirit of the Lord came upon him (Judges 11:29),
and he asked God to give him victory over the Ammonites. Sadly,
as a part of his request, Jephthah made a foolish vow that ultimately
cost his daughter's life. Still, the Lord gave him the victory.

God uses outcasts and flawed people to accomplish His will. Some
of us have committed big sins, others have had big sins committed
against us. Whatever your case, don't let it stop you from answering
God's call. He's been in control the entire time, and He will use your
experiences to strengthen you. Just be obedient.

SOLOMON: "GIVE ME DISCERNMENT, LORD"

Then God said to him: "Because you have asked this thing, and have not asked long life for yourself, nor have asked riches for yourself, nor have asked the life of your enemies, but have asked for yourself understanding to discern justice, behold, I have done according to your words."

1 KINGS 3:11–12 NKJV

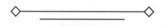

If the Lord appeared to you in a dream and asked you, "What shall I give you?" how would you respond? If you are young, you might ask for a beautiful wife. If you are middle-aged, you might ask for a larger 401k. If you are older, you might ask for a longer life.

None of those things are inherently bad, but when the Lord appeared to Solomon in a dream and asked him that very question, Solomon's answer was better: "Now, O LORD my God, You have made Your servant king instead of my father David, but I am a little child; I do not know how to go out or come in. And Your servant is in the midst of Your people whom You have chosen, a great people, too numerous to be numbered or counted. Therefore give to Your servant an understanding heart to judge Your people, that I may discern between good and evil" (1 Kings 3:7–9 NKJV).

Although Solomon wasn't really a child, because he lacked understanding he felt like one. So he asked God for discernment, and God was pleased.

God may never appear to you in a dream. But He would be just as pleased as He was with Solomon if you asked Him for discernment.

CLASSICS: CHARLES SPURGEON

ASA: THE BATTLE BELONGS TO THE LORD

And Asa had an army of men that bare targets and spears. . . . And there came out against them Zerah the Ethiopian with an host of a thousand thousand, and three hundred chariots; and came unto Mareshah. Then Asa went out against him. . . . And Asa cried unto the LORD his God, and said, LORD, it is nothing with thee to help, whether with many, or with them that have no power: help us, O LORD our God; for we rest on thee, and in thy name we go against this multitude. O LORD, thou art our God; let no man prevail against thee.

2 CHRONICLES 14:8–11 KJV

In the middle of his reign Asa was put to the test by a very serious trial. He was attacked by the Ethiopians, and they came against him in mighty swarms. What a host to be arrayed against poor little Judah—an army of a million footmen and three hundred thousand chariots! All the host that Asa could muster—and he did his best—was but small compared to this mighty band; and it appeared as if the whole land would be eaten up, for the people seemed sufficient to carry away Judea by handfuls.

But Asa believed in God, and therefore when he had mustered his little band he committed the battle to the Lord his God. Read attentively that earnest believing prayer which he offered (verse 11). How grandly he threw all his burden upon God! He declared that he rested in the Most High and believed that God could as well achieve the victory by a few and feeble folk as by a vast army; after this prayer he marched to the battle with holy confidence, and God gave him the victory.

JOSEPH: GOD'S PLAN ALWAYS PREVAILS

"Joseph is still alive! In fact, he is ruler of all Egypt."
GENESIS 45:26 NIV

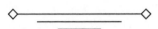

One can't help but wonder at the life of Joseph, the favored son of Jacob and firstborn son of Rachel. God led Joseph through a roller coaster of ups and downs which were instrumental in the creation of the nation of Israel.

Because of his status as privileged son, Joseph was sold into slavery by his jealous brothers. But God brought prosperity to Joseph by leading him to become the servant of an Egyptian official.

Then a false accusation landed Joseph in prison. Still, God was with Joseph. When God inspired him to interpret Pharaoh's dream, he was raised to the second highest position in Egypt. There, God used Joseph not only to prepare Egypt for an upcoming famine but also to provide a place for nascent Israel to prosper and grow into a nation.

Joseph's rise to greatness seemed unlikely, yet God was at work, guiding events in order to provide not only for Joseph but for God's people at large. So when you're going through rough times, don't despair. Remember Joseph's words to his brothers: "You intended to harm me, but God intended it for good" (Genesis 50:20 NIV).

God's plan always prevails.

PAUL: GOD'S REWARDS
ARE MUCH BETTER

*For it seems to me that God has put us apostles on display
at the end of the procession, like those condemned to die in
the arena. We have been made a spectacle to the whole
universe, to angels as well as to human beings.*

1 CORINTHIANS 4:9 NIV

What is the sign of God's blessing on a Christian leader? What do we look for in the experts we trust for spiritual advice? As Paul sought to correct the perceptions of the Corinthian church, he evoked graphic images of prisoners being led to die in the arena at the hands of gladiators or wild animals. Paul argued that the apostles who founded the church were not talented speakers or respectable individuals that you'd put on display. Rather, they were the ones you'd toss into the arena for sport and entertainment.

In a single sentence, Paul removes the glamor from the work of ministry. However, there is an encouraging truth in his message: We need not be wise teachers, experienced orators, flashy miracle workers, or skilled writers in order to share the Gospel message. In fact, Paul was criticized for being a boring speaker! Rather than trying to impress the Corinthians with his skill, Paul said that God uses plain, simple people who commit to doing the hard work of ministry day in and day out. They aren't recognized and they don't stand out.

While anyone can do the essential work of ministry, there are few, if any, earthly accolades for faithfulness and effectiveness. Fortunately, God's rewards are much better—and they'll last forever.

CLASSICS: D. L. MOODY

FOLLOWERS OF JESUS: OUR ROLE IN HIS WORK

Jesus said, Take ye away the stone. Martha, the sister of him that was dead, saith unto him, Lord, by this time he stinketh: for he hath been dead four days.

JOHN 11:39 KJV

Before the act of raising Lazarus could be performed, the disciples had their part to do. Christ could have removed the stone with a word. It would have been very easy for Him to have commanded it to roll away, and it would have obeyed His voice, as the dead Lazarus did when He called him back to life. But the Lord would have His children learn this lesson: that they have something to do towards raising the spiritually dead. The disciples had not only to take away the stone, but after Christ had raised Lazarus they had to "loose and let him go."

It is a question if any man on the face of the earth has ever been converted, without God using some human instrument, in some way. God could easily convert men without us; but that is not His way.

HABAKKUK: WHEN YOU'RE DISMAYED

O LORD my God, my Holy One, you who are eternal—surely you do not plan to wipe us out? O LORD, our Rock, you have sent these Babylonians to correct us, to punish us for our many sins.

<small>HABAKKUK 1:12 NLT</small>

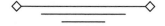

Habakkuk urged his readers to trust the Lord even when evil over-ran their world. The prophet captured a unique dialogue between himself—the Old Testament's "doubting Thomas"—and God.

How long, Habakkuk asked, would God allow the southern king-dom of Judah to perpetrate wickedness before He judged it (1:1–4)? The Lord replied that He was already raising up the Babylonians to carry the people of Judah into exile (1:5–11).

The answer astonished the prophet. Habakkuk asked how God could plan to use such a vile and pagan nation to judge Judah (1:12–2:1). The Lord replied that He would take care of the Babylonians later. Habakkuk must continue to place his faith in God (2:2–20).

That instruction turns out to be the most important message from the Lord to Habakkuk—and all of us. After all, consider who the Lord is. In the words of today's scripture, He is "my God." He's personal—that's why He could have a dialogue with Habakkuk in the first place. Second, the Lord is "my Holy One, you who are eternal." The Lord is eternally and infinitely holy, just, pure, and righteous. He always does what is right. Finally, He is "our Rock"—that is, to the faithful, not to the obstinate, wicked, and rebellious.

When world events dismay us (and they will), the Lord is our Rock, indeed.

MATTHIAS:
DEPENDENCE ON PRAYER

*"Therefore it is necessary to choose one of the men who have
been with us the whole time the Lord Jesus was living
among us, beginning from John's baptism to the time
when Jesus was taken up from us. For one of these must
become a witness with us of his resurrection."*

ACTS 1:21–22 NIV

Imagine how differently the Church would be had prayer been absent
during its infancy!

Judas had hanged himself, leaving a gap in the twelve apostles
originally chosen by Jesus. However, after Jesus' ascension—and after
much prayer by His 120 followers—the apostle Peter recognized
that Psalm 109:8 prophesied a replacement for Judas. So they prayed
again and cast lots on two candidates: Joseph called Barsabbas
(also known as Justus), and Matthias, who had seen Jesus' ministry
firsthand—His baptism, His miracles, and His ascension. The lot
fell Matthias's way and he was added to the eleven.

According to tradition, Matthias later preached the Gospel in
Judea before being martyred. The Book of Common Prayer celebrates
his life on February 24, offering the following prayer: "Grant that
your Church, being delivered from false apostles, may always be
guided and governed by faithful and true pastors. . ."

The apostles, as well as countless other Christians throughout
history, prayed earnestly for the purity of Christ's Church. Do you?

CLASSICS: CHARLES SPURGEON

MANASSEH: FORGIVEN MUCH

And prayed unto him: and he was intreated of him, and heard his supplication, and brought him again to Jerusalem into his kingdom. Then Manasseh knew that the LORD he was God.

2 CHRONICLES 33:13 KJV

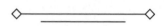

Manasseh is one of the most remarkable characters whose history is written in the sacred pages.

We are accustomed to mention his name in the list of those who greatly sinned, and yet found great mercy. Side by side with Saul of Tarsus, with that great sinner who washed the feet of Jesus with her tears and wiped them with the hairs of her head, and with the thief that died upon the cross—a forgiven sinner at the eleventh hour—we are wont to write the name of Manasseh, who "shed innocent blood very much" and, notwithstanding that, was forgiven and pardoned, finding mercy through the blood of a Savior who had not then died, but whom God foresaw should die, and the merits of whose sacrifice He therefore imputed to so great a transgressor as Manasseh.

JAIRUS: GOD IS ALWAYS FAITHFUL

*Then a man named Jairus, a synagogue leader, came and fell
at Jesus' feet, pleading with him to come to his house because
his only daughter, a girl of about twelve, was dying.*

LUKE 8:41–42 NIV

◇———◇

A parent will do almost anything to prevent a child from dying.

As an official of the synagogue, Jairus undoubtedly knew that
the Pharisees were at odds with Jesus. But his daughter's desperate
condition drove him to seek the healer. Jairus's act of humility at Jesus'
feet—and his faith that Jesus could help—was a sharp contrast to the
Pharisees' arrogance.

As Jesus journeyed toward Jairus's house, He gave a further reason
for faith by healing a woman of a longtime affliction. The timing was
impeccable: mere seconds later, Jairus would need stronger faith.

Immediately afterward, word came that there was no point in
taking up the Master's time—the girl had died. Imagine the grief that
overwhelmed Jairus. But Jesus told him to stop being afraid. "Only
believe," He said, "and she will be made well."

Despite the ridicule of people at his home, Jesus restored the
girl to life.

When we need great faith, we do well to remember the times
God has already shown Himself faithful—just like He did with Jairus.

PAUL: BE A HARD WORKER

We work hard with our own hands. When we are cursed, we bless; when we are persecuted, we endure it; when we are slandered, we answer kindly. We have become the scum of the earth, the garbage of the world—right up to this moment.

1 CORINTHIANS 4:12–13 NIV

Working hard is an admirable trait. Consider the apostle Paul, who worked tirelessly for the Gospel of Christ: He spent years on the mission, covering thousands of miles by foot and by boat. He started, encouraged, and corrected churches. Along the way, he wrote several books of the New Testament—much of the time while facing intense persecution.

Paul's work on behalf of the Gospel was obvious. But he also labored less visibly to shape his character to be more like Jesus. "I do not run like someone running aimlessly," he told the Corinthian Christians, "I do not fight like a boxer beating the air. No, I strike a blow to my body and make it my slave so that after I have preached to others, I myself will not be disqualified for the prize" (1 Corinthians 9:26–27 NIV).

Paul's life and teaching demand that we also work hard, not only outwardly but inwardly. When we do the "heavy lifting" to shape our hearts and minds to become more like Christ, we'll find ourselves stronger when the inevitable troubles of life come on us. We'll be able, like the apostle, to weather our trials with grace.

ELIPHAZ, BILDAD, AND ZOPHAR: WHEN FRIENDS DISAPPOINT YOU

*"If I were you, I would appeal to God; I would lay
my cause before him. . . . We have examined this,
and it is true. So hear it and apply it to yourself."*

JOB 5:8, 27 NIV

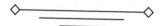

Job's friends, Eliphaz, Bildad, and Zophar certainly meant well. Their hearts were in the right place—they saw their friend was in trouble and went to him to offer help. But in each case, the help they offered moved quickly from godly compassion to a kind of self-absorbed religious rhetoric. You may know the kind: words that make the speaker feel good about his own deep well of wisdom, but don't help the unfortunate hearer at all.

It's critical to remember that scripture says Job was "blameless and upright." As his difficult situation spun further and further out of control, it must have become increasingly challenging to maintain focus on God. We may find ourselves in similar situations: surrounded by difficulties that are only made worse by the careless words of friends and loved ones.

When the storms of life blow their hardest, take hope in the perfect wisdom and love of God. Cling tightly to the undeniable goodness and love of your Savior. "A bruised reed he will not break, and a smoldering wick he will not snuff out," the prophet Isaiah wrote. "In faithfulness he will bring forth justice" (Isaiah 42:3 NIV).

CLASSICS: CHARLES SPURGEON

JOAB: LAYING HOLD OF THE ALTAR

Then tidings came to Joab: for Joab had turned after Adonijah,
though he turned not after Absalom. And Joab fled unto the
tabernacle of the LORD, and caught hold on the horns of the
altar. . . . And Benaiah came to the tabernacle of the LORD, and
said unto him, Thus saith the king, Come forth. And he said,
Nay; but I will die here. And Benaiah brought the king word
again, saying, Thus said Joab, and thus he answered me.

1 KINGS 2:28, 30 KJV

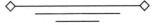

I have two lessons which I am anxious to teach at this time. The first is derived from the fact that Joab found no benefit of sanctuary even though he laid hold upon the horns of the altar of God's house, from which I gather this lesson—that outward ordinances will avail nothing. Before the living God, who is greater and wiser than Solomon, it will be of no avail to any man to lay hold upon the horns of the altar.

But, second, there is an altar—a spiritual altar—whereof if a man do but lay hold upon the horns and say, "Nay; but I will die here," he shall never die; but he shall be safe against the sword of justice forever; for the Lord has appointed an altar in the person of His own dear Son, Jesus Christ, where there shall be shelter for the very vilest of sinners if they do but come and lay hold thereon.

SETH: IMPACTING GENERATIONS TO COME

When Adam had lived 130 years, he had a son in his own likeness, in his own image; and he named him Seth.

Genesis 5:3 niv

Seth was the third son of Adam and Eve—at least the third one mentioned. The Bible is clear that after Cain killed Abel, Seth would be a sort of replacement son for Adam and Eve. The act of murder left one son in the ground and another estranged from his family. The birth of Seth almost seemed like a new start to parenting for the first couple.

Among his descendants were Enoch (whom God took to heaven before he died), Methuselah (who lived 969 years), and Noah (who built the ark). Even Jesus is linked to the line of Seth.

Little more is known about Seth. But given these details about his family line, it's easy to assume that he took what his parents taught him about God and intentionally passed it along.

If you grew up in a Christian home, use what you know to continue impacting your family for Jesus. If you didn't, use what you're learning about Jesus now to begin impacting future generations.

BARNABAS: MODEL OF ENCOURAGEMENT

When [Saul] came to Jerusalem, he tried to join the disciples, but they were all afraid of him, not believing that he really was a disciple. But Barnabas took him and brought him to the apostles.

ACTS 9:26–27 NIV

Barnabas makes for an interesting study. His real name was Joseph, and he came from the Mediterranean island of Cyprus, about 250 miles from Jerusalem. He was part of the Jewish tribe of Levi, which produced Israel's priests, and first appears in Acts 4 shortly after the Holy Spirit's arrival at Pentecost. As a member of the generous early Church, Joseph sold a field and handed the proceeds over to the apostles, who gave him the nickname *Barnabas*: "son of encouragement."

The next time he appears in scripture, Barnabas is encouraging an unlikely new believer named Saul—the same Saul who had once rabidly persecuted Christians before Jesus transformed him on the road to Damascus. The believers' understandable fear of Saul changed when Barnabas stood up for him, bringing the future apostle to the Church leadership for a proper introduction.

God places Barnabases in strategic locations to encourage His people at just the right times. A Barnabas may have already helped you, or one might be coming into your life right now. Either way, be willing to accept the encouragement he provides, and always look for ways to be a Barnabas yourself.

CLASSICS: CHARLES SPURGEON

OLD TESTAMENT SAINTS: EMBRACING FAITH

These all died in faith, not having received the promises, but having seen them afar off, and were persuaded of them, and embraced them, and confessed that they were strangers and pilgrims on the earth.

HEBREWS 11:13 KJV

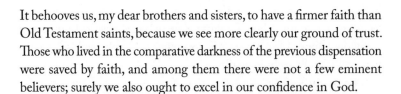

It behooves us, my dear brothers and sisters, to have a firmer faith than Old Testament saints, because we see more clearly our ground of trust. Those who lived in the comparative darkness of the previous dispensation were saved by faith, and among them there were not a few eminent believers; surely we also ought to excel in our confidence in God.

Let the eleventh of Hebrews stand as a triumphal arch with the names of ancient believers recorded thereon: these all died in faith, and they were no mean men; but inasmuch as we enjoy a brighter light and are living under a better economy, we are called upon to be their superiors in faith. Our faith should be clearer, calmer, stronger, more effectual in working; we should do greater things than these in the name of Jesus.

Being endowed more richly with the Spirit of God, the modern church should attempt grander works than Israel ever thought upon, and so there should be a shining more and more unto the perfect day.

JESUS: FORETASTES OF HEAVEN

*"Go back and report to John what you have seen and
heard: The blind receive sight, the lame walk, those who
have leprosy are cleansed, the deaf hear, the dead are
raised, and the good news is proclaimed to the poor."*

LUKE 7:22 NIV

Two thousand years ago, Jesus Christ's earthly ministry gave the
believing men, women, youth, and children around Him amazing
foretastes of eternity. Those foretastes cover a wide horizon: from seeing
individuals raised from the dead to seeing others healed spiritually,
physically, and psychologically.

Let's not assume, however, that these wonderful foretastes of
heaven aren't ours to experience *today*. As followers of Jesus Christ,
all our sins—past, present, and future—are already forgiven, yet we
experience it anew each time we confess them. Immediately afterward,
we want to slow down and savor that experience of being forgiven. If
we do, we enjoy a delicious foretaste of heaven.

Even though our salvation is all-encompassing, it doesn't mean
we don't sin—any more than it means we never get sick, suffer trials,
wrestle with temptation, fail, and die. While we're on this planet, aren't
these means helping us to continue longing for heaven?

We never want to miss our critical need to slow down and savor
each specific foretaste on this side of eternity. In a real sense, these
are Jesus Christ's rich and valuable gifts to us.

JUDE: COMMITTED TO GOD'S TRUTH

*But you, dear friends, by building yourselves up in your
most holy faith and praying in the Holy Spirit, keep
yourselves in God's love as you wait for the mercy of
our Lord Jesus Christ to bring you to eternal life.*

Jude 20–21 niv

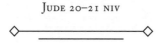

The New Testament letter of Jude bears some striking similarities to 2 Peter. Jude—believed by many to be a half brother of Jesus (Matthew 13:55; Mark 6:3)—actually quoted Peter in verses 17 and 18: "But, dear friends, remember what the apostles of our Lord Jesus Christ foretold. They said to you, 'In the last times there will be scoffers who will follow their own ungodly desires'" (2 Peter 3:3). And Jude made several other allusions found in the second chapter of 2 Peter: about the imprisonment of fallen angels; the destruction of Sodom and Gomorrah; proud sinners who speak evil of "celestial beings," and false teachers and their condemnation. Jude even echoed some of Peter's descriptions of false teachers: compare "mists driven by a storm" (2 Peter 2:17) and "clouds without rain, blown along by the wind" (Jude 12).

In today's world, some might accuse Jude of plagiarism. But we can assume that God was simply directing Jude to confirm and fortify the important message Peter had shared.

False teaching destroys lives. Careful study, good doctrine, and obedience to God's Word makes us strong, ready for any and every attack of the world, the flesh, and the devil. We can, as Jude urges in today's scripture, build ourselves up in the faith and keep ourselves in God's love. But to do so, we must commit ourselves to God's truth.

CLASSICS: ANDREW MURRAY

PAUL: A PATTERN FOR SINFUL MEN

Wherefore I beseech you, be ye followers of me.
1 CORINTHIANS 4:16 KJV

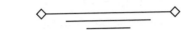

Our Lord took Paul, a man of like passions with ourselves, and made him a pattern of what He could do for one who was the chief of sinners. And Paul, the man who, more than any other, has set his mark on the church, has ever been appealed to as a pattern man.

In his mastery of divine truth and his teaching of it; in his devotion to his Lord and his self-consuming zeal in His service; in his deep experience of the power of the indwelling Christ and the fellowship of His cross; in the sincerity of his humility and the simplicity and boldness of his faith; in his missionary enthusiasm and endurance—in all this, and so much more, "the grace of our Lord Jesus was exceeding abundant in him."

DAVID: FAITHFUL IN HOLDING BACK

*"The LORD rewards everyone for their righteousness and
faithfulness. The LORD delivered you into my hands today,
but I would not lay a hand on the LORD's anointed."*

1 SAMUEL 26:23 NIV

Sometimes, faithfulness means inaction.

When Saul got wind of the fact that David was hiding from him
in the wilderness of Ziph (1 Samuel 26:2–3), he took three thousand
men in search of him. But David outfoxed him, showing up at Saul's
camp early one morning while everybody was sleeping. His cousin
Abishai wanted to kill Saul on the spot, but David, recognizing that
Saul was God's anointed, restrained Abishai.

For the second time, David's faithfulness to the Lord out-
weighed an opportunity to kill his oppressor. The Hebrew word
rendered "faithfulness" in this verse means "moral fidelity." To kill
Saul would have been equal to being unfaithful to God, and David
wouldn't do that. He had other moral failings over the course of
his life, but here he saw his situation through spiritual eyes, and it
made all the difference.

Are you on the cusp of making a seemingly justified decision
that you know deep down would mean unfaithfulness to God? Stop
and look at the situation through spiritual eyes. Don't take any action
that God's Word prohibits.

SAMSON: BAD ATTITUDE, STILL BLESSED

Now he was suddenly very thirsty. He called out to GOD, "You have given your servant this great victory. Are you going to abandon me to die of thirst and fall into the hands of the uncircumcised?" So God split open the rock basin in Lehi; water gushed out and Samson drank.

JUDGES 15:18–19 MSG

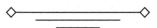

After taking out a group of Philistine soldiers with a makeshift weapon, Samson sang a brief song: "With a donkey's jawbone I made heaps of donkeys of them. With a donkey's jawbone I killed an entire company" (Judges 15:16 MSG). Suddenly, he realized he was thirsty.

Samson's thirst was "a natural effect of the great pains he had taken," John Wesley wrote. "And perhaps there was the hand of God therein, to chastise him for not making mention of God in his song, and to keep him from being proud of his strength."

Even Samson's prayer afterward has an edge to it. He seemed exasperated by his thirst and God's "abandonment." In His mercy, God miraculously provided water.

That's the amazing thing about God: He often blesses us with good things even when we fail Him—when our hearts are cold and distracted, when we've consciously chosen to sin. Let's be sure to acknowledge His blessings, but also to root out our attitudes and actions that separate us from God. If we can consistently do that, we'll be spiritually stronger than Samson ever was.

EZRA: APPALLED BY SIN

*When I heard this, I tore my tunic and cloak, pulled hair
from my head and beard and sat down appalled. Then
everyone who trembled at the words of the God of Israel
gathered around me because of this unfaithfulness of the
exiles. And I sat there appalled until the evening sacrifice.*

EZRA 9:3–4 NIV

Ezra was a real bad-news-bearer for the Jews who still lived in Jerusalem. As an exile, he had been far away from the homeland and the temple ruins—so he now valued them all the more. As a descendant of Aaron, he was a dedicated student of the Law.

Many Jews in Jerusalem, he found, seemed to value none of these things. Familiarity had bred contempt. They had diluted their faith and way of life to a point where they were hardly recognizable as Jews. By marrying foreign women, they were, in effect, destroying their heritage—since "Jewishness" was traditionally passed through the maternal line. These women also worshiped pagan gods and would raise their children to do the same. No wonder Ezra was appalled.

If Jesus came back today, would He think we had diluted His message? Maybe we need to give that some thought before the Lord shows up, like Ezra, pulling His beard in frustration.

CLASSICS: MATTHEW HENRY

ISAAC: PRIORITIZING PRAYER

And Isaac went out to meditate in the field at
the eventide: and he lifted up his eyes, and saw,
and, behold, the camels were coming.

GENESIS 24:63 KJV

Some think Isaac expected the return of his servants about this time
and went out on purpose to meet them. But, it should seem, he went
out to take the advantage of a silent evening and a solitary field for
meditation and prayer.

Our walks in the field are then truly pleasant when in them we
apply ourselves to meditation and prayer. We there have a free and
open prospect of the heavens above us and the earth around us, and
the host and riches of both, by the view of which we should be led to
the contemplation of the Maker and owner of all. Merciful providences
are then doubly comfortable when they find us in the way of our duty.

Some think Isaac was now praying for good success in this affair
and meditating upon that which was proper to encourage his hope in
God concerning it; and now when he sets himself, as it were, upon his
watchtower, to see what God would answer him, *he sees the camels coming.*

EUTYCHUS: STAY ALERT

Seated in a window was a young man named Eutychus,
who was sinking into a deep sleep as Paul talked on
and on. When he was sound asleep, he fell to the ground
from the third story and was picked up dead.

ACTS 20:9 NIV

If you have ever felt yourself dozing off during a church service, then you might have some sympathy toward young Eutychus.

When the apostle Paul had arrived in Troas, Eutychus and many others gathered excitedly in a third-floor room to hear the great man speak. Paul, of course, had plenty to say and was still speaking at midnight. Eutychus, who had probably been working all day, dozed off and tumbled from the window ledge he had been sitting on!

Thankfully, someone noticed and raised the alarm. But the fall from the third floor had a predictable outcome: Eutychus was dead. Paul, however, ran downstairs, threw his arms around him, restored him to life, had a snack. . .and carried on preaching.

If your preacher goes on and on, it might be because he has something worth saying. Like Paul, he might be speaking words of life. Eutychus got to experience the power of those words firsthand. But you and I don't need to fall out a window to benefit from a sermon. We only need to stay alert, listen, and believe.

ONESIMUS: "NOW HE IS VERY USEFUL"

I appeal to you to show kindness to my child, Onesimus. . . .
Onesimus hasn't been of much use to you in the
past, but now he is very useful to both of us.

PHILEMON 10–11 NLT

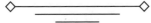

When Onesimus ran away from his owner in Colosse, his flight took him to Rome. In seeking his own security, Onesimus made a remarkable discovery: the man who had converted his master to Christianity, Paul, was in the city too. But their roles were now reversed. Paul was under house arrest awaiting trial while Onesimus could visit him freely.

Onesimus became a Christian and began doing for Paul many of the same tasks he had done for his owner, Philemon. Eventually, Paul decided Onesimus and Philemon needed to be reconciled.

Onesimus would return to a city where he had been neither a Christian nor a dependable slave. He must have wondered how the Colossians could be certain of his transformed life. Paul reassured Onesimus in two ways: First, he sent Tychicus to accompany him. Second, he praised Onesimus in the general letter to the Colossians and in the personal one of Philemon, writing one sentence in both letters with his own hand to prove their authenticity (Colossians 4:18; Philemon 19).

There was a time when all of us, like Onesimus, hadn't "been of much use" to God or other people. But when we accepted Jesus Christ as Lord and Savior, we became "very useful." Today, let's commit to serving God and mankind with every power our Lord gives us.

CLASSICS: MATTHEW HENRY

JOB: FRESH GLORY

My root was spread out by the waters, and the dew lay all night upon my branch. My glory was fresh in me, and my bow was renewed in my hand.

JOB 29:19–20 KJV

Job was like a tree whose root is not only spread out, which fixes it and keeps it firm, so that it is in no danger of being overturned, but *spread out by the waters,* which feed it and make it fruitful and flourishing, so that it is in no danger of withering. And, as he thought himself blessed with the fatness of the earth, so also with the kind influences of heaven too, for the *dew lay all night upon his branch.*

Providence favored him and made all his enjoyments comfortable and all his enterprises successful. Let none think to support their prosperity with what they draw from this earth without that blessing which is derived from above. God's favor being continued to Job, in the virtue of that his glory was still fresh in him. Those about him had still something new to say in his praise and needed not to repeat the old stories: and it is only by constant goodness that men's glory is thus preserved fresh and kept from withering and growing stale.

DAVID: PRAYING THE PRAYER OF THE IMPERFECT

Don't put your servant on trial, for no one is innocent before you.
PSALM 143:2 NLT

Have you ever felt like your prayer life was awkward? If so, you might have been tempted to quit.

When King David tried to speak the pain in his heart, he understood that his moral shortcomings caused him to speak imperfectly to a perfect God. But he didn't give up. He kept praying the prayer of the imperfect, and God changed the king's status.

Through prayer, the guilty can stand before the Innocent, asking for and accepting God's forgiveness—despite personal failure.

Even when you are guilty, God can declare you "not guilty" when you confess your inadequacy and acknowledge His perfection. This declaration has nothing to do with your goodness and everything to do with God's gift of grace.

Your prayer life will improve when you start seeing your imperfection as the starting point of God's plan for transformation.

CLASSICS: D. L. MOODY

PETER: REPENTANCE AND RESTORATION

*But Peter, standing up with the eleven, lifted up his voice,
and said unto them, Ye men of Judaea, and all ye that dwell
at Jerusalem, be this known unto you, and hearken to my
words. . . . And it shall come to pass in the last days, saith
God, I will pour out of my Spirit upon all flesh: and your
sons and your daughters shall prophesy, and your young men
shall see visions, and your old men shall dream dreams.*

ACTS 2:14, 17 KJV

◇——————◇

When Peter denied his Master, he was a very different man from what
he was on the day of Pentecost. He got out of communion with his
Lord, and the word of a servant nearly frightened him out of his life.
He denied his Master with oaths and cursing.

How terribly a man falls when he loses faith and courage. But he
was restored; look at him on the day of Pentecost. If that maid had
been present and heard him preach the marvelous sermon recorded
in the Acts, I can imagine she would be the most amazed person in
all Jerusalem. "Why," she says, "I saw him a few days ago, and he was
terribly alarmed at being called a disciple of Christ; now he stands
up boldly for this same Christ; he has no shame now."

God used him mightily on the day of Pentecost, as he preached
to that vast congregation, some of whom were the very murderers of
his Lord and Master. But he could not use Peter till he had repented
of his cowardice and had been restored to faith and courage.

PAUL: CHANGED TO SERVE OTHERS

When I was with the Jews, I lived like a Jew to bring the Jews to Christ. . . . When I am with the Gentiles who do not follow the Jewish law, I too live apart from that law so I can bring them to Christ. But I do not ignore the law of God; I obey the law of Christ.

1 CORINTHIANS 9:20–21 NLT

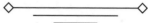

Paul first appears in the New Testament as Saul of Tarsus, a zealous Jew who tried to stamp out the Christian faith. Following a heart-to-heart talk with Jesus on the road to Damascus, Saul was baptized. After his conversion, the apostles in Jerusalem accepted him, but some Christians looked upon him with suspicion. He eventually went to Tarsus. Later, Barnabas went there and rescued Saul from obscurity, and the Holy Spirit sent them on a missionary journey.

On the island of Cyprus, Saul made his first recorded Gentile convert: Sergius Paulus, the Roman governor. After this success, Saul became known as Paul, derived from the Latin family name, Paulus. Apparently, Paul's name change signified his desire to embrace his role as an apostle to the Gentiles (Acts 13:7–9, 13).

With the new birth and baptism, a person leaves behind a past of hate, rage, and sin to embrace a better life—and to better the lives of others. How are you serving others, both the Christians and non-believers around you? Today, ask God to lead you into the most effective ministry for His glory.

DAVID: WALK BY FAITH

"You go out and come in with me in the army and it is good in my eyes. I have found nothing wrong in you from the day you came to me until this day. But you are not pleasing in the eyes of the leaders."

1 Samuel 29:6 NLV

David found himself in a real dilemma when the Philistine king, Achish, called him to fight against Israel. On the run from King Saul, David and his men had found refuge with the enemy Philistines. Now it was time to show David's true allegiance.

Bible commentator Adam Clarke points out that if David had gone into battle, he would have had his choice between two sins: fight for the Philistines (thereby opposing God's chosen people) or deceive and oppose Achish (who had treated David hospitably).

However, other Philistine leaders, knowing that David was a celebrated warrior of Israel, objected. So Achish ultimately sent David away from the battlefield.

"God, therefore," Clarke wrote, "so ordered it in His mercy that he was not permitted to go to a battle in which he was sure to be disgraced, whatever side he took, or with what success so ever he might be crowned."

David was in a pickle of his own making, but God still delivered him.

The lesson isn't to behave recklessly and wait for God to sort things out. But know that even when you sin, He is gracious and ready to forgive. Whatever dilemmas you may face, trust God to show you the way as you walk by faith.

CLASSICS: CHARLES SPURGEON

JESUS: LOVING TO THE UTTERMOST

*Are not two sparrows sold for a farthing? and one of them
shall not fall on the ground without your Father. But
the very hairs of your head are all numbered. Fear ye not
therefore, ye are of more value than many sparrows.*

MATTHEW 10:29–31 KJV

It is most delightful to see how familiarly our Lord Jesus talked with
His disciples. He was very great, and yet He was among them as one
that serveth; He was very wise, but He was gentle as a nurse with her
children; He was very holy and far above their sinful infirmities, but
He condescended to men of low estate; He was their Master and Lord,
and yet their friend and servant. He talked with them, not as a superior
who domineers, but as a brother full of tenderness and sympathy.

You know how sweetly He once said to them, "If it were not so, I
would have told you"; and thus He proved that He had hidden nothing
from them that was profitable to them. He laid bare His very heart
to them: His secret was with them. He loved them to the uttermost
and caused the full river of His life to flow for their behalf.

GAIUS: HONORABLE MENTION

*I thank God that I did not baptize any of
you except Crispus and Gaius.*

1 CORINTHIANS 1:14 NIV

It's encouraging to be noticed, but we often want more than that.

When some of the Corinthian believers were bragging about who had brought the Gospel to them or who had baptized them, Paul took them to task like a frustrated parent, asking who did the work in them. Was it Paul or Cephas, or was it the Messiah?

Gaius is one of the few Corinthians Paul baptized. And apparently, Paul was confident he wasn't going to brag about who dipped him. Gaius was more than just noticed—He was found trustworthy, thus earning himself an honorable mention.

Gaius showed up later as Paul's host on his third missionary journey. In fact, he was host to the entire local church, which met in Gaius's home. He was still trustworthy and had now shown himself hospitable and concerned with the well-being of his fellow believers.

As believers, many of us don't serve in ways that others notice, yet what we do is vitally important. Whether we quietly provide hospitality, give money, or pray faithfully, we—like Gaius—will certainly receive an honorable mention from God. What could be better than hearing our Lord's "well done, good and faithful servant"?

MORDECAI: FAITHFUL IN ALL THINGS

Mordecai the Jew was second in rank to King Xerxes, preeminent among the Jews, and held in high esteem by his many fellow Jews, because he worked for the good of his people and spoke up for the welfare of all the Jews.

ESTHER 10:3 NIV

There are a couple of reasons that the Old Testament hero Mordecai rose in rank. First, he providentially foiled an assassination attempt on King Xerxes' life, which (equally providentially) was brought to Xerxes's mind just before the Jews themselves were set to be killed. Second, Mordecai inspired Queen Esther to do the right thing—to stand up for her people even though she herself faced death. That couldn't have been easy for Mordecai, given that he had raised his younger cousin as if she had been his daughter.

Mordecai always did the right thing, even though it was difficult. He chose integrity and courage over comfort and security. As he did so, God not only strengthened Mordecai's resolve but elevated him to a place of greater influence.

The small stands you make right now could lead to better opportunities, both for yourself and God's kingdom, down the road. Know that as you do the right thing, no matter who is watching or what others think, God notices. . .and He gives you the strength you need to press on.

Jesus once said, "He that is faithful in that which is least is faithful also in much: and he that is unjust in the least is unjust also in much" (Luke 16:10 KJV). Commit today to be faithful in all things.

JESUS: A CALL TO SACRIFICE

He that findeth his life shall lose it: and he that
loseth his life for my sake shall find it.

MATTHEW 10:39 KJV

When the Lord told His disciples they must take up the cross and follow Him, they could have little understanding of His meaning. He wished to rouse them to earnest thought and so prepare them for the time when they should see Him carrying His cross.

From the Jordan, where He had presented Himself to be baptized and reckoned among sinners, onward, He carried the cross always in His heart. That is to say, He was always conscious that the sentence of death, because of sin, rested on Him and that He must bear it to the uttermost.

As the disciples thought on this and wondered what He meant by it, one thing only helped them—it was the thought of a man who was sentenced to death and carries his cross to the appointed place. Christ had said at the same time: "He that loseth his life shall find it."

HEZEKIAH: ONE MAN'S DECISIONS

He in the first year of his reign, in the first month, opened
the doors of the house of the LORD, and repaired them.

2 CHRONICLES 29:3 KJV

Hezekiah's father, Ahaz, was a horrible example. After being defeated in battle, he decided the gods of the enemy had brought them victory. So he set up altars to those gods all over Judah.

But when Hezekiah became king at the age of twenty-five, he immediately turned the hearts of his people toward the true God. Beginning with repairing the temple doors, he put the Levites to work cleaning the neglected place of worship and restoring its furnishings to their former splendor. He gathered the rulers of Jerusalem to the temple to offer a sacrifice. Many came to see and take part in the worship.

Later, Hezekiah sent messages throughout the land that all should come to Jerusalem to keep the Passover, which had not been observed for a long time. The joy that flowed during these celebrations released the nations' suppressed longing for fellowship with their God.

Because of Hezekiah's willingness to follow God instead of walking in his father's sins, the whole nation benefited. Sometimes, just one man's decisions can change an entire generation.

JAMES: THE VALUE OF HARDSHIP

Therefore, get rid of all moral filth and the evil that is so prevalent and humbly accept the word planted in you, which can save you.

JAMES 1:21 NIV

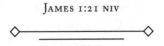

James, who was probably writing to Jewish converts to Christianity who were dispersed abroad (James 1:1), wanted them to understand that their trials could produce lasting spiritual results.

Building on that thought, he told them to get rid of all filthiness and other forms of wickedness as they humbly accepted the Word of God. Disposing of wickedness isn't something we can do in our flesh, which cries out for wickedness. Instead, it comes as we hear, read, meditate on, and submit to the Word of God. Humbly accepting God's Word means we don't argue against it or justify our sin when scripture confronts it. Rather, we recognize the darkness of our hearts, confessing and repenting.

You will never fully escape the pull of wickedness in this world, but the degree to which you struggle with it is inversely proportional to the amount of time you spend interacting with and submitting to the Word of God. If the world's pull feels stronger than it should, find more time to hide the Word in your heart so that you won't sin against God (Psalm 119:11).

CALEB: GOD-INSPIRED OPTIMISM

"On that day Moses swore to me, 'The land. . .will be
your inheritance. . .forever, because you have followed
the LORD my God wholeheartedly.'. . . The LORD
helping me, I will drive them out just as he said."

JOSHUA 14:9, 12 NIV

A negative spirit is always a mark of self-reliance. To follow God wholeheartedly, as Caleb did, requires an unwavering trust in God's encouragement and empowerment. Along with that comes a confident optimism in God's presence and His power in our lives—an eagerness to engage with God in His mission.

Caleb, forty-five years earlier, exuded this confident optimism. And now, at eighty-five years old, he welcomed the challenge to engage in battle against the Anakites.

"Been there, done that" never entered Caleb's lexicon. He refused to leave the battle for the young men of his clan. Seeing the finish line of the race he started decades earlier, he redoubled his effort and charged into the hill country, confident in *God's* ability, not his own.

Imagine the Anakites, shaking in their size 25 boots as Caleb approached, weapons drawn. They never stood a chance in the face of Caleb's divinely empowered onslaught. In fact, Caleb's story was still being told years later (Judges 1:20).

Are there challenges you've been waiting years to accomplish? Are you ready to reengage, confident you're accomplishing what God has called you to do? Follow Caleb's example of faith, and leave a legacy worthy of God's warriors.

TIMOTHY: FIGHT THE GOOD FIGHT

*Fight the good fight of the faith. Take hold of the eternal
life to which you were called when you made your good
confession in the presence of many witnesses.*

1 TIMOTHY 6:12 NIV

Timothy was called both to minister and to put off the cares of this world—namely, the love of money that leads so many astray (1 Timothy 6:10). He was to fight the good fight of faith, advancing the Gospel.

Timothy's vocational calling might have differed from yours, but his spiritual calling was quite similar. You're to be in the world, but not of it (John 17:15–17). You're to set your mind on things above, not on the things of this earth (Colossians 3:2). You're to be transformed by the renewing of your mind, not conformed to this world (Romans 12:2). As such, you're called to fight the good fight as well.

How is your fight going? If you don't sense a battle, then you probably aren't engaged in one. If, however, you feel the tension between this world and the next and are actively engaged in overcoming your sinful habits, then you're right where God wants you. Don't stop now. The world needs to see your witness. Wrestle, fight, and pray—eternity is at stake for all of humanity.

CLASSICS: MATTHEW HENRY

MOSES: FOLLOWING GOD'S DIRECTIONS

*And Moses reared up the tabernacle, and fastened his
sockets, and set up the boards thereof, and put in the bars
thereof, and reared up his pillars. And he spread abroad
the tent over the tabernacle, and put the covering of the
tent above upon it; as the LORD commanded Moses.*

EXODUS 40:18–19 KJV

Moses not only did all that God directed him to do, but in the order
that God appointed for God will be sought in the due order. To each
particular there is added an express reference to the divine appointment,
which Moses governed himself by as carefully and conscientiously
as the workmen did and therefore, as before, so here it is repeated, *as
the LORD commanded Moses,* seven times in less than fourteen verses
(Exodus 40:19–33).

Moses himself, as great a man as he was, would not pretend to vary
from the institution, neither to add to it nor diminish from it, in the
least punctilio. Those that command others must remember that their
Master also is in heaven, and they must do as they are commanded.

JOSEPH: TRUSTING GOD'S PROMISES

*Then Joseph said to his brothers, "I am about to die. But God will
surely come to your aid and take you up out of this land to the land
he promised on oath to Abraham, Isaac and Jacob." And Joseph
made the Israelites swear an oath and said, "God will surely come
to your aid, and then you must carry my bones up from this place."*

<small>GENESIS 50:24–25 NIV</small>

Joseph spent most of his life in Egypt, far from the land that God had
promised to his father, Jacob; yet on his deathbed, at the age of 110,
Joseph was confident that God would bring His people back to the
Promised Land. How did Joseph have such faith? Perhaps because
he experienced God's work firsthand multiple times.

God had raised Joseph from slavery to prosperity as a servant of
the captain of Pharaoh's guard, then from prison to the second most
powerful position in Egypt. Joseph had been in hard places before,
but he had seen how God was faithful. So at his deathbed, Joseph
fully expected God to be faithful to the promises He had made to
his forefathers.

While God promises many blessings to believers, He doesn't
say our life on this earth will be easy. In fact, the Bible teaches that
believers will experience troubles and even persecution. But no matter
how difficult life may be, we can rest assured that "in all things God
works for the good of those who love him" (Romans 8:28 NIV). God
is with us even in times of trials, and He will be faithful.

DAVID: NOT ONE TO GLOAT

When David was told that it was the men from Jabesh
Gilead who had buried Saul, he sent messengers to them
to say to them, "The LORD bless you for showing this
kindness to Saul your master by burying him."

2 SAMUEL 2:4–5 NIV

After David was anointed king of Israel in Hebron, he learned that
the men of Jabesh-gilead had buried King Saul. Perhaps the men of
Judah wanted to point the finger at the men of Jabesh-gilead, thinking
David might be displeased by their actions. But either way, David,
who had likely inquired about Saul's body because he wanted to honor
him with a proper burial, sent a blessing back to them.

Regardless of how far Saul had gone astray, he was the Lord's
anointed and was worthy of respect. David always had a firm understanding of this concept, even when he was on the run from Saul,
fearing for his life. This is consistent with Proverbs 24:17–18 (NIV):
"Do not gloat when your enemy falls; when they stumble, do not let
your heart rejoice, or the LORD will see and disapprove and turn his
wrath away from them."

How do you respond when one of your enemies falls—either
literally or figuratively? Do you gloat? Or do you, like David, send
your blessings and prayers?

ZECHARIAH: LOOK TO THE FUTURE WITH HOPE

In the eighth month of the second year of Darius,
the word of the LORD came to Zechariah the son of
Berechiah, the son of Iddo the prophet, saying, "The
LORD has been very angry with your fathers."

ZECHARIAH 1:1–2 NKJV

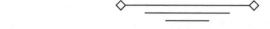

It was business as usual in Israel: the people were following the bad example of their forefathers. The rebuilding of the Temple had faltered for years before stopping altogether.

But neither the prophet Zechariah nor the Lord wanted it to stay that way. That's why God spoke again to His people. The people needed encouragement to build again, so God not only told them that their fathers were wrong but also called them to repent.

Zechariah's message looked forward—and it included numerous references to the work God would do in his own generation and beyond, culminating in the Messiah's salvation.

Like the people of Zechariah's age, we too will face terrible trials. Are you faltering? Remember that God did not desert Zechariah's people, and He will not forget you either. Look to the future with hope.

◇— *Day 218* —◇

PAUL: THE REWARD WILL COME

*And let us not be weary in well doing: for in due
season we shall reap, if we faint not.*
GALATIANS 6:9 KJV

Don't let anybody fool you: the Christian life is tough. If it weren't,
why would the apostle Paul write what he did in Galatians 6:9?

There is a weariness in well doing. There are those moments when
we feel like fainting—or giving up, as newer translations of the Bible
say. In the context, Paul was describing the difficulties of restoring
a fellow Christian who's fallen into sin. We are to carry each other's
burden to fulfill the law of Christ (verse 2). But we must beware of
the danger of falling into sin ourselves, perhaps by thinking we are
better than our sinning brother (verses 1, 4).

This is the well-known passage that describes sowing and reaping,
spiritually speaking: "Be not deceived; God is not mocked: for whatsoever a man soweth, that shall he also reap" (verse 7). It's all work!
Sowing, reaping, restoring fellow believers who stumble. . .

The good news is in verse 9, where Paul—speaking for God—
promises a harvest. There will be a payoff for the hard work we put
into our Christian lives. But we can't faint. We don't dare give up.
Stay on task, do your work faithfully, allow God to provide the strength
. . .and then wait for the reward. It will come.

CLASSICS: D. L. MOODY

ABRAHAM: SIMPLY A SOJOURNER

*By faith Abraham, when he was called to go out into
a place which he should after receive for an inheritance,
obeyed; and he went out, not knowing whither he went.
By faith he sojourned in the land of promise, as in a strange
country, dwelling in tabernacles with Isaac and Jacob, the
heirs with him of the same promise: for he looked for a city
which hath foundations, whose builder and maker is God.*

HEBREWS 11:8–10 KJV

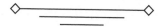

When Abraham once caught sight of the holy city with the eyes of
his understanding, which were opened to see its glories, then it was
that he "confessed that he was a stranger and a pilgrim on the earth,
and that he looked for a city which hath foundations, whose builder
and maker is God." He had no desire to stay here—heaven was his
home—so much brighter, so much better than anything he could
find here below.

We must all feel we are but pilgrims and sojourners here; our home
is above. Our feet are often weary and our hearts heavy; but never
mind that, let us look forward to that "city which hath foundations."
Weary we may be, and often are, but, blessed be God! There is a place
of rest. "There is rest for the weary there."

GAMALIEL: SURRENDER THE SITUATION

"Therefore, in the present case I advise you: Leave these men alone!
Let them go! For if their purpose or activity is of human origin,
it will fail. But if it is from God, you will not be able to stop
these men; you will only find yourselves fighting against God."

ACTS 5:38–39 NIV

Gamaliel had seen this before: Theudas and then Judas the Galilean claimed to be men of significance. They were killed and their followers scattered.

But with Jesus' apostles it was different. Long after Jesus' death on a cross, His followers were bolder than ever. This prompted Gamaliel, a Pharisee and "a teacher of the law, who was honored by all the people" (Acts 5:34 NIV), to advise the Sanhedrin to leave Peter and the apostles alone. If God was with these men, they would prevail no matter what the Sanhedrin wanted to do about them.

Gamaliel is mentioned only briefly in scripture, but his message is profound, even in our day. Instead of taking matters into our own hands, using whatever social, political, or spiritual clout we think we have, trust that God knows best.

This is an act of surrender and deep trust in our heavenly Father. Whatever we might think we can do to get out of a difficult situation, it's best to simply give it over to God to do with as He wills. As the apostle Paul said, "when I am weak, then I am strong" (2 Corinthians 12:10 NIV). It is only in trusting God's strength that we truly find ours.

ABRAHAM: PERSISTENT INTERCESSION

*The men turned away and went toward Sodom,
but Abraham remained standing before the LORD.*

GENESIS 18:22 NIV

The sin in the city of Sodom had reached such a grievous level that God told Abraham He intended to destroy the city. But instead of giving up on Sodom, where his nephew Lot and his family lived, Abraham began bargaining with God for the city's destiny.

Abraham's prayer of intercession began with him pleading with God to spare Sodom on account of fifty righteous people. From there, he asked God if He would have mercy on the city for forty-five righteous people. . .then forty. . .then thirty-five. . .then thirty. . .then twenty. . .then finally ten.

From a human perspective, it's easy to wonder if God might have grown impatient with Abraham's haggling. But He didn't. In fact, He assured Abraham that He would indeed spare the city if just ten righteous people could be found there. In doing so, He showed that He wants His people to intercede on behalf of others.

Intercession is a special kind of prayer. It's opening your heart and standing in the gap (Ezekiel 22:30) for someone—and doing it consistently until you see results. But here's the wonderful truth about this kind of prayer: God loves hearing and answering it, and He is in no way put off when we refuse to quit.

Day 222

CLASSICS: CHARLES SPURGEON

SAMUEL: COMMEMORATING GOD'S WORK

Then Samuel took a stone, and set it between Mizpeh and Shen, and called the name of it Ebenezer, saying, Hitherto hath the LORD helped us.

1 SAMUEL 7:12 KJV

It is certainly a very delightful thing to mark the hand of God in the lives of ancient saints. How profitable an occupation to observe God's goodness in delivering David out of the jaw of the lion and the paw of the bear; His mercy in passing by the transgression, iniquity and sin of Manasseh; His faithfulness in keeping the covenant made with Abraham; or His interposition on the behalf of the dying Hezekiah.

But, beloved, would it not be even more interesting and profitable for us to mark the hand of God in our own lives? Ought we not to look upon our own history as being at least as full of God, as full of His goodness and His truth, as much a proof of His faithfulness and veracity as the lives of any of the saints who have gone before?

I think we do our Lord an injustice when we suppose that He wrought all His mighty acts in days of yore and showed Himself strong for those in the early time, but doth not perform wonders or lay bare His arm for the saints that are now upon the earth.

AMOS: LACKING CREDENTIALS

*Amos answered Amaziah, "I was neither a prophet
nor the son of a prophet, but I was a shepherd,
and I also took care of sycamore-fig trees."*

AMOS 7:14 NIV

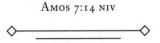

If God's kingdom had a human resources department that carefully went over résumés and contacted every reference, Amos probably wouldn't have gotten far in the hiring process.

Before God called him to be a prophet, Amos made his living as a shepherd and a fruit picker—probably like thousands of other men of Judah at the time. Honorable work, but it didn't provide the kind of professional experience most would think necessary for preaching to an entire nation.

But that's the way God works, isn't it?

Amos was one of many people God used to speak His truth without the "right" credentials. Think of Moses, a man who wasn't much of a public speaker. And how about Gideon, who was petrified with fear? Then there's the apostle Peter, a common fisherman with an often misdirected passion. And the apostle Paul? Forget it! With his past, he wouldn't even have passed a background check.

Amos was like so many other men God used to speak to the people of his time—unqualified, by the world's standards at least. Yet he preached a message that lives on to this day.

So don't worry if you feel unworthy of being God's instrument— the only credential God cares about is your willingness to serve Him.

JETHRO AND MOSES: WISE ADVICE, ACCEPTED

And Moses' father in law said unto him,
The thing that thou doest is not good.

Exodus 18:17 kjv

Jethro traveled from his home area to bring his daughter Zipporah and her two sons back to his son-in-law Moses. After a joyful meeting, Moses told Jethro all that God had done to Egypt's pharaoh and for Israel. Jethro praised God and recognized that He was above all other gods.

In coming days, as Jethro saw all the judicial work Moses performed—sitting before the people and settling disputes all day, every day but the Sabbath—he realized that the effort was too much for one man. Jethro told Moses that he should appoint leaders over groups of one thousand, one hundred, fifty, and ten. Furthermore, Moses should continue to teach the people God's Laws but let the leaders settle all but the most important disputes—which Moses would handle himself. These new leaders, Jethro said, should be men "such as fear God, men of truth, hating covetousness" (Exodus 18:21 kjv).

Moses immediately acted on Jethro's advice—a wise change of procedure made possible only by the long relationship of trust and respect that he and his father-in-law shared.

Be thankful for the trustworthy people in your life, and carefully consider their advice. After God, they'll be your greatest help.

CLASSICS: D. L. MOODY

JESUS: YOU ARE
SAFE IN HIS HANDS

And I give unto them eternal life; and they shall never perish, neither shall any man pluck them out of my hand.

JOHN 10:28 KJV

It is the work of the shepherd to care for the sheep, to feed them and protect them.

"I am the Good Shepherd." "My sheep hear My voice." "I lay down My life for the sheep." In that wonderful tenth chapter of John, Christ uses the personal pronoun no less than twenty-eight times, in declaring what He is and what He will do. In verse 28 He says, "They shall never perish; neither shall any *man* pluck them out of My hand." But notice the word *man* is in italics. See how the verse really reads: "Neither shall any pluck them out of My hand"—no devil or man shall be able to do it. In another place the scripture declares, "Your life is hid with Christ in God" (Colossians 3:3).

How safe and how secure!

ELIJAH: DEALING WITH DEPRESSION

*Then he went on alone into the wilderness, traveling all day.
He sat down under a solitary broom tree and prayed that he
might die. "I have had enough, LORD," he said. "Take my life,
for I am no better than my ancestors who have already died."*

1 KINGS 19:4 NLT

A mighty prophet helped prove that there was a God in Israel, one
who could choose when it would rain. The demonstration was glorious,
impressive, and definitive. Yet when adversity came and the prophet
felt threatened, he told God he'd had enough. Now, he wanted to die.

But the God of all had other plans for Elijah. So when God heard
his prayer, He said no.

Elijah's prayer sprung from a place of depression, not victory. He
was living as a pessimist, refusing to recall the glory God had just
shown. It would not have been loving or kind for God to have said yes
to this prayer, given that all this prophet needed was encouragement,
rest, and a little more time to see what God would do.

And that's exactly what God provided to Elijah. He does the same
for us, so when you're feeling down and out, hang on. Keep praying.
Know that God is always with you, and has your best interests at heart.

PAUL: NEVER DESPAIR

We are hard pressed on every side, but not crushed;
perplexed, but not in despair; persecuted, but not
abandoned; struck down, but not destroyed.

2 Corinthians 4:8–9 niv

Adam's sin bent every man, woman, and child toward the choice to sin (Romans 5:12). This means people—including you—will make choices that intentionally or unintentionally bring trouble into their lives. Jesus said, "In this world you will have trouble. But take heart! I have overcome the world" (John 16:33 niv).

The apostle Paul experienced trouble. He was beaten, imprisoned, and hated by many. But when trouble came, Paul could say he wasn't distressed, didn't despair, didn't feel abandoned, and wasn't destroyed. Some who had witnessed Paul's distressing circumstances might have thought his words betrayed an advanced case of insanity.

But the reason Paul could honestly say these things is the same reason *you* can. Romans 8:28 (niv) provides the perspective: "And we know that in all things God works for the good of those who love him, who have been called according to his purpose."

Having been called into God's service, Paul loved God and had absolute assurance that the One who accompanied him to the storm would hold an umbrella. Wise men realize that the toughest of times are temporary when compared to eternity, and that God never forsakes His own (Hebrews 13:5).

CLASSICS: D. L. MOODY

STEPHEN: WELCOMED BY JESUS

But he, being full of the Holy Ghost, looked up stedfastly into heaven, and saw the glory of God, and Jesus standing on the right hand of God, and said, Behold, I see the heavens opened, and the Son of man standing on the right hand of God.

ACTS 7:55–56 KJV

When Stephen was being stoned he lifted up his eyes, and it seemed as if God rolled back the curtain of time and allowed him to look into the eternal city and see Christ standing at the right hand of God.

When Jesus Christ went on high He led captivity captive and took His seat, for His work was done; but when Stephen saw Him He was standing up, and I can imagine He saw that martyr fighting, as it were, singlehanded and alone, the first martyr, though many were to come after him. You can hear the tramp of the millions coming after him, to lay down their lives for the Son of God.

But Stephen led the van; he was the first martyr, and as he was dying for the Lord Jesus Christ he looked up; Christ was standing to give him a welcome, and the Holy Ghost came down to bear witness that Christ was there. How then can we doubt it?

JACOB: HOLD ON TO GOD

So Jacob was left alone, and a man wrestled with him till daybreak.
When the man saw that he could not overpower him, he touched
the socket of Jacob's hip so that his hip was wrenched as he wrestled
with the man. Then the man said, "Let me go, for it is daybreak."
But Jacob replied, "I will not let you go unless you bless me."
<small>GENESIS 32:24–26 NIV</small>

Jacob knew that on the next morning, he would come face-to-face with his twin brother, Esau—the man he had cheated nearly fifteen years earlier. Jacob was obeying God's instruction to return to his homeland, but he dreaded the next day.

Apparently unable to sleep, Jacob prayed for God's protection. Then he went off alone to plot ways of appeasing Esau, to "pacify him with. . .gifts" (Genesis 32:20 NIV).

Late in the night, a mysterious "man" confronted and wrestled with Jacob. Many exhausting hours later, the fight had reached a stalemate. As daybreak arrived, this angel of God, whom Jacob identified later as God Himself (Genesis 32:30), tried to disengage and leave. But Jacob held on longer, insisting on a blessing.

He had learned, after years of relying on his own strength and cunning, that all he truly needed to face Esau was God's blessing. Jacob held tightly to the Lord, understanding what would later be written in Psalm 55:22: "Cast your cares on the LORD and he will sustain you; he will never let the righteous be shaken" (NIV).

SHADRACH, MESHACH, AND ABEDNEGO: NO COMPROMISE, NO MATTER WHAT

*"If we are thrown into the blazing furnace, the God we serve
is able to deliver us from it, and he will deliver us from Your
Majesty's hand. But even if he does not. . .we will not serve
your gods or worship the image of gold you have set up."*

DANIEL 3:17–18 NIV

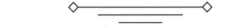

Modern thinking holds that compromise is always a virtue, that holding strongly to any conviction or belief brands you as "narrow minded," "unbending," or "intolerant."

The world today probably wouldn't think much of Shadrach, Meshach, and Abednego, three young Hebrew men who served in the court of Nebuchadnezzar, king of the Babylonian Empire. These men held a special place in the kingdom, right up until the moment they refused a "bow or die" order straight from the king himself. How did they respond? "We won't bow to your idols, even if it means being burned to a crisp in your furnace."

These three young friends knew full well that their God was more than able to save them from death at the hands of Nebuchadnezzar's men. But they also knew that whether or not God saved them, they would never dishonor Him nor defile themselves by bending the knee to the king's golden idol.

Life is filled with situations where compromise seems the wiser choice. But when compromise means dishonoring God by putting His standards in second place, then "we won't bow" is our only true response.

CLASSICS: ANDREW MURRAY

JESUS: ASKING OF GOD

But I know, that even now, whatsoever thou
wilt ask of God, God will give it thee.

JOHN 11:22 KJV

Jesus says, "Father! I will." On the ground of His right as Son, and the Father's promise to Him, and His finished work, He might do so. The Father had said to Him, "Ask of Me, and I will give Thee." He simply availed Himself of the Father's promise.

Jesus has given us a like promise: "Whatsoever ye will shall be done unto you." He asks me in His name to say what I will. Abiding in Him, in a living union with Him in which man is nothing and Christ all, the believer has the liberty to take up that word of His High Priest and, in answer to the question, "What wilt thou?" to say, "Father! I will all that Thou hast promised."

This is nothing but true faith; this is honoring God: to be assured that such confidence in saying what I will is indeed acceptable to Him.

BOAZ: NO SCHEMING NECESSARY

*"The LORD bless you, my daughter," he replied. "This kindness
is greater than that which you showed earlier: You have
not run after the younger men, whether rich or poor."*

RUTH 3:10 NIV

The first time he saw her, it seems Boaz was taken with Ruth (Ruth
2:5). Most likely considerably older, Boaz went out of his way to
accommodate Ruth, even warning his men not to lay a hand on her.
Imagine his surprise when he went to sleep in the threshing floor one
night and woke up to find Ruth lying at his feet! She informed Boaz
that he was her guardian-redeemer.

It would have been easy for Boaz to make Ruth his wife right
away, even though scripture doesn't say whether he was tempted to
do so. However, knowing he wasn't the nearest guardian-redeemer,
Boaz invited the other man to step in and then trusted God for the
results. You probably know the rest of the story: the closer relative
said no, so Boaz ended up marrying Ruth.

Boaz and Ruth both acted honorably, exhibiting high moral
character and a humble reliance on God when it would have been
easy to act on impulse. We know—from the Bible and from personal
experience—that God provides exactly what we need, when we need
it. Remember that truth and trust Him to provide what you need.
He'll sometimes provide what you want as well.

DAVID: STEPPING UP TO BATTLE

*That was the beginning of a long war between those
who were loyal to Saul and those loyal to David.
As time passed David became stronger and stronger,
while Saul's dynasty became weaker and weaker.*

2 SAMUEL 3:1 NLT

Saul and his son Jonathan—David's beloved friend—were killed by the Philistines, and David was anointed king of Judah. But Saul's men in the northern sections of Israel remained faithful to Saul, going so far as to anoint Ishbosheth, another son of Saul, as king. War ensued.

Just as David was God's chosen king for Israel, we as Christians are given a kingdom too (Luke 12:32). But David still had to fight for his realm, and we too must fight many battles before we find peace and comfort.

However, the apostle Paul assured us that our hardships will be worth it: "Since we are [God's] children, we are his heirs. In fact, together with Christ we are heirs of God's glory. But if we are to share his glory, we must also share his suffering. Yet what we suffer now is nothing compared to the glory he will reveal to us later" (Romans 8:17–18 NLT).

If God calls us to "share" in Jesus' suffering, He will provide the power to do so. And He promises rewards we can hardly imagine.

So step up to the battle lines!

CLASSICS: D. L. MOODY

PAUL: OUR AFFLICTIONS ARE LIGHT

*For our light affliction, which is but for a moment, worketh
for us a far more exceeding and eternal weight of glory.*

2 CORINTHIANS 4:17 KJV

Look at "Paul the aged," old and feeble, being led up the streets of
Rome to his death. Ah! Rome never in all her days of triumphant
warfare had known such a conqueror as this man, who is going quietly
to his death; faithful to God, even to death.

"Paul, don't you tremble now? What has all your preaching done
for you? For you are going to be put to death. Come now, give it up,
and perchance they'll let you off. Are not you afraid?"

"Afraid?" says the aged apostle, "No, indeed! I have had stripes,
imprisonments, beatings with rods, stonings, shipwrecks three times,
perils of fire, perils of sword, but none of these things move me. This
light affliction, which is but for a moment, worketh out for me a far
more exceeding and eternal weight of glory. Afraid? No! I press toward
the mark of the prize of the high calling in Christ Jesus. What the
world may or may not do to my poor body, matters not to me—the
sooner the better; I press forward. When absent from the body I shall
be present with the Lord," says he.

JOSHUA: DOING THINGS GOD'S WAY

*Then the LORD said to Joshua, "See, I have delivered Jericho
into your hands, along with its king and its fighting men."*
JOSHUA 6:2 NIV

Imagine this: Having been commissioned by God to take the Promised Land as Israel's rightful inheritance, you are near a locked-down Jericho (Joshua 6:1–2), pondering your next move. Suddenly, a heavenly being—the commander of God's army—appears and tells you he has delivered the city into your hands. He goes on to give you specific marching orders about how to take the city, and the plan works exactly the way he says.

This is what Joshua, the son of Nun, experienced as he transitioned from Moses' faithful aide to Israel's faithful leader. Joshua listened to God, and he didn't question God's plan for taking Jericho—not even the strange command to march around the city for seven days. He didn't run ahead of God, charging the city gates. Instead, he obeyed God's instructions and watched the city walls fall.

We all face battles in life, and sometimes God's instructions seem strange. Forgive people? Pray for our enemies? Give sacrificially? Give thanks in everything? Hard as it is for the human mind to accept, God's ways are always the right ways. Obey them, like Joshua did, and wait to see how the Lord works things out.

CLASSICS: MATTHEW HENRY

SOLOMON: BLESSINGS PHYSICAL AND SPIRITUAL

Judah and Israel were many, as the sand which is by the sea in multitude, eating and drinking, and making merry.

1 KINGS 4:20 KJV

Solomon did not only keep a good table himself but enabled all his subjects, according to their rank, to do so too and taught them that God gave them their abundance that they might use it soberly and pleasantly, not that they might hoard it up.

There is nothing better than for a man to *eat the labour of his hands* (Ecclesiastes 2:24), and that *with a merry heart* (Ecclesiastes 9:7). His father, in the psalms, had led his people into the comforts of communion with God, and now he led them into the comfortable use of the good things of this life. This pleasant posture of Israel's affairs extended, in place, from Dan to Beersheba—no part of the country was exposed nor upon any account uneasy; and it continued a long time, *all the days of Solomon,* without any material interruption. Go where you would, you might see all the marks of plenty, peace, and satisfaction.

The spiritual peace and joy and holy security of all the faithful subjects of the Lord Jesus were typified by this. *The kingdom of God is not,* as Solomon's was, *meat and drink,* but, what is infinitely better, *righteousness and peace and joy in the Holy Ghost.*

JESUS: COME AND FIND REST

*Then Jesus said, "Come to me, all of you who are weary
and carry heavy burdens, and I will give you rest."*
MATTHEW 11:28 NLT

When you carry heavy burdens, when you grow weary, when you long for rest, and when you wonder if you can take one more step, Jesus calls you to Himself. He doesn't demand any particular action or mindset. He knows full well that you're weary, so the invitation is spare and simple.

When Jesus calls you, He tells you to come as you are. Isn't that a relief? Rather than telling you to get your act together or to wait until you're ready for a greater commitment, He tells you to come at your worst. When you're tired, hopeless, or weighed down with many worries, Jesus tells you to stop waiting around. Come as you are, right now.

While He doesn't guarantee solutions or the removal of your burdens, He promises that you will find rest. If you come to Jesus, things will get better, even if the burdens remain.

You don't have to keep soldiering on. Weariness and burdens are your "qualifications" for coming to Jesus for rest and restoration. Perhaps coming to the end of yourself is the only way to prepare for transformation.

PAGAN KINGS: NO MATCH FOR GOD

I, Nebuchadnezzar, raised my eyes toward heaven, and my sanity was restored. Then I praised the Most High; I honored and glorified him who lives forever. His dominion is an eternal dominion; his kingdom endures from generation to generation. . . . Now I, Nebuchadnezzar, praise and exalt and glorify the King of heaven, because everything he does is right and all his ways are just. And those who walk in pride he is able to humble.

DANIEL 4:34, 37 NIV

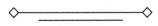

Today's verse is the end of the story of Nebuchadnezzar. The powerful, prideful king of Babylon had brought God's judgment upon himself by some ill-advised self-glory, and spent seven years in a state of insanity, living with wild animals and eating grass like an ox. But the Lord was gracious to restore the king's mind, and the last time we hear of Nebuchadnezzar in scripture, he is speaking God's praise to his kingdom and beyond.

Two generations later, Darius the Mede made a similar statement of praise to God, sending it to the people of every race and nation and language throughout his empire, which comprised at least 120 provinces (Daniel 6:25–27). And a third powerful biblical king, Cyrus the Great, issued his own statement in praise to the Lord, the God of heaven, throughout the provinces as well (2 Chronicles 36:22–23; Ezra 1:1–4).

These men, powerful as they might have been, were nothing in comparison to the one true God. In His hand, "the king's heart is a stream of water that he channels toward all who please him" (Proverbs 21:1 NIV).

And, Christian, He is on *your* side.

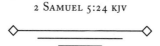

Day 239

CLASSICS: CHARLES SPURGEON

DAVID: NEVER GO BEFORE PROVIDENCE

And let it be, when thou hearest the sound of a going in the tops of the mulberry trees, that then thou shalt bestir thyself: for then shall the LORD go out before thee, to smite the host of the Philistines.

2 SAMUEL 5:24 KJV

My brethren, let us learn from David to take no steps without God. The last time you moved, or went into another business, or changed your situation in life, you asked God's help and then did it, and you were blessed in the doing of it. You have been up to this time a successful man; you have always sought God, but do not think that the stream of providence necessarily runs in a continuous current; remember, you may tomorrow without seeking God's advice venture upon a step which you will regret but once, and that will be until you die.

You have been wise hitherto; it may be because you have trusted in the Lord with all your heart and have not leaned to your own understanding (Proverbs 3:5–6). If Providence tarries, tarry till Providence comes; never go before it. He goes on a fool's errand who goes before God, but he walks in a blessed path who sees the footsteps of Providence and reads the map of scripture and so discovers, "This is the way wherein I am to walk."

ANDREW: BRINGING PEOPLE TO JESUS

*Andrew, Simon Peter's brother, was one of the two who
heard what John had said and who had followed Jesus.
The first thing Andrew did was to find his brother
Simon and tell him, "We have found the Messiah."*

JOHN 1:40–41 NIV

◇———————◇

When we spend time with Jesus, it's only natural that we want to do whatever we can to bring others to Him so that they can spend time with Him too.

Andrew, who would become one of Jesus' twelve apostles, had been a follower of John the Baptist. But after hearing John proclaim Jesus as "the lamb of God"—and then spending the day with Him—he could barely contain his excitement. He went to find his brother Simon (whom Jesus later renamed Peter) so that he could bring him to meet Jesus.

The Gospel of John reports that this wasn't the last time he brought people to meet the Lord. By the Sea of Galilee, Andrew brought a boy to Jesus, who then performed a tremendous miracle with the boy's small amount of food (John 6:8–13). And in Jerusalem, he and Philip introduced Jesus to a group of curious Greeks (John 12:20–22).

Andrew is far from the most prominent apostle in the four Gospel accounts. But his time with Jesus teaches us an important message: being used of God to bring others into His kingdom isn't always a matter of teaching, preaching, or facilitating. Sometimes, it's as simple as finding opportunities to bring people to Jesus.

PHARAOH'S CUPBEARER: TOO EASILY DISTRACTED

And the chief butler told his dream to Joseph, and said to him, In my dream, behold, a vine was before me; and in the vine were three branches: and it was as though it budded, and her blossoms shot forth; and the clusters thereof brought forth ripe grapes.

GENESIS 40:9–10 KJV

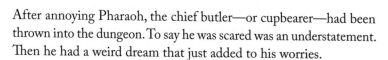

After annoying Pharaoh, the chief butler—or cupbearer—had been thrown into the dungeon. To say he was scared was an understatement. Then he had a weird dream that just added to his worries.

Thankfully, a fellow prisoner named Joseph was willing to ask God to interpret the dream. He reassured the cupbearer that he would soon be free.

The cupbearer had never really understood how good he had it. His exalted position in Pharaoh's court was a blessing, and even the wine he served was a gift from God. However, only by losing it all did he become prepared to even listen to God.

Joseph asked one favor in return for his help: "Don't forget me!" But once the good times returned, the cupbearer got distracted. He didn't recall Joseph for two full years.

Does that ring any bells? When hard times come along, we beg God to help us out. Once restored. . .we often forget Him again. Thankfully, the cupbearer finally remembered to help Joseph, but let's not take our chances. Remember to praise God in the good times and the bad, because He never forgets us.

CLASSICS: D. L. MOODY

PAUL: DEALING WITH THORNS IN THE FLESH

*Lest I should be exalted above measure through the abundance of the
revelations, there was given to me a thorn in the flesh, the messenger
of Satan to buffet me, lest I should be exalted above measure. For
this thing I besought the Lord thrice, that it might depart from me.
And he said unto me, My grace is sufficient for thee: for my strength
is made perfect in weakness. Most gladly therefore will I rather
glory in my infirmities, that the power of Christ may rest upon me.*

2 Corinthians 12:7–9 KJV

As Moses takes up more room in the Old Testament than any other
character, so it is with Paul in the New Testament, except, perhaps,
the Lord Himself. Yet Paul did not know how to pray for himself. He
besought the Lord to take away "the thorn in the flesh." His request
was not granted; but the Lord bestowed upon him a greater blessing.
He gave him more grace.

It may be we have some trial—some thorn in the flesh. If it is
not God's will to take it away, let us ask Him to give us more grace
in order to bear it. We find that Paul gloried in his reverses and his
infirmities, because all the more the power of God rested upon him.

It may be there are some of us who feel as if everything is against
us. May God give us grace to take Paul's platform and say: "All things
work together for good to them that love God" (Romans 8:28 KJV).
So when we pray to God we must be submissive and say, "Thy will
be done."

JOHN THE BAPTIST: ONE PURPOSE ONLY

Verily I say unto you, Among them that are born of women there hath not risen a greater than John the Baptist: notwithstanding he that is least in the kingdom of heaven is greater than he.

MATTHEW 11:11 KJV

The day John was born, his father, Zacharias, foretold that he would prepare the way of the Lord. Zacharias also made clear that the Lord's purpose in coming was to "give knowledge of salvation unto his people by the remission of their sins" (Luke 1:77 KJV).

We're told that John grew strong in the Spirit and spent his time in deserted areas until he started preaching. He knew the scriptures about the Messiah and knew that he, John, was the one Isaiah spoke of as crying in the wilderness, "Make straight the way of the Lord" (Isaiah 40:3 KJV).

John set himself to his task with single-minded determination. He spoke to crowds about the need to turn away from sin and obey God's commands. He told the people to look at Jesus and trust Him to take away their sin.

John's life was never about himself. He had neither wife nor family. He was not rich. He didn't live long. His parents were aged when he was born and may have died before he even began preaching. John came into the world for only one purpose—to point the way to the Savior. There is no better purpose.

JOSEPH: CHOOSING TO TRUST ANYWAY

*Joseph, to whom she was engaged, was a righteous man and did not want
to disgrace her publicly, so he decided to break the engagement quietly.
As he considered this, an angel of the Lord appeared to him in a dream.
"Joseph, son of David," the angel said, "do not be afraid to take Mary as
your wife. For the child within her was conceived by the Holy Spirit."*

MATTHEW 1:19–20 NLT

Joseph, a working-class man, didn't expect drama when he invited Mary to be his wife. Then Mary got pregnant and Joseph found himself in a frightening situation.

If Mary was unfaithful in their engagement, might she be unfaithful during their marriage? Would the community assume Joseph had had premarital sexual relations? What if the baby looked nothing like Joseph? Mary's infidelity might become obvious, and people would shun the couple. Joseph's livelihood in carpentry might be jeopardized.

So he decided to break things off. If Joseph did that publicly, Mary's infidelity would be punishable by death. If he divorced her quietly, she would be shamed, but live. Joseph held Mary's life—and the life of her unborn child—in his hands.

Then an angel appeared. Joseph was to marry Mary as planned. He was to trust God over the evidence of Mary's seeming infidelity.

And Joseph did trust God. He took Mary as his wife and adopted Jesus as his son. Jesus' life was saved so He could save the entire world from sin.

Perhaps the angel's request—God's request—seemed unfair to Joseph. There will be times when God's expectations of us will be tough too. Will we choose to trust anyway? Joseph did. So can we.

JABEZ: HOW TO PRAY

Jabez cried out to the God of Israel, "Oh, that you would bless me and enlarge my territory! Let your hand be with me, and keep me from harm so that I will be free from pain." And God granted his request.

1 CHRONICLES 4:10 NIV

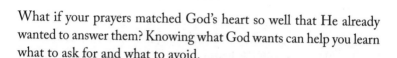

What if your prayers matched God's heart so well that He already wanted to answer them? Knowing what God wants can help you learn what to ask for and what to avoid.

Jabez's prayer seems simple, specific, and bold. . .maybe even a bit presumptuous. Yet God answered it.

You should never assume that God's response will be better if you are bossy and demanding. The intensity of Jabez's cry to God indicates he was passionate about his request. Maybe he spent a lot of time deliberating on it before he uttered the words.

It's clear that Jabez followed God and that his request matched God's heart. How do we know this? God answered his prayer.

CLASSICS: CHARLES SPURGEON

DAVID: HOLY SELF-DENIAL

For thou, O LORD of hosts, God of Israel, hast revealed to thy
servant, saying, I will build thee an house: therefore hath thy
servant found in his heart to pray this prayer unto thee.

2 SAMUEL 7:27 KJV

David had first found it in his heart to build a house for God. He resolved that the ark of God should no longer abide under curtains but should be more suitably housed. The Lord, however, did not design that David should build His temple, though He declared it was well that it was in his heart.

Our intentions to serve the Lord in a certain manner may be thoroughly good and acceptable, and yet we may not be permitted to carry them out. We may have the will but not the power: the aspiration but not the qualification. We may have to stand aside and see another do the task we had chosen for ourselves, and yet we may be nonetheless pleasing to the Lord, who in His great love accepts the will for the deed.

It is a holy self-denial which in such cases rejoices to see the Lord glorified by others and at the Captain's bidding cheerfully stands back in the rear when zeal had urged it to rush to the front. It is as true service not to do as to do when the Lord's word prescribes it.

PAUL AND SILAS: THANKFULNESS IS A CHOICE

Be thankful in all circumstances, for this is God's will for you who belong to Christ Jesus.

1 THESSALONIANS 5:18 NLT

Being thankful in good times is easy enough, but it is God's will for us to be thankful in bad times too. Since no one is immune to struggle, we all have a choice to make: Will we obey the words of 1 Thessalonians 5:18 or not?

The apostle Paul, who wrote today's scripture, lived up to his own command. Acts 16:16–34 describes his experience in Philippi, where he and his missionary companion Silas were jailed for casting a demon from a fortune-telling slave girl. Though unjustly imprisoned, Paul and Silas prayed and sang hymns in their cell. As a result of this obedience, their chains fell off—as did the chains of everyone in that prison! Paul and Silas even got to share the Gospel with the jailer, who gladly accepted Christ.

Would any of these positive things have happened if Paul and Silas had been complaining in their cell? Had they been bemoaning their hardships and the unfairness of life? It's doubtful.

Choose to be thankful. In doing so, you fulfill God's will for your life. And when you fulfill His will, He will certainly give you whatever strength you need—"in all circumstances."

METHUSELAH: WHAT LIFE IS ALL ABOUT

Methuselah lived 969 years, and then he died.
GENESIS 5:27 NLT

Genesis 5 records the long lives of many of the early patriarchs. Of these, Methuselah is noted for his lifespan—at 969 years, it's the longest recorded in the Bible—but little else.

Adam lived 930 years and was still alive at Methuselah's birth. Did Adam talk to Methuselah and confess his and Eve's role in the fall? Did Methuselah listen to Adam's description of his walks in the Garden with God? Surely Adam or Enoch, Methuselah's father, told him about the disastrous consequences of failing to follow God's direction.

A long lifespan gives a person ample time to improve his life. . .or sink deeper into sin. With such a long life, did Methuselah pray every day to become a better person? Or did he, like many in his generation (Genesis 6:5), plot how to achieve his own selfish desires?

None of us know how long our lives will last, and even the longest life on earth ends surprisingly quickly. Let's make it our goal, every day, to draw closer to God and walk more perfectly in His way. That's really what this life is all about.

EZEKIEL: A MESSAGE OF CONSOLATION

"Yet I will remember the covenant I made with you when you were young, and I will establish an everlasting covenant with you."
EZEKIEL 16:60 NLT

After listing the shocking number of sins and transgressions that the people of Judah had committed against the Lord, Ezekiel offered a message of consolation. After reaping what they had sown, the people learned that God had planned far beyond their sin. God's covenant with them was not contingent on their faithfulness.

When God thinks of you, He isn't ultimately focused on the ways you have let Him down. While sin must be dealt with, God's covenant—which has been given through Jesus' ministry—still stands. No matter how many times you let go, God won't abandon His child. There's always space for a new beginning.

Perhaps you aren't shocked by God's mercy in the past, but you may have a hard time accepting it for yourself in the present. Is God *really* that merciful? The pages of scripture leave no doubt: God's covenant stands, and you can only miss out on it if you walk away. His mercies truly are new every morning.

THE ISLANDERS OF MALTA: GOD'S SURPRISING HELPERS

Once safely on shore, we found out that the island was called Malta. The islanders showed us unusual kindness. They built a fire and welcomed us all because it was raining and cold.

ACTS 28:1–2 NIV

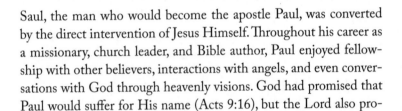

Saul, the man who would become the apostle Paul, was converted by the direct intervention of Jesus Himself. Throughout his career as a missionary, church leader, and Bible author, Paul enjoyed fellowship with other believers, interactions with angels, and even conversations with God through heavenly visions. God had promised that Paul would suffer for His name (Acts 9:16), but the Lord also provided strong supports for his servant.

In the last chapter of Acts, we see Paul getting support from a surprising source—the pagan inhabitants of the island of Malta. Though these people didn't know the one true God (they thought Paul himself was a god when a snakebite didn't kill him), they were compassionate to the great missionary and his traveling companions, whose ship had broken apart in a storm.

That's just like God, who can use any person or nation or situation to accomplish His will. Think of the Persian king, Cyrus, restoring the Jewish nation. Or Jonah's fish. Or even the horrible choices of Judas Iscariot that led to Jesus' death on the cross. . .and the salvation of everyone who believes.

When life is hard, as is often the case, be ready for God to help— from the expected sources or even from the surprising ones.

CLASSICS: MATTHEW HENRY

JESUS: TEARS OF COMPASSION

Jesus wept.
JOHN 11:35 KJV

◇——————◇

A very short verse, but it affords many useful instructions:

(1) That Jesus Christ was really and truly man, and partook with the children, not only of flesh and blood, but of a human soul, susceptible of the impressions of joy, and grief, and other affections. He could weep, and, as a merciful man, He *would weep*, before He gave this proof of His divinity.

(2) That He was *a man of sorrows*, and *acquainted with grief*, as was foretold (Isaiah 53:3). We never read that He laughed, but more than once we have Him in tears. Thus He shows not only that a mournful state will consist with the love of God, but that those who sow to the Spirit must sow in tears.

(3) Tears of compassion well become Christians, and make them most to resemble Christ.

PETER AND JOHN: BOLDNESS FOR JESUS

Now when they saw the boldness of Peter and John, and perceived that they were uneducated and untrained men, they marveled. And they realized that they had been with Jesus.

ACTS 4:13 NKJV

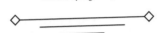

When Peter and John healed the lame man outside the temple, the man did what came naturally to him—he joined Peter and John in the temple, "walking, leaping, and praising God" (Acts 3:8 NKJV). The people inside marveled, giving Peter an opportunity to point out that the man was healed in the name of Jesus—the One this very people had denied.

That landed them in the custody of the Sanhedrin, who weren't all that fond of what Peter and John were saying. As Peter testified at their trial, he boldly and accurately portrayed Jesus as the chief cornerstone in whom salvation is found (Acts 4:11–12). That's when the religious leaders began to realize that these two uneducated men had been in Jesus' presence. Their time with Jesus had changed them, giving them a boldness they never had before.

How have you been changed by spending time with Jesus? The more you're in His presence, through prayer, Bible reading, and meditation on His Word, the more you'll find yourself speaking out with the boldness of Peter and John.

LUKE: OUR GOD-GIVEN SKILLS

Our dear friend Luke, the doctor, and Demas send greetings.
COLOSSIANS 4:14 NIV

Luke, the author of the Gospel of Luke and the book of Acts, was a Greek physician from Antioch who became a Christian and later accompanied Paul on his missionary travels, as evidenced by the verse above (2 Timothy 4:11; Philemon 1:24). Tradition holds that he was also an artist, with some paintings attributed to him still in existence, including "Black Madonna of Częstochowa," housed at a monastery in Poland and "Salvation of the Roman People" at the Basilica of St. Mary Major in Rome.

As a writer, physician, and possibly a painter, Luke was clearly an observer—someone who pays special attention to detail. Good creative types of all sorts feel an obligation to depict truth as accurately as possible. It should be no surprise that we read such a person's inspired account of our Savior's birth from Luke 2 every Christmas.

Maybe God has wired you, like Luke, to be a creative type. Or maybe you're more of a nuts-and-bolts kind of guy. However you're wired, evaluate how well you're using those traits for God's glory. Then get to work!

CLASSICS: ANDREW MURRAY

ABRAHAM: THE INTERCESSOR

*And it came to pass, when God destroyed the
cities of the plain, that God remembered Abraham,
and sent Lot out of the midst of the overthrow,
when he overthrew the cities in the which Lot dwelt.*

GENESIS 19:29 KJV

Think of Abraham as he pleads for Sodom. Time after time he renews his prayer until the sixth time he has to say, "Let not my LORD be angry." He does not cease until he has learned to know God's condescension in each time consenting to his petition, until he has learned how far he can go, has entered into God's mind and now rests in God's will. And for his sake Lot was saved. "God remembered Abraham, and delivered Lot out of the midst of the overthrow."

And shall not we, who have a redemption and promises for the heathen which Abraham never knew, begin to plead more with God on their behalf?

PAUL: BECOMING A GOD PLEASER

I am not trying to please people. I want to please God.
Do you think I am trying to please people? If I were
doing that, I would not be a servant of Christ.

GALATIANS 1:10 CEV

At one point in his life, the apostle Paul was indeed a people pleaser. As a Pharisee, he studied to show himself approved by men. As a persecutor of those who followed Jesus, he pleased men by holding the coats of the men who stoned Stephen to death (Acts 7:58). He even approached the high priest at one point for permission to persecute Christians (Acts 9:1–2).

Post conversion, Paul became a God pleaser, contending for the Gospel at all cost, no matter what human beings thought. After hearing that the Galatian church was straying from God and the Gospel, he wrote a letter to them as a warning. "I pray," he said sharply, "that God will punish anyone who preaches anything different from our message to you! It doesn't matter if that person is one of us or an angel from heaven" (Galatians 1:8 CEV).

As believers, we are called to humbly love our neighbors as ourselves. But when a false gospel is presented, we must speak the truth as lovingly—yet firmly—as possible. Souls are at stake, so we cannot afford to be people pleasers when it comes to the Gospel. To compromise in this area is to forfeit our status as servants of Christ.

ENOCH: GOD WANTED HIM HOME

And Enoch walked with God after he begat Methuselah three hundred years, and begat sons and daughters: and all the days of Enoch were three hundred sixty and five years: and Enoch walked with God: and he was not; for God took him.

GENESIS 5:22–24 KJV

The generations of Adam in the book of Genesis don't just say how long each descendant lived. They emphatically state that each of them died. Except for Enoch.

After a short life—compared to others on the list—Enoch was taken by God. Everyone else died, but Enoch simply vanished off the face of the earth. Why? Frustratingly, the writer doesn't say.

But we are given a hint in the book of Hebrews: "Before his translation he had this testimony: that he pleased God" (Hebrews 11:5 KJV).

Despite the fact that God is everywhere, we're separated from Him by original sin. Jesus died to close this gap. But imagine living a life so pleasing to God that He just can't wait to have you in His company—so He doesn't even wait for you to die!

Even more impressively, Enoch lived eight generations after the Fall and only two generations before the Flood. Difficult times to be a man of God.

Plenty of people will tell you that these are difficult and godless days. What better time to follow the example of Enoch, the man God didn't want to be without?

CLASSICS: CHARLES SPURGEON

JOSIAH: GOD WANTS HUMBLE MEN

Because thine heart was tender, and thou didst humble thyself before God, when thou heardest his words against this place, and against the inhabitants thereof, and humbledst thyself before me, and didst rend thy clothes, and weep before me; I have even heard thee also, saith the LORD.

2 CHRONICLES 34:27 KJV

God had much love towards Josiah, and, having honored him to rebuild the Temple, He knew the natural tendency of the human heart to pride, and therefore, with a holy jealousy for one whom He loved so well, He sent him this discovery of the book of the law, to keep him humble at the time when otherwise he might have been exposed to peril by the lifting up of his heart.

You and I, in the midst of a career of success from God, when our heart is most pure and most right, must not therefore expect that all things will go smoothly, but may rather for that very reason expect to experience humiliating circumstances. Like Paul, when favored with an abundance of revelations, we may expect a "thorn in the flesh," lest we should be exalted above measure.

Disclosures of our own weakness and sinfulness are often made to us at the very time when God is honoring us most. In order that our vessel may be able to endure a strong and fair wind of divine favor, the Lord in infinite wisdom causes us to be ballasted with grief or trial.

SOLOMON: WHEN YOU'RE FEELING EMPTY

"Meaningless! Meaningless!" says the Teacher.
"Utterly meaningless! Everything is meaningless."
ECCLESIASTES 1:2 NIV

Solomon was the wisest man who ever lived (1 Kings 3:12). But after a lifetime of trying everything under the sun to fill the deepest longings of his heart, the conclusion he drew is shocking: "When I surveyed all that my hands had done and what I had toiled to achieve, everything was meaningless, a chasing after the wind; nothing was gained under the sun" (Ecclesiastes 2:11 NIV).

Solomon had everything this world has to offer. *Everything.* But even a casual reading of Ecclesiastes makes it painfully clear that he was not happy. Something was missing, and Solomon knew it. No matter what he tried, all his attempts at finding happiness were nothing more than chasing after the wind.

This, of course, should come as no surprise. Nothing this world offers is big enough to fill the all-consuming hole in our hearts. Sin created the void. Only Jesus can fill it.

Even when we know Jesus, we will sometimes find ourselves struggling with the emptiness Solomon felt. Unlike him, though, we have the Holy Spirit living permanently within us. As Jesus said, "I will pray the Father, and he shall give you another Comforter, that he may abide with you for ever" (John 14:16 KJV).

In seasons of emptiness, you have the entire Trinity working on your behalf. Pray! God will bring you through.

NEHEMIAH: FOLLOWING
GOD'S LEADING

*So I arrived in Jerusalem. Three days later, I slipped out during
the night, taking only a few others with me. I had not told
anyone about the plans God had put in my heart for Jerusalem.*

NEHEMIAH 2:11–12 NLT

Nehemiah, an Israelite who served as cupbearer for the Persian king,
wanted to rebuild Jerusalem, which still lay in ruins decades after
the Babylonian invasion. Because "the gracious hand of God was on"
Nehemiah (verse 8 NLT), Artaxerxes allowed him to pursue his desire
and even promised him materials for the job.

Once in Jerusalem, Nehemiah slipped out during the night to
inspect the city's broken walls and burned gates. In one spot, the
rubble was so bad that his donkey couldn't advance.

Then, with a full, personal knowledge of the need, Nehemiah
went to the city officials and religious leaders in Jerusalem. "You
know very well what trouble we are in," he told them. "Let us rebuild
the wall of Jerusalem and end this disgrace!" (verse 17). Telling the
others about his interaction with King Artaxerxes as well as the many
blessings of God along the way, Nehemiah got the others to commit
to the work. "Yes, let's rebuilt the wall!" they said (verse 18). And
they did—under Nehemiah's leadership, the job was completed in a
miraculous fifty-two days.

There's no way Nehemiah could have rebuilt the walls of Jerusalem
by himself. But when he followed "the plans God had put in [his]
heart," studying the need and assembling a good team, success was
sure to follow. This pattern never fails.

JESUS: SHINING THE LIGHT

Jesus replied, "My light will shine for you just a little longer.
Walk in the light while you can, so the darkness will not
overtake you. Those who walk in the darkness cannot see where
they are going. Put your trust in the light while there is still
time; then you will become children of the light." After saying
these things, Jesus went away and was hidden from them.

JOHN 12:35–36 NLT

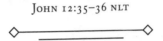

Jesus was speaking to a crowd of people in Jerusalem when they asked Him how the Son of God could possibly die. He explained to them that He would only be with them in person for a short time and urged them to take advantage of His presence on earth. He was the light of the world, trying to show them how to walk out of darkness. If they followed Him, they would enjoy eternal salvation with His Father in heaven.

As a Christian, God wants you to bear Christ's light to the world. He wants you to let your light shine for others to see. Can those around you see Christ in you? Has your light dimmed, or is it still shining brightly?

Today, commit to spreading the Word of the Lord. Be a shining light for someone else to see. Inspire people to come to the Lord by blessing them and illuminating the world around you.

Day 261

CLASSICS: CHARLES SPURGEON

PAUL: SET APART FROM BIRTH

But when it pleased God, who separated me from my mother's womb, and called me by his grace, to reveal his Son in me, that I might preach him among the heathen; immediately I conferred not with flesh and blood: neither went I up to Jerusalem to them which were apostles before me; but I went into Arabia, and returned again unto Damascus.

GALATIANS 1:15–17 KJV

Paul's conversion is generally considered so very remarkable for its suddenness and distinctness, and truly it is; yet, at the same time, it is no exception to the general rule of conversions, but is rather a type, or model, or pattern of the way in which God shows forth His longsuffering to them that are led to believe on Him.

It appears from my text, however, that there is another part of Paul's history which deserves our attention; namely, the fact that although he was suddenly converted, yet God had had thoughts of mercy towards him from his very birth. God did not begin to work with him when he was on the road to Damascus. That was not the first occasion on which eyes of love had darted upon this chief of sinners, but he declares that God had separated him and set him apart even from his mother's womb, that he might by-and-by be called by grace and have Jesus Christ revealed in him.

DAVID: VICTORY BELONGS TO GOD

So the LORD made David victorious wherever he went.

2 SAMUEL 8:6 NLT

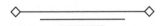

Saul's dislike of David began shortly after the king appointed the young man as a military commander. Once, as the army returned from a battle victory, women from the towns of Israel came out to meet King Saul, dancing and proclaiming, "Saul has killed his thousands, and David his ten thousands!" (1 Samuel 18:7 NLT). Saul was not happy.

What the king failed to realize was that David's successes on the battlefield had little to do with David himself and everything to do with God. The Lord was with David, making him victorious wherever he went. The words of today's scripture are repeated in 2 Samuel 8:14.

We know that David wasn't perfect. In fact, later in life, he would commit adultery and ultimately arrange the death of the woman's husband. But he'd been chosen by God to be king, and the Lord described him as a man after His own heart (1 Samuel 13:14; Acts 13:22).

All of us have flaws, but God still chooses to work through us, empowering us to accomplish what He wills. Keep your focus on the Lord through prayer and time in His Word. Deny yourself and take up your cross each day (Matthew 16:24). Humbly wait on the Lord and His victory—whatever form that takes.

FAITHFUL STEWARDS: REWARDED BY GOD

Then came the first, saying, Lord, thy pound hath gained ten pounds. And he said unto him, Well, thou good servant: because thou hast been faithful in a very little, have thou authority over ten cities.

LUKE 19:16–17 KJV

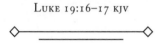

In His wisdom and for His own purposes, God gives people varying abilities. But whether a Christian sweeps the streets or serves as ruler of his country, he is expected to do his best.

Jesus told similar parables in Luke 19 and Matthew 25, describing a wealthy man planning a trip to a "far country." Knowing that he would be away for some time, he called his servants together and distributed money for them to use in conducting business. In Matthew, one servant received five talents (an amount of gold or silver) and gained an additional five; one servant received two talents, and gained two more. In Luke, several servants each received a pound (about a hundred days' wages), with one man gaining an impressive ten in return, and the next, five. In both stories, when the wealthy man returned home to collect his money, he commended the industrious servants for being "faithful in a very little." They were rewarded with much larger opportunities.

The beauty of these stories is that God doesn't expect us to match outcomes with more gifted people. He simply wants us to do our best. And that's possible for any of us. When we do, we put ourselves in line for His greater blessing.

JESUS: GUARD YOURSELF AGAINST GREED

Jesus replied, "Friend, who made me a judge over you to decide such things as that?" Then he said, "Beware! Guard against every kind of greed. Life is not measured by how much you own."

LUKE 12:14–15 NLT

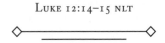

In a culture where the firstborn son enjoyed immense benefits and privileges, a younger brother pleaded with Jesus for a more equal distribution of the family's inheritance. His argument certainly appears reasonable to us today, but Jesus wasn't looking at this matter from a financial standpoint.

Jesus saw that the younger brother had become obsessed with wealth, allowing greed to determine the value of his life. By refusing to arbitrate a settlement in this family, Jesus may have saved this young man from his desires. We shouldn't think that Jesus deprived this young man of something reasonable; rather, Jesus most likely gave him the hard truth that he needed the most.

Today, it's common to treat money as the solution to almost all of our problems. Even if our desire for money often risks becoming a never-ending pit of greed and self-indulgence, we rarely treat it as a threat to our spiritual or relational well-being.

Jesus didn't mince words in this story: He treated greed as a threat that you must always remain aware of. Every time you pray for more money (or "provision"), you should also pray for God's protection from greed.

CLASSICS: MATTHEW HENRY

HEZEKIAH: SPEAKING A GOOD WORD

And he set captains of war over the people, and gathered them together
to him in the street of the gate of the city, and spake comfortably to
them, saying, Be strong and courageous, be not afraid nor dismayed for
the king of Assyria, nor for all the multitude that is with him: for there
be more with us than with him: with him is an arm of flesh; but with
us is the LORD our God to help us, and to fight our battles. And the
people rested themselves upon the words of Hezekiah king of Judah.

2 CHRONICLES 32:6–8 KJV

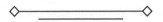

Hezekiah endeavored to keep up their faith, in order to the silencing
and suppressing of their fears. "Sennacherib has a multitude with
him, and yet there are more with us than with him; for we have God
with us, and how many do you reckon Him for? With our enemy is
an arm of flesh, which he trusts to; but with us is the LORD, whose
power is irresistible, our God, whose promise is inviolable, a God
in covenant with us, to help us and to fight our battles, not only to
help us to fight them, but to fight them for us if He please": and so
He did here.

A believing confidence in God will raise us above the prevailing
fear of man. He that feareth the fury of the oppressor forgetteth the
LORD his Maker (Isaiah 51:12–13). It is probable that Hezekiah said
more to this purport and that the people rested themselves upon
what he said, not merely upon his word, but on the things he said
concerning the presence of God with them and His power to relieve
them, the belief of which made them easy. Let the good subjects and
soldiers of Jesus Christ rest thus upon His word and boldly say, Since
God is for us, who can be against us?

MORDECAI: DO THE RIGHT THING

One day as Mordecai was on duty at the king's gate, two of the king's eunuchs, Bigthana and Teresh—who were guards at the door of the king's private quarters—became angry at King Xerxes and plotted to assassinate him. But Mordecai heard about the plot and gave the information to Queen Esther. She then told the king about it and gave Mordecai credit for the report.

ESTHER 2:21–22 NLT

◇———————◇

We aren't sure what role Mordecai had in King Xerxes' court at this point in Esther's story. Some believe he was an officer of some sort, since he was present at the king's gate. Whatever his duty, God placed Mordecai in the right place at the right time. He overheard talk of an assassination attempt, and his response saved the king's life.

"Mordecai was not rewarded at the time, but a remembrance was written," says the old-time Bible commentator Matthew Henry. "Thus, with respect to those who serve Christ, though their recompence is not till the resurrection of the just, yet an account is kept of their work of faith and labor of love, which God is not unrighteous to forget. The servant of God must be faithful to every trust."

In this life, we see many people cheating, stealing, lying, and hurting others. Though it may seem like they "get away with murder," and that a committed Christian just can't get ahead, take encouragement from the story of Mordecai. Do the right thing and trust God to handle the rest. He can, and He will.

CLASSICS: CHARLES SPURGEON

JESUS: THE ONLY WAY

*Jesus saith unto him, I am the way, the truth, and the
life: no man cometh unto the Father, but by me.*

JOHN 14:6 KJV

Never try to draw near to God in prayer or praise or meditation or
scripture reading or holy service apart from Jesus Christ, or your
attempt must be a failure. Through the wall of fire which surrounds
the throne you can only pass by way of the one door, namely, the body
and blood of our great Mediator, Sacrifice and Substitute. Is not that
door sufficient? Why should we climb up some other way?

If I am very heavy of heart, do not let me try to raise my spirits,
and so come in the power of human courage; but let me come just
as I am, made bold through Him whose comforts delight my soul. If
I feel that I have been sinning, do not let me try to get rid of my sin
by some other process and then draw near to God; but let me come,
sinner as I am, in the name of the sinner's Savior, and so draw near to
God, having washed my robes and made them white in the blood of
the Lamb. Jesus saith, "I am the way": why should we seek another?

UZZIAH: BEWARE OF PRIDE

Uzziah sought God during the days of Zechariah, who taught him to fear God. And as long as the king sought guidance from the LORD, God gave him success.

2 CHRONICLES 26:5 NLT

Judah had a new king. He came to the throne at sixteen years of age, and he had much to learn. While other teenage boys were learning a trade, Uzziah was facing something a bit more important. Fortunately, he had a godly mentor named Zechariah who taught him to honor God and seek His direction. As long as he listened, Uzziah experienced multiple blessings.

For example, Uzziah managed to upgrade the army's weapons of war, defeat the Philistines, fortify the city of Jerusalem, and offer safety and security to his people—even as northern Israel's kings came and went.

However, Uzziah began to believe he was pretty special. He wrongly assumed he could go into the temple's sanctuary and burn incense. But this was not his job: he hadn't been set apart to manage this sacred duty. The priests reacted to him with righteous anger, and in response to Uzziah's unrepentant heart, God caused leprosy to break out on the king's forehead. Uzziah would suffer from the disease for the rest of his life.

No matter what God allows us to accomplish, we should never think we are above humbly obeying Him.

BARAK: DON'T MISS THE FULL BLESSING

Barak said to her, "If you go with me, I will go; but if you don't go
with me, I won't go." "Certainly I will go with you," said Deborah.
"But because of the course you are taking, the honor will not be yours,
for the LORD will deliver Sisera into the hands of a woman."

JUDGES 4:8–9 NIV

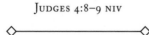

The Bible depicts Barak, a military leader during the time of Israel's judges, as a great man of faith—so great that he is mentioned by name in the Faith Hall of Fame in Hebrews 11 (verse 32).

Barak courageously united the warriors from the tribes of Israel and led them to victory over their Canaanite enemies. He also respected the authority of the judge Deborah, setting himself apart as a man who honored the leadership of a woman—something virtually unheard of in those days.

But Barak, as courageous as he was, had a moment of doubt, and it prevented him from receiving the full blessing God had chosen him to receive. Barak had enough faith to take on the task God had set before him—but under one condition that God never intended. By placing his faith not in God alone but also in Deborah's leadership, he lost some of the blessing God had intended for him.

Doing great things for God requires faith. When we place our faith in God alone, He allows us the full blessing He intends. But we must have the courage to believe Him.

JESUS' DISCIPLES: LEARNING ABOUT LOVE

Now before the feast of the passover, when Jesus knew that his hour was come that he should depart out of this world unto the Father, having loved his own which were in the world, he loved them unto the end.

JOHN 13:1 KJV

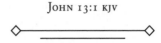

Just when Jesus Christ was about to be parted from His disciples and led away to Calvary: "having loved His own which were in the world, He loved them unto the end." He knew one of His disciples would betray Him; yet He loved Judas. He knew another disciple would deny Him and swear he never knew Him; and yet He loved Peter. It was Christ's love for Peter that broke his heart and brought him back in penitence to the feet of his Lord.

For three years Jesus had been with the disciples trying to teach them His love, not only by His life and words, but by His works. And, on the night of His betrayal, He takes a basin of water, girds Himself with a towel and, taking the place of a servant, washes their feet; He wanted to convince them of His unchanging love.

PAUL: WALK WORTHY

As a prisoner for the Lord, then, I urge you to live a life worthy
of the calling you have received. Be completely humble and gentle;
be patient, bearing with one another in love. Make every effort
to keep the unity of the Spirit through the bond of peace.

EPHESIANS 4:1–3 NIV

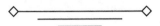

The apostle Paul was a prisoner in Rome as he penned this epistle to the church in Ephesus. As such, he could have asked for any number of things—a visit, support, prayer—but under the inspiration of the Holy Spirit, he had something else on his mind: he wanted Christians in this church to walk in a manner worthy of their calling.

Paul then spelled out what that calling looks like: humility, gentleness, patience, tolerance, love, and unity. Some of these qualities are often viewed as aspects of certain personality types, but Paul said they are basic callings for every Christian. What better way to distinguish a Christian from the world and to show the world what a redeemed life looks like?

How are you doing in these areas? If you've fallen short in your calling, confess that to the Lord and then rely on the sanctifying work of the Holy Spirit to change you.

EHUD: GOOD INFLUENCE

*And it came to pass, when he was come, that he blew a trumpet in
the mountain of Ephraim, and the children of Israel went down
with him from the mount, and he before them. And he said unto
them, Follow after me: for the LORD hath delivered your enemies
the Moabites into your hand. . . . And they slew of Moab at that
time about ten thousand men, all lusty, and all men of valour;
and there escaped not a man. So Moab was subdued that day
under the hand of Israel. And the land had rest fourscore years.*

JUDGES 3:27–30 KJV

◇——————◇

Ehud, having slain the king of Moab, gave a total rout to the forces
of the Moabites that were among them and so effectually shook off
the yoke of their oppression. There escaped not a man of them. And
they were the best and choicest of all the king of Moab's forces, all
lusty men, men of bulk and stature, and not only able-bodied, but
high spirited too, and men of valor. But neither their strength nor
their courage stood them in any stead when the set time had come
for God to deliver them into the hand of Israel.

The consequence of this victory was that the power of the Moabites
was wholly broken in the land of Israel. The country was cleared of
these oppressors, and the land had rest eighty years. We may hope
that there was likewise a reformation among them, and a check
given to idolatry, by the influence of Ehud which continued a good
part of this time. It was a great while for the land to rest, fourscore
years; yet what is that to the saints' everlasting rest in the heavenly
Canaan?

NOAH: BELIEVING AND ACTING

*By faith Noah, when warned about things not yet
seen, in holy fear built an ark to save his family.*
HEBREWS 11:7 NIV

The unknown writer of Hebrews opens the eleventh chapter of his
epistle by defining faith as "confidence in what we hope for and assurance about what we do not see" (Hebrews 11:1 NIV). He then goes on
to show what that means through several Old Testament examples.

One of those examples is Noah, who, in obedience to God's
command, built a giant ship called an ark to prevent him, his family,
and representatives of every living creature from perishing during
the Flood.

Noah's story showcases his amazing faith. As God relayed His
instructions to Noah (Genesis 6:12–22), he didn't question or test
God even once. The end of this passage simply explains, "Noah did
everything just as God commanded him." (Genesis 6:22 NIV). And
because of his faith and obedience in the face of something he couldn't
yet see, his family and all the animals were saved.

The apostle James tells us that even evil spirits believe in God—
and tremble in fear (James 2:19). Faith, therefore, means not just
believing in God, but believing and then *acting* on His word. . .even
if it doesn't make any earthly sense.

DAVID: REFUSING VENGEANCE

*"Is there not still someone of the house of Saul,
to whom I may show the kindness of God?"*

2 SAMUEL 9:3 NKJV

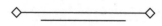

After God's Spirit departed from Israel's first king, Saul hunted his replacement—the young shepherd who once killed a giant and now played peaceful harmonies to lull Saul's troubled soul. David lived on the run for years, refusing to fight back against God's anointed, even when presented with two ideal opportunities to end Saul's life.

Not only did David pass up revenge, but after Saul died in battle, he sought out Saul's remaining descendants—not to kill them and consolidate his power but to see if he could show them kindness.

In David's day, mercy was seen as weakness. Refusing to retaliate to preserve your honor tainted you as unreliable. The whole turning-the-other-cheek that Jesus later taught would have been ridiculous to most people.

But as David demonstrated, the higher virtue lies in being able to avenge yourself but refusing to do so. It takes faith to refrain—a belief that when God says vengeance belongs to Him (Proverbs 25:21–22; Romans 12:19), He means it. Not only will He hold you accountable for all you've said and done, He'll do the same for everyone else. Have the faith to let Him.

MEPHIBOSHETH: THE WELL-TREATED "DEAD DOG"

*Mephibosheth bowed down and said, "What is your
servant, that you should notice a dead dog like me?"*

2 SAMUEL 9:8 NIV

Crippled Mephibosheth saw himself as a "dead dog"—unworthy of
being noticed by anybody, let alone King David. But David didn't
see him that way, especially since he was the son of his best friend,
Jonathan. So David sought to show him kindness, even going so far as
to restore the land that belonged to Saul, his grandfather, and inviting
him to eat at the king's table.

In Mephibosheth's time, wild dogs ran amok in the east and
people often showed contempt for them. Given his physical condition,
Mephibosheth would have been accustomed to this reaction as well. And
then, out of nowhere, David offered him mercy beyond imagination.

Do you remember how you felt the moment the Holy Spirit
revealed that you were a sinner in God's sight with no hope for eternity
apart from Him? You felt the weight of your condition for the first
time; but then, a moment later, you recognized that Jesus had paid
the full price to remove your burden and redeem your soul.

Yes, you are a redeemed Mephibosheth. As such, you are invited
to dine at the marriage supper of the Lamb (Revelation 19:6–9).

JONAH AND JESUS: COMPARISON AND CONTRAST

"This is a wicked generation. It asks for a sign, but none will be given it except the sign of Jonah. For as Jonah was a sign to the Ninevites, so also will the Son of Man be to this generation."

LUKE 11:29–30 NIV

When certain people asked Jesus for a sign, Jesus referred to the "sign of Jonah." Jonah was an Israelite prophet whom God had called to go to the city of Nineveh and preach against the residents' wickedness. Jonah, however, disobeyed God and tried to flee in a ship. Consequently, he ended up being thrown into the sea and swallowed by a great fish, where he remained for three days. During that time, Jonah appealed to God for salvation, and God heard his prayers. After three days, He caused the fish to cast Jonah upon dry land.

This was the sign to which Jesus referred, though Jesus' humble obedience stood in contrast to Jonah's disobedience. Jesus, offering Himself as a sacrifice in order to save many, was beaten, crucified, and laid in a tomb for three days. But after those three days, God raised Him from the dead.

What a comfort to know that we can rest in Christ's obedience. Unlike reluctant Jonah, Jesus *willingly* gave his life for us. May we also obey God and be used for His purposes.

CLASSICS: CHARLES SPURGEON

SAMSON: GUARD YOUR LOCKS

*Howbeit the hair of his head began to grow
again after he was shaven.*

JUDGES 16:22 KJV

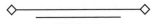

Though Samson's hair grew again, and his strength came back, and he died gloriously fighting against the Philistines, yet he never recovered his eyes, or his liberty, or his living power in Israel! Short and effective was his last stroke against the adversary, but it cost him his life. He could not again rise to be the man he had been before; and though God did give him a great victory over the Philistine people, yet it was but as the flicker of an expiring candle; he was never again a lamp of hope to Israel. His usefulness was abated, and even brought to an end, through his folly.

Whatever the grace of God may do for us, it cannot make sin a right thing, or a safe thing, or a permissible thing. It is evil, only evil, and that continually. O children of God, be not enslaved by fleshly lusts! O Nazarites unto God, guard your locks, lest they be cut away by sin while you are sleeping in the lap of pleasure! O servants of Jehovah, serve the Lord with heart and soul by His grace even to the end, and keep yourselves unshorn by the world!

THE WIDOW OF NAIN'S SON: RAISED TO NEW LIFE

And when He came near the gate of the city, behold, a dead man
was being carried out, the only son of his mother; and she was
a widow. And a large crowd from the city was with her.

LUKE 7:12 NKJV

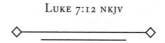

As her son was carried out of the city gate, the widow stared destitution in the face. As an older woman, she had no career opportunities to speak of and no one to care for her from then on.

Jesus saw the situation and had compassion. "Do not weep," he told the grieving mother. He touched the young man's coffin and told him to rise. Immediately, the boy sat up and began to speak. Jesus reunited mother and son as the crowd glorified God and praised Jesus as a prophet.

If the crowds and the widow were amazed, imagine what the son must have felt! Reunited with his needy mother, he must have wondered why Jesus had chosen him, out of all the people who had died that day, for resurrection,

We too have been raised to new life. And like the widow's son, we might wonder why Jesus chose us instead of someone else. But God's choice is always for a reason—all we must do is make the most of the days He has given us.

CLASSICS: ANDREW MURRAY

PRAYING CHRISTIANS: RISING TO THE OCCASION

Peter therefore was kept in prison: but prayer was made without ceasing of the church unto God for him. . . . And, behold, the angel of the Lord came upon him, and a light shined in the prison: and he smote Peter on the side, and raised him up, saying, Arise up quickly. And his chains fell off from his hands. And the angel said unto him, Gird thyself, and bind on thy sandals. And so he did. And he saith unto him, Cast thy garment about thee, and follow me.

ACTS 12:5–8 KJV

◇——————◇

We have the story of Peter in prison on the eve of execution. The death of James had aroused the Church to a sense of real danger, and the thought of losing Peter too wakened up all its energies. It betook itself to prayer.

That prayer availed much; Peter was delivered. When he came to the house of Mary, he found "many gathered together praying." Stone walls and double chains, soldiers and keepers, and the iron gate, all gave way before the power from heaven that prayer brought down to his rescue.

The whole power of the Roman Empire, as represented by Herod, was impotent in the presence of the power the Church of the Holy Spirit wielded in prayer.

ABEL: IT'S OKAY TO FINISH LAST

*Abel also brought an offering—fat portions from some of the
firstborn of his flock. The LORD looked with favor on Abel and
his offering, but on Cain and his offering he did not look with
favor. So Cain was very angry, and his face was downcast.*

<small>GENESIS 4:4–5 NIV</small>

After reading the story of Abel and his brother Cain, you might be
tempted to think that "nice guys finish last." But you'd be mistaken.

Abel, second son of Adam and Eve, was the family "good boy."
He may have consistently done what his parents asked. Certainly,
he loved God deeply, for when it came time to make an offering, he
brought his heavenly Father the best he had. And God smiled on him.

Cain, the elder son, may have thought, *Mom always loves you
best—and Dad does too. Now, even God is taking your side.* Quickly,
sibling rivalry overcame brotherly love. Feeling unloved and unac-
cepted because God knew that his sacrifice wasn't from the heart,
Cain took out his anger on his brother. As a result, he committed
the first murder in history and was condemned to wander the earth
for the rest of his days.

Abel didn't have a long life, but judging from the joy that accompanied his sacrifice to God, it was a successful one. Jesus commended
Abel as a righteous man (Matthew 23:35). Though Cain lived on for
many more barren years after killing his brother, who can possibly
say those years were better?

If finishing last means eternal joy, maybe being last is the first
thing we should aim for.

ELIJAH: HOW TO (REALLY) SERVE GOD

And after six days Jesus taketh Peter, James, and John his brother, and bringeth them up into an high mountain apart, and was transfigured before them: and his face did shine as the sun, and his raiment was white as the light. And, behold, there appeared unto them Moses and Elias talking with him.

MATTHEW 17:1–3 KJV

Elijah is one of the few figures in the Bible who seem to transcend ordinary life. As if his work on earth wasn't spectacular enough, this man seems to have kept busy even after he was taken up to heaven.

Elijah and Moses appeared at Jesus' transfiguration. As the three met (and shone) on the top of a high mountain, the disciples saw them deep in conversation. Elijah was still deeply involved in the Lord's work even centuries after his departure.

The book of Malachi promises that Elijah will herald that "great and terrible day" when Christ will return in all His glory. So apparently, his work isn't done yet.

What a way to serve God. . .walking so closely with Him that this life and the next blend seamlessly into one!

JESUS: PRESENT WITH HIS OWN

"No, I will not abandon you as orphans—I will come to you. Soon the world will no longer see me, but you will see me. Since I live, you also will live. When I am raised to life again, you will know that I am in my Father, and you are in me, and I am in you."

JOHN 14:18–20 NLT

◇——————◇

If you haven't had a crisis of faith—wondering if your prayers are just bouncing off the ceiling or if you're the only one struggling with doubts—you will at *some* point. In fact, Jesus' disciples frequently wrestled with doubts and confusion. If you feel like living by faith each day is a bit beyond you, you're in good company.

Jesus recognized this struggle in His followers and assured them He would remain closer to them than they could even imagine. While His followers feared being left behind like orphans, Jesus assured them that He would come live within them. This mystery isn't something you'll figure out from a sermon or a prayer retreat. This is a lifelong assurance that you can cling to and experience on deeper levels through the highs and lows of life.

Although you probably won't see Jesus walking alongside you, He is within you, much like He and the Father are one. This union with God will keep your faith alive until you see Him face-to-face.

PAUL: A MODEL FOR SUFFERING

*For to you it has been granted on behalf of Christ, not
only to believe in Him, but also to suffer for His sake.*
PHILIPPIANS 1:29 NKJV

Paul knew what it meant to suffer for Christ. He chronicles many of
his perils in 2 Corinthians 11:24–27. They include five lashings from
the Jews, three beatings with rods, one stoning, and more. He was
in constant danger and always in need of food, shelter, and clothing.

Writing from a Roman prison, he wanted the believers in Philippi
to understand that they too were called to suffer for Christ. Since the
church in Philippi was known for its generosity, even sending Paul
supplies when he was ministering to other churches (Philippians
4:15), he wanted to hear only good reports about this church, even if
he couldn't be with them (Philippians 1:27). Therefore, he prepared
them to not fear their adversaries. Suffering for Christ had been
granted to them by God; it was a privilege.

How can we see it any differently in our own lives? Many of us,
as modern Christians, tend to get caught up in our comfort, often
forgetting that we are destined to suffer for Christ. We aren't called
to seek trouble, but we are called to endure it when it comes. Are you
preparing yourself and your family accordingly?

CLASSICS: ANDREW MURRAY

ABRAHAM: OBEDIENCE PLEASES GOD

*And said, By myself have I sworn, saith the L*ORD*, for because thou hast done this thing, and hast not withheld thy son, thine only son: that in blessing I will bless thee, and in multiplying I will multiply thy seed as the stars of the heaven, and as the sand which is upon the sea shore; and thy seed shall possess the gate of his enemies; and in thy seed shall all the nations of the earth be blessed; because thou hast obeyed my voice.*

GENESIS 22:16–18 KJV

Think of Abraham, the father of the chosen race. "By faith Abraham *obeyed*." When he had been forty years in this school of faith-obedience, God came to perfect his faith and to crown it with His fullest blessing. Nothing could fit him for this but a crowning act of obedience.

When he had bound his son on the altar, God came and said, "By Myself have I sworn, in blessing I will bless thee, and in multiplying I will multiply thee; and in thy seed shall all nations be blessed, because thou hast obeyed My voice." And to Isaac He spake, "I will perform the oath which I sware to Abraham, because that Abraham obeyed My voice" (Genesis 26:3, 5).

Oh, when shall we learn how unspeakably pleasing obedience is in God's sight, and how unspeakable is the reward He bestows upon it. The way to be a blessing to the world is to be men of obedience; known by God and the world by this one mark—a will utterly given up to God's will.

BARZILLAI: FAITHFUL NO MATTER WHAT

Now Barzillai was very old, eighty years of age.
He had provided for the king during his stay in
Mahanaim, for he was a very wealthy man.

2 SAMUEL 19:32 NIV

Barzillai is one of the lesser-known men of Old Testament times, but his story can teach us something about standing strong for what's right, no matter the risk.

David's son, Absalom, had turned public opinion against his father, to the point where the king had to run for his life. Fortunately, Barzillai used his own wealth to provide shelter for David during this time.

The Bible doesn't tell us whether Barzillai knew David personally, but he definitely understood that David was truly a man after God's own heart. So even though his decision to support David wouldn't have fared well in public opinion polls, he never hesitated in standing up for God's anointed leader of Israel.

We live in a time when identifying ourselves with Jesus Christ isn't as popular as it once was—now, standing for God's principles opens us up to scorn and rejection. But God calls us to be modern-day Barzillais—people who will stand up for Him despite the risks.

DAVID: SUPERNATURAL STRENGTH

*"In your strength I can crush an army;
with my God I can scale any wall."*

2 SAMUEL 22:30 NLT

David was a bundle of contradictions. He was a great sinner, but he was also a man after God's own heart. He could be patient, but sometimes he acted in haste. He could show great mercy—as he did with Jonathan's disabled son, Mephibosheth—or be utterly ruthless. He was a warrior as well as a poet. The latter may have made him especially sensitive to understanding his ultimate identity before a holy God: a weak vessel.

Three times in 2 Samuel 22—David's song of praise to the Lord—he mentioned that God strengthened him. He sang about God as his rock, fortress, shield, savior, and more.

We too are bundles of contradictions. We sin much while also chasing after God. We are impatient with others but also try to show compassion. But when God works in us, we can only do good. And once we've tasted of His power, how can we do anything else but praise Him like David did?

CLASSICS: D. L. MOODY

JOSEPH: GOD WAS WITH HIM

And the patriarchs, moved with envy, sold
Joseph into Egypt: but God was with him.
ACTS 7:9 KJV

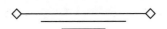

Joseph was another of those great men who walked in fellowship with God. His brethren tried to get rid of him; Satan attempted to put him down; but they could not, although he lay so long in the Egyptian prison.

The skeptical and unbelieving of that day might have said, "Look at that man; he serves the God of his fathers, the God of Abraham, and Isaac, and Jacob; he will not turn aside a hair's breadth from the worship of the unknown God: yet see how his God serves him! He is in prison!" But wait God's time.

It is better to be in prison with God than in a palace without Him. It is said that he was in prison; but—and I like that expression—"God was with him."

JESUS: MEET HIM AT THE COMMUNION TABLE

And he said to them, "I have eagerly desired to eat this Passover with you before I suffer. For I tell you, I will not eat it again until it finds fulfillment in the kingdom of God."

LUKE 22:15–16 NIV

Jesus spoke these words to men who had failed Him. His disciples had argued over who would be the greatest, often misunderstood His teaching, failed to cast out demons in His name, and even fell asleep when He asked them to pray for Him. And yet Jesus eagerly desired to eat the Passover meal with this band of misfits before He suffered.

Christ's sacrificial death on the cross led the apostle Paul to refer to him as "Christ, our Passover lamb" (1 Corinthians 5:7)—the old had passed away, and the new had come. The Passover meal gave way to the institution of the Lord's Supper (1 Corinthians 11), in which we proclaim the Lord's death until He returns.

Do you approach the communion table at your church with the same vigor and desire as Jesus? Are you eager to settle your account with God in a corporate worship setting, knowing other believers around you are doing the same thing? If not, you may need to check your faith. If Jesus earnestly desired to celebrate the Passover, knowing it would spell the beginning of His suffering, how much more should we yearn to commemorate His sacrifice?

JOSEPH OF ARIMATHEA: THE REWARDS ARE UNENDING

Now Joseph was a disciple of Jesus, but secretly because he feared the Jewish leaders.

JOHN 19:38 NIV

Everything we know about Joseph of Arimathea comes from just a handful of verses in each Gospel. He was a rich disciple of Jesus (Matthew 27:57), a prominent member of the Sanhedrin (Mark 15:43), a good and upright man who had not consented to the Sanhedrin's decision to crucify Jesus (Luke 23:50–51), and a man who kept his devotion to Jesus a secret (John 19:38). This was an unusual combination of traits in Joseph's time.

Jesus had taught how hard it was for a rich man to enter heaven, yet here was one who had given his heart to Him. It's no wonder Joseph kept his true beliefs a secret: he would have faced scandal and perhaps death had the Sanhedrin found out.

However, there can be no doubt about Joseph's devotion to Jesus in the end. After Jesus' death, Joseph personally petitioned for the body, prepared it with expensive perfume, and laid it in his own tomb. He sacrificed material goods and risked his position to honor the King of kings.

Following Jesus is inherently risky, because the world hates Him and anyone who aligns with Him. But any risks are short-term, while the rewards are unending.

PAUL: AN EXAMPLE OF INTEGRITY

Join together in following my example.
PHILIPPIANS 3:17 NIV

Paul realized that he was leading the way and that others were following him, so he behaved accordingly.

First, Paul knew how much his example mattered, and he took that responsibility seriously. Second, he told others to become like them: "Keep your eyes on those who live as we do" (Philippians 3:17). Third, he stressed the consequences that will come to those who follow the wrong example. And finally, Paul led with integrity, handling his flaws and failures with grace and humility.

But Paul wasn't alone in his position: every man who seeks a great adventure in God is leading the way for others. The question is: What kind of example are you setting? Are you living up to the life of Christ in you, or you slipping back into old habits and patterns? Integrity isn't about putting your best foot forward or presenting a handsome veneer that hides the truth—it's about consistently handling challenges and temptations in a Christ-like manner.

The world has plenty of hypocrites. It's men of true integrity that are in short supply.

JEREMIAH: SHARING GOD'S SWEETNESS

*Thy words were found, and I did eat them; and thy
word was unto me the joy and rejoicing of mine heart:
for I am called by thy name, O LORD God of hosts.*

JEREMIAH 15:16 KJV

Jeremiah had been greatly persecuted for his faithfulness in delivering the Word of God. He tells us the reason for his continuance in a work which brought him so sorrowful a reward. He gives us to understand that he had been faithful in delivering God's Word, because that Word had been overpoweringly precious to his own soul.

God's Word came with such sweetness to his own soul and filled his heart with such ravishing joy and delight that he could not do otherwise than go and tell out among his fellowmen what had been so delightful to himself.

JOSHUA: LONG OBEDIENCE

Joshua waged war against all these kings for a long time. . . . For it was the LORD himself who hardened their hearts to wage war against Israel.

JOSHUA 11:18–20 NIV

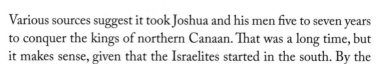

Various sources suggest it took Joshua and his men five to seven years to conquer the kings of northern Canaan. That was a long time, but it makes sense, given that the Israelites started in the south. By the time they reached the north, the enemy kings—having heard of the Israelites' advance—had probably dug in and formed alliances.

Notice that the Lord himself hardened the kings' hearts, causing them to wage war against Israel. But these nations in the north were destined to fall. In Deuteronomy 31:8, Moses made a comforting promise to Joshua: "The LORD himself goes before you and will be with you; he will never leave you nor forsake you. Do not be afraid; do not be discouraged" (NIV). Still, it took Joshua and his army *years* to conquer their enemies. Not even a promised victory was instantaneous. That's often the case for us too.

Have you been fighting a spiritual battle for years, only to become discouraged by your lack of victory? As soldiers in the fight, our job is to obey our Commander and leave the result to Him—no matter how long it takes.

Today, take heart. God goes before you and He will be with you.

ZACCHAEUS: WHEN YOU WANT TO BE SEEN

Jesus said to him, "Today salvation has come to this house, because this man, too, is a son of Abraham. For the Son of Man came to seek and to save the lost."

LUKE 19:9–10 NIV

Zacchaeus was a small man with large ambitions.

He didn't have many friends—not because he was short but because he was small at heart. As a tax collector, he sometimes charged more than he was asked to collect, earning himself the money to support a high-end lifestyle. . .but also a sour reputation around town.

But when Zacchaeus heard Jesus had come to Jericho, he was intrigued. Knowing the crowds would block his view, he scaled a nearby tree and watched the famed teacher and healer coming closer. Then Jesus stopped, looked up, and said, "Zacchaeus, come down immediately. I must stay at your house today" (Luke 19:5 NIV).

Jesus knew Zacchaeus by name, and He invited Himself to lunch! The tax collector was eager to oblige. This encounter with Jesus began an internal change in the small-hearted man. As he issued generous tax refunds for his overcharges, he discovered that what he most wanted in life was simply to be found.

Discrimination is not a part of God's love language. Bring your height, body shape, emotional baggage, and broken dreams. As with Zacchaeus, it's guaranteed that you'll be found.

CLASSICS: ANDREW MURRAY

JACOB: FORCING GOD TO BLESS US

And he said, Let me go, for the day breaketh. And he said, I will not let thee go, except thou bless me. And he said unto him, What is thy name? And he said, Jacob. And he said, Thy name shall be called no more Jacob, but Israel: for as a prince hast thou power with God and with men, and hast prevailed.

GENESIS 32:26–28 KJV

Think of Jacob, when he feared to meet Esau. The angel of the Lord met him in the dark and wrestled with him. And when the angel saw that he prevailed not, he said, "Let me go." And Jacob said, "I will not let thee go." And he blessed him there.

And that boldness that said, "I will not," and forced from the reluctant angel the blessing was so pleasing in God's sight that a new name was there given to him: "Israel, he who striveth with God, for thou hast striven with God and with men, and hast prevailed."

And through all the ages God's children have understood what Christ's two parables teach, that God holds Himself back and seeks to get away from us until what is of flesh and self and sloth in us is overcome, and we so prevail with Him that He can and must bless us.

THE RICH FOOL:
A WARNING PARABLE

"But God said to him, 'Fool! This night your soul will be required of you; then whose will those things be which you have provided?'"

LUKE 12:20 NKJV

Andrew Carnegie believed "the man who dies thus rich dies disgraced." In Luke 12:13–21, it appears we have a man who didn't quite subscribe to that philosophy.

Quite possibly, this fellow wasn't even miserly; he may have been quite generous to others as God blessed him. But he still became all too comfortable, all too self-satisfied, all too self-absorbed. He may have hit a point in his life when he no longer cared much about giving. He had all he needed and then some. Why bother? He was preoccupied with how he would store all his excess.

We're told that God had something to say to this man. It began with, "Fool!" Having another person call you a fool is one thing. Having God call you a fool is quite another.

Why was God so harsh? For one thing, this man was "goods-centered" instead of God-centered. It isn't wicked to be rich, but it is wicked to be selfish. This man never thought to ask the One responsible for all his blessings what he should do with his wealth. He failed to acknowledge that only God can fill the void within us. He also failed to prepare for eternity. He clearly had only this life in view.

Jesus warns us, "So is he who lays up treasure for himself, and is not rich toward God" (Luke 12:21 NKJV).

ELIPHAZ THE TEMANITE: ACCEPTING UNCERTAINTIES

Then Eliphaz the Temanite replied: "If someone ventures a word with you, will you be impatient? But who can keep from speaking?"

JOB 4:1–2 NIV

While Job sits in his misery, the unwitting subject of a challenge between God and the devil, four friends come to comfort him. They love him and their intentions are sincere—but each tackles the situation from his own perspective.

Eliphaz the Temanite is perhaps the loudest voice in the group. He believes in God but has a rationalist approach to how God works. God punishes the wicked, he insists, so it would be in Job's own interest to examine his soul, confess his sin, and be restored.

Like rationalists everywhere, Eliphaz makes a convincing case. But he is hidebound by his own thought process. When Job insists he has done nothing wrong and points out that God doesn't always strike down the wicked, Eliphaz's patience rapidly runs out.

His stance is attractive to many. We like to figure things out; we are comforted by cause and effect, reassured by the thought that there is always a rational answer. Job's attitude is more difficult to adopt. His uncertainty causes him great distress, yet he still trusts.

Just as Eliphaz would have done better to sit with his friend in uncertainty rather than seeking explanations, we should resist the urge to hastily judge another's misfortunes.

ABRAHAM: BELIEVING FOR OTHERS TOO

And the LORD appeared unto him the same night, and said, I am the God of Abraham thy father: fear not, for I am with thee, and will bless thee, and multiply thy seed for my servant Abraham's sake.

GENESIS 26:24 KJV

Abraham had not believed for himself alone, but for his child; the faith that was counted for righteousness had entirely reference to God's promise about his child; as a father he had believed and received the child in faith from God; the sign of circumcision in the child was the seal to the child of the father's faith.

God dealt with father and child as one; the father believed for himself and his child as one; the child had the same place in the covenant, and the same claim on the seal of the covenant, as the father. And as he grew up it would be to him a seal not only of the faith his father had, but of God's promise waiting for his faith too, the remembrancer of the one thing required by God, the one thing counted righteousness by Him, the one thing well-pleasing to Him, and by which he in turn could pass the blessing on to his seed again.

LYSIAS: PURSUING JUSTICE

[Paul] also hath gone about to profane the temple: whom we took, and would have judged according to our law. But the chief captain Lysias came upon us, and with great violence took him away out of our hands.

Acts 24:6–7 KJV

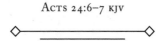

When Lysias, who was Greek by birth, purchased his Roman citizenship (Acts 22:28), he probably received the forename Claudius. His role as a commander in the Roman army likely put him in charge over more than a thousand men.

Paul, on the other hand, was a Roman citizen by birth. As such, he had the full rights of citizenship, including the right to a Roman trial. When Paul ran afoul of the Jewish leaders in Jerusalem, they falsely accused him of being a troublemaker who stirred up rebellions against his own government and defiled the temple.

But once Lysias sorted out the details and learned that Paul was a Roman citizen, he and his men removed Paul by force so that he could get a fair trial.

Despite the people's opposition, Lysias was determined to do the right thing—even if it required force. That's what genuine leadership looks like. Is there a situation in your life that may require a similar response, even if it means taking a forceful stand?

JESUS: WITH US IN SPIRIT

*"But the Advocate, the Holy Spirit, whom the Father will
send in my name, will teach you all things and will remind
you of everything I have said to you. Peace I leave with you;
my peace I give you. I do not give to you as the world gives.
Do not let your hearts be troubled and do not be afraid."*

JOHN 14:26–27 NIV

◇━━━━━━━━◇

Mere hours before His arrest and crucifixion, Jesus promised to send His Holy Spirit to comfort and instruct His followers. Even after Jesus' resurrection in a few days, they would have great need of the Spirit's peace and direction once Jesus ascended into heaven. Despite the shock of seeing Jesus leave, the Spirit would prevent fear from taking root in their hearts.

Jesus assures us too that we can seek the Holy Spirit's direction, wisdom, and peace. We will surely face situations where fear appears to be more than warranted. But in Jesus, we can choose to turn to the Holy Spirit.

This does not guarantee our problems will be resolved or we'll suddenly have incredible wisdom to make the best choices. Rather, the Spirit will reassure us that whatever may happen tomorrow, we are not alone—God remains with us. The Spirit guards our souls and keeps us close to Jesus, even when every other source of peace appears to be far away.

THE ETHIOPIAN EUNUCH: WILLING TO ASK QUESTIONS

*And the eunuch answered Philip, and said, I pray thee,
of whom speaketh the prophet this? of himself, or of some
other man? Then Philip opened his mouth, and began at
the same scripture, and preached unto him Jesus.*

ACTS 8:34–35 KJV

The Ethiopian eunuch didn't need spectacles—he needed a new perspective. And God perfectly positioned Philip to provide it.

A high official of the queen in Ethiopia, the eunuch had traveled to Jerusalem to worship God. Philip saw him reading scripture in his chariot, just like you might read the Bible in your car or on a train.

In modern times, we know that the Old Testament refers to Christ many times (in Isaiah 53, for example), but for the people in that day, the Messiah's identity was a mystery. The eunuch was obviously confused by what he read. So Philip, with his firsthand knowledge, took the old words and gave them new life, explaining to the eunuch that the suffering Savior had fulfilled these centuries-old prophecies.

All those confusing verses now made sense! Jesus was the missing piece in the puzzle. The eunuch looked around, saw some water, and asked to be baptized. His life was changed, forever, because he was willing to humble himself and ask questions.

How about you?

HUNGRY LEPERS: FOLLOWING THEIR CONSCIENCE

Now there were four men with leprosy at the entrance of the city gate. They said to each other, "Why stay here until we die?"

2 Kings 7:3 NIV

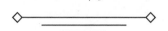

With Samaria hunkered down inside its city walls in fear of the Arameans, its people were starving. The situation for four Samarian lepers on the outside of the city walls was even more dire. Even if they violated cleanliness laws by entering the city, they wouldn't find any food. But if they went into the Arameans' camp in search of food, they could be killed. They took a risk and chose the latter.

The men had no idea that God had gone before them, chasing the Arameans out of the camp with the sounds of chariots, horses, and a great army. When they reached the camp and realized that it was abandoned, the lepers ate, drank, and began to store up goods for themselves. Then their conscience got the best of them, prompting them to report their findings to the king so that the rest of the city could partake.

God provided for His people through four unclean men who, despite being in self-preservation mode, still had the integrity to do what was right when nobody was watching. As we seek to overcome our own impurities and limitations, we too will be faced with the opportunity to do what is right. May we choose well.

THE DEMONIAC OF GADARA: NEVER TOO FAR GONE

Then they came to Jesus, and saw the one who
had been demon-possessed and had the legion,
sitting and clothed and in his right mind.

MARK 5:15 NKJV

Is there a more desperate biblical figure than the out-of-control, demon-possessed man of Gadara? Infiltrated by a horde of demons, who called themselves "Legion" (Mark 5:9), he had been reduced to a humiliating state and separated from home and friends. It's likely that this unhappy fellow had toyed with sin until it had a stranglehold on him.

It has been said that whenever Jesus confronted demons, they did what even the religious leaders of the day refused to do: They acknowledged Him to be the Son of God. It was no different in this case.

From the start, Jesus was in control of the entire situation, demons and all. Imagine the freedom the man felt when the demons left him! Once the man's sanity was restored, Jesus and the apostles clothed him. He begged to go with Jesus, but the Master sent him home to share the message of his healing (Mark 5:19).

This man keenly knew what he had been saved from. Many of us keenly feel the guilt of our own sin. But if Jesus could cleanse and save the demoniac of Gadara, He can certainly do the same for us. No one is ever too far gone for our Lord.

BARNABAS: STANDING UP FOR OTHERS

But Barnabas took him and brought him to the apostles. He
told them how Saul on his journey had seen the Lord and
that the Lord had spoken to him, and how in Damascus
he had preached fearlessly in the name of Jesus.

ACTS 9:27 NIV

After encountering Jesus on the Damascus Road, Saul would become the most famous and influential missionary of all time. However, even though he was a changed man with a new purpose, the Christians of Jerusalem were understandably suspicious and even fearful.

Saul had a well-earned reputation as a man who hated the Church, having made it his life's goal to stop this new movement we now call Christianity. This he had done by viciously persecuting every Christian who crossed his path.

But Saul had an earthly advocate, a Jewish Christian from Cyprus named Barnabas. While the Jerusalem Christians wanted nothing to do with Saul, Barnabas embraced him as a "new creation" in Jesus Christ. He also took a personal interest in mentoring him, knowing that God had called this man to do great things for the kingdom of God.

Barnabas seemingly took a big risk by hitching his wagon to Saul. In the same way, let's be on the lookout for new brothers and sisters in Christ—some of them from very rough backgrounds—and mentor and stand up for them so that they can become all God intends them to be.

CLASSICS: ANDREW MURRAY

JESUS: WHAT LOVE IS

And I have declared unto them thy name, and will
declare it: that the love wherewith thou hast
loved me may be in them, and I in them.

JOHN 17:26 KJV

Do you want to know what love is? Oh, my heart cannot take it in, nor my tongue express it; my thoughts cannot reach to all its fullness. Love means—giving all!

It is that with God, and it is that with us too. If you are to have love, it means you are to give up everything to God; everything. God cannot be limited. With God love means giving His life to His Son, and with that giving everything! That is the love of God to Christ.

My friends, as you think of the love of God, has it ever said to you that you must die? The highest point of God's love is that He invites us to die utterly to self, to be like Himself and His Son, perfect in love. God's love to Christ means death. May we have grace to say: I would enter into the death of Jesus, I would be nothing in myself, O my God! May Thy love consent to accept of me to be nothing.

PETER: THE ULTIMATE PAYBACK

Don't repay evil for evil. Don't retaliate with insults when people insult you. Instead, pay them back with a blessing. That is what God has called you to do, and he will grant you his blessing.

1 PETER 3:9 NLT

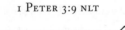

In the heat of an argument or frustrating situation, it's hard to resist giving someone a piece of our mind. As social media makes it easier to argue without seeing someone face-to-face, we often display the ugliest parts of our anger and discord without the filter of empathy or understanding.

Peter challenges us to bless those who insult us and to avoid any kind of retaliation. Although he was writing to Christians who were being actively marginalized and persecuted for their faith, his message remains powerful to anyone who seeks to infuse the world with God's hope.

You gain very little from insulting others, and even the act of receiving an insult can be good for you. Sure, insults tend to undermine your ego, but when you release your anger and offer blessings instead, you bring another person one step closer to God. . .while reminding yourself of your identity as His beloved child.

THE CENTURION: FORGIVENESS IS FOR EVERYONE

Now when the centurion, and they that were with him, watching Jesus, saw the earthquake, and those things that were done, they feared greatly, saying, Truly this was the Son of God.

MATTHEW 27:54 KJV

Scared? Well, there's one person who can tell you about scared—this centurion.

He didn't just turn up at the conclusion of the crucifixion and proclaim some immortal words. In all likelihood, he was in charge of the "soldiers of the governor" who whipped, spat on, and mocked Jesus. He likely gave the orders to drive the nails through His hands and feet.

Then, as the sky darkened and the earth shook, he realized that he had just "killed" the Son of a powerful God! It would have terrified the bravest of men. Hopefully, someone had a quiet word with him afterward. Having recognized Jesus for who He really was, all he had to do to find eternal peace was accept Him as his Savior.

We don't always give our Lord the respect He deserves. Some of us, through the way we live our lives, treat Him pretty shabbily. None of us, however, have treated Him the way the centurion did, and yet even he was given a second chance.

Don't be scared. Find solace in the love and forgiveness of the Son of God.

JESUS: DEALING WITH THE WILDERNESS

Jesus was led by the Holy Spirit to a desert. There He was tempted by the devil. Jesus went without food for forty days and forty nights. After that He was hungry.

MATTHEW 4:1–2 NLV

Immediately following His baptism, Jesus was led to the wilderness. It seems like a strange way to begin His earthly ministry: the heavens had just opened and declared Jesus to be God's Son in whom He was well pleased. Jesus could have immediately started healing the sick and cleaning out the temple, but the Holy Spirit led Him into the wastelands, where He would encounter hardship, hunger, and temptation.

Life is sometimes like that. We can experience a spiritual high on Sunday, when it feels like the heavens opened and God declared His love for us. Then Monday, back in the regular routine, we feel hungry, spiritually bereft, and tempted by the devil to lay aside our mission.

If Jesus experienced such wilderness moments, shouldn't we as His followers expect to encounter them as well? And since Jesus overcame His trials, we can claim His victory too. We can respond to temptation with God's truth. Our spiritual hunger is satisfied by His Word. Our hardships end when we follow Him home.

In this life, there's always a wilderness. But it plays a valuable role in our growth. Once we learn that the source of our strength is not in ourselves but the power of God's Word, we will be ready for the ministry God has prepared for us.

CLASSICS: D. L. MOODY

PAUL: CONSTANTLY GIVING THANKS

Be careful for nothing; but in every thing by prayer and
supplication with thanksgiving let your requests be made known
unto God. And the peace of God, which passeth all understanding,
shall keep your hearts and minds through Christ Jesus.

PHILIPPIANS 4:6–7 KJV

Among all the apostles none suffered so much as Paul; but none of
them do we find so often giving thanks as he.

Take his letter to the Philippians. Remember what he suffered
at Philippi; how they laid many stripes upon him and cast him into
prison. Yet every chapter in that Epistle speaks of rejoicing and giving
thanks. There is that well-known passage: "Be careful for nothing, but
in everything, by prayer and supplication, with thanksgiving, let your
requests be made known unto God." As someone has said, there are
here three precious ideas: "Careful for nothing; prayerful for everything; and thankful for anything."

We always get more by being thankful for what God has done
for us. Paul says again: "We give thanks to God and the Father of
our Lord Jesus Christ, praying always for you" (Colossians 1:3 KJV).
So he was constantly giving thanks. Take up any one of his Epistles,
and you will find them full of praise to God.

THE MAN BORN BLIND:
TAKING ONE SMALL STEP

After saying this, he spit on the ground, made some mud
with the saliva, and put it on the man's eyes. "Go," he told
him, "wash in the Pool of Siloam" (this word means "Sent").
So the man went and washed, and came home seeing.

JOHN 9:6–7 NIV

The account in John 9 of Jesus healing the blind man in Jerusalem raises some questions: Why did Jesus rub mud in the blind man's eyes? Why did He tell him to go wash himself in a nearby pool? Couldn't Jesus have just pronounced him healed and sent him on his way like He had so many others?

It's possible that Jesus healed him this way so that the blind man would have a small part in the process. He never asked Jesus for help, so Jesus gave him the opportunity to receive healing by trusting in Jesus' unusual methods and then taking one small step of obedience. All this, Jesus said, happened for the purpose of glorifying God.

Sometimes, God performs miracles without our even knowing; other times, He may ask us to take some small step toward making it happen, thereby increasing our faith and bringing more glory to Himself.

Are you willing to take that step?

CALEB: FOLLOWING WHOLEHEARTEDLY

From Hebron Caleb drove out the three Anakites—
Sheshai, Ahiman and Talmai, the sons of Anak.

JOSHUA 15:14 NIV

We can't read the book of Joshua without considering the life of Caleb.

In Joshua 14, we learn Caleb followed God "wholeheartedly" (verses 8, 9, 14). In this, Caleb followed the formula for prosperity and success that we read about in Joshua 1:8.

Joshua 14 tells us of Caleb's desire to take his inheritance (which Moses promised him) in Hebron, even at eighty-five years old. This octogenarian was still itching for a fight—the same fight he had been eager to engage in as a forty-year-old, the first time he encountered these giants. At that time, his confidence in God's power overflowed: "We should go up and take possession of the land, for we can certainly do it" (Numbers 13:30 NIV).

What was Caleb's secret? He still relied—wholeheartedly—on God's strength, not his own. Even after forty-five years, Caleb believed that God's promises would be fulfilled. He knew his role in this mission, and he was eager to advance against his enemies and prove God's power once again.

This message is for you too, whether you're eighty-five, forty, or twenty. Patience, trust, and wholehearted devotion prepare you to take on life's most difficult challenges and pursue God's mission. When you follow God as Caleb did, you become ready to move forward in faith, no matter when God calls.

CLASSICS: ANDREW MURRAY

DAVID: A PERFECT HEART

*For it came to pass, when Solomon was old, that his
wives turned away his heart after other gods:
and his heart was not perfect with the L*ORD *his
God, as was the heart of David his father.*

1 KINGS 11:4 KJV

We know how sadly David sinned. And yet the heart of David was
perfect with the Lord his God. In God's record of the lives of His
servants there are some of whom it is written: his heart was perfect
with the Lord his God.

Is this, let each reader ask, what God sees and says of me? Does
my life, in the sight of God, bear the mark of intense, wholehearted
consecration to God's will and service? Of a burning desire to be as
perfect as it is possible for grace to make me?

Let us yield ourselves to the searching light of this question.
Let us believe that with this word *perfect* God means something
very real and true. Let us not evade its force or hide ourselves from
its condemning power by the vain subterfuge that we do not fully
know what it means. We must first accept it and give up our lives to
it before we can understand it.

ANANIAS: OBEYING EVEN WHEN AFRAID

Then Ananias went to the house and entered it. Placing his hands on Saul, he said, "Brother Saul, the Lord—Jesus, who appeared to you on the road as you were coming here—has sent me so that you may see again and be filled with the Holy Spirit." Immediately, something like scales fell from Saul's eyes, and he could see again. He got up and was baptized, and after taking some food, he regained his strength.

ACTS 9:17–19 NIV

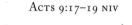

Saul's conversion on the road to Damascus is pivotal in Church history. Soon to be called Paul, the former persecutor of Christians would go on to write much of the New Testament. These books detail the early Church's victories and defeats, explain deep truths about God and Jesus, and provide a template for godly living.

Can you imagine what might have happened if Ananias—who knew that Saul had persecuted and scattered thousands of Christians throughout the Roman world—had given in to fear and refused the Spirit's command to visit him? The Christian Church and our Bibles would look much different today.

The good news is that, in God's perfect plan and will, Ananias did obey—even though he was afraid.

Fear can be paralyzing, but God is in the habit of healing paralysis! When He commands, through either His Word or the nudging of His Spirit, just go. God has infinite power to take care of the rest.

CLASSICS: CHARLES SPURGEON

JESUS: HOW FAR HE STOOPED—FOR US

Then cried they all again, saying, Not this man, but Barabbas. Now Barabbas was a robber.

JOHN 18:40 KJV

This episode in the Savior's history shows that in the judgment of the people, Jesus Christ was a greater offender than Barabbas; and, for once, I may venture to say, that *vox populi* (the voice of the people), which in itself was a most infamous injustice, if it be read in the light of the imputation of our sins to Christ, was *vox Dei* (the voice of God).

Christ, as He stood covered with His people's sins, had more sin laid upon Him than that which rested upon Barabbas. In Him was no sin; He was altogether incapable of becoming a sinner: holy, harmless, and undefiled is Christ Jesus, but He takes the whole load of His people's guilt upon Himself by imputation, and as Jehovah looks upon Him, He sees more guilt lying upon the Savior than even upon this atrocious sinner, Barabbas. Barabbas goes free—innocent—in comparison with the tremendous weight which rests upon the Savior.

Think, beloved, then, how low your Lord and Master stooped to be thus numbered with the transgressors.

MOSES: GOD EQUIPS

"My grace is all you need. My power works best in weakness."
2 Corinthians 12:9 nlt

Imagine this: a potential employee is being interviewed for a job, and the employee's first question is, "Who are you?" His second question: "Who am I?" When told he will be a salesman, the candidate says, "What if the customers don't believe me? I have poor speaking skills." As the interview concludes, he asks, "Why don't you hire someone else?"

Do you think he would get a callback interview?

During God's conversation with Moses at the burning bush, Moses asked similar questions (Exodus 3:1–22, 4:1–17). When God said He would rescue His people from oppression in Egypt, Moses probably rejoiced. . .until he learned that he would be the one to challenge Pharaoh.

Forty years had passed since Moses had fled Egypt. He'd made a new life for himself in Midian. He was so far removed from his people, in fact, that he hadn't circumcised his own son (Exodus 4:25). At first, he resisted his call to greatness. But God overcame all of Moses' objections one by one and then sent him toward Egypt to face his destiny.

Moses learned that God would equip him to carry out his assignments. God will do the same for us.

ELIJAH: YOU'RE NEVER ALONE

"Lord, they have killed your prophets and torn down your altars;
I am the only one left, and they are trying to kill me?" And
what was God's answer to him? "I have reserved for myself
seven thousand who have not bowed the knee to Baal."

ROMANS 11:3–4 NIV

In 1 Kings 18, the prophet Elijah challenged 450 priests of Baal to a showdown of epic proportions. With all Israel watching, Elijah called down fire from heaven, devouring a massive, water-soaked offering in divine fashion. The people fell on their faces, confessing God, and then dispatched the pagan priests. Furious, Queen Jezebel swore to kill Elijah. He ran away, hid in a cave and, completely discouraged, poured out his complaint to God.

How did God encourage Elijah during his spiritual depression? By telling him about the anonymous men who had resisted the pressure of their times—ordinary men who were faithful day after day. Elijah may have been the star of this epic, but this remnant of unknown men was working behind the scenes, being used by God to encourage one of the most powerful prophets in the Bible.

Few of us will ever face the pressures Elijah did. But at times we will undoubtedly feel alone. The happy truth is that we're never alone—God Himself walks with us, and He has reserved many others for His purposes. They will encourage you. . .and you can encourage them by remaining faithful to your Lord.

CLASSICS: ANDREW MURRAY

ABRAHAM: EVERYTHING BY FAITH

*Thou art the LORD the God, who didst choose Abram, and
broughtest him forth out of Ur of the Chaldees, and gavest him
the name of Abraham; and foundest his heart faithful before
thee, and madest a covenant with him to give the land of the
Canaanites, the Hittites, the Amorites, and the Perizzites,
and the Jebusites, and the Girgashites, to give it, I say, to his
seed, and hast performed thy words; for thou art righteous.*

NEHEMIAH 9:7–8 KJV

By faith Abraham saw the unseen; in hope he lived in the future.
He had his heart as little in Canaan as in Haran; it was in heaven;
it was with God.

And we, who have been called to enter into the true tabernacle
which God hath pitched—oh, shall we not obey and go out, even
though it be not knowing whither we go. Let us separate ourselves
entirely from the world and its spirit; let us, like the Son, die to the
creature, that we may live to God.

A worldly spirit in the church or the Christian is a deadly disease:
it makes the life of faith impossible. Let us count it our worst enemy
and live as foreigners, who seek the city which is to come. Let us hear
the voice calling us out to Himself, to close fellowship, to obedience as
of the angels in heaven, to be a testimony and a blessing for the world.

CORNELIUS: SIMPLE OBEDIENCE

While Peter yet spake these words, the Holy Ghost fell on all them which heard the word. And they of the circumcision which believed were astonished, as many as came with Peter, because that on the Gentiles also was poured out the gift of the Holy Ghost.

<small>ACTS 10:44–45 KJV</small>

We who are Gentiles owe a huge debt of gratitude to a man we might rarely think about.

Jesus had commanded His disciples to preach the Gospel to people of every nation (Mark 16:15), but after His resurrection, the disciples took awhile to actually do that. In the meantime, faith was taking root in the hearts of the most unlikely people.

Cornelius of Caesarea was a centurion in the occupying Roman army. He had devoted his heart to God and was well respected among the Jews. . .but he was a Gentile. The disciples—all Jewish—didn't really know how to deal with such a man. God, of course, did. He sent a vision to Peter declaring that the old ideas of "clean" and "unclean" people had no place in His new kingdom. The Gentiles were to be welcomed in. In other words, Jesus loved the whole world!

The Lord told Cornelius to seek out Peter, and he obeyed and was saved—the first of countless millions of Gentiles who would follow Jesus through the succeeding centuries.

Cornelius could never have imagined what his simple obedience would set in motion. Who knows what your simple obedience today might accomplish?

PAUL: ABLE TO DO ALL THINGS—THROUGH CHRIST

I can do all things through Christ who strengthens me.
PHILIPPIANS 4:13 NKJV

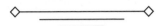

After condemning and even murdering Christians, the apostle Paul was brought to Christianity, eventually dedicating his life to serving Jesus. His journey led him through abundant wealth, extreme poverty, and everything in between. He was imprisoned for several years but still wrote the joyful letter of Philippians from prison.

When Paul says he "can do all things through Christ," he's not talking about a superhuman ability to satisfy his selfish purposes. Paul learned to get by with whatever he had—even if he had nothing. He focused on what he knew he should do—serve the Lord—instead of what he might think he should have. Paul set his priorities in order and was grateful for all that God gave him. He faced many trials, but he found joy in spreading God's Word and was not deterred by any trouble he encountered along the way.

You also "can do all things through Christ." You can accomplish any task, overcome any adversity, and survive any trouble if you come to the Lord and ask Him to strengthen you. As you build your relationship with Him, He will help you every step of the way.

NAAMAN: ALLOWING GOD TO WORK IN HEARTS

So Naaman said, ". . .Yet in this thing may the Lord pardon your servant: when my master goes into the temple of Rimmon to worship there, and he leans on my hand, and I bow down in the temple of Rimmon—when I bow down in the temple of Rimmon, may the Lord please pardon your servant in this thing."

2 KINGS 5:17–18 NKJV

◇═══════════◇

Naaman was an able and valiant military commander for the king of Syria. He was also a leper. In ancient times, leprosy was an incurable, dread disease that disfigured the body.

Happily for Naaman, a young Israelite woman captured by Syrian raiders was serving in his home. This young woman believed the prophet Elisha could cure Naaman and said as much to her mistress. When Naaman was told, he went off to see Elisha.

When Naaman arrived at Elisha's house, the prophet sent out a servant to tell him to bathe in the Jordan seven times. This wasn't good enough for Naaman, who was expecting much more. Leaving in a purple rage, he finally relented, when persuaded by his aides, and heeded the prophet's counsel. Dunking seven times in the Jordan, he was cured of his leprosy. Overwhelmed by his cure, Naaman vowed to worship no god but the God of Israel.

If we commit to walk with God, we cannot hold on to any sin. Only God can enable us to make that kind of commitment, as He likely did for Naaman.

PETER: "SERVE ONE ANOTHER"

God has given each of you a gift from his great variety of
spiritual gifts. Use them well to serve one another.

1 PETER 4:10 NLT

◇─────────────◇

When Peter penned these words, the destruction of Israel and the Jewish temple was at hand (1 Peter 4:7). With persecution imminent, Peter wanted believers to maintain their focus, stay earnest and disciplined in their prayers, and show their love by opening their homes to one another (verses 7–9). In addition, they were to serve one another by using their God-given spiritual gifts.

In our troubled times, many sense (even fear) that the end is near. Some respond with anger, getting caught up in heated doctrinal or political exchanges. Others struggle to stay engaged, feeling a pull toward isolation. Either way, the wrong attitudes can render our witness ineffective. That's why Peter wrote his first letter. His advice included opening your home to fellow believers, praying, studying, laughing, and weeping with them. We should serve our fellow believers by using our spiritual gifts.

If you aren't sure about your own spiritual gift, talk to a leader at church to help you identify it. Then put it into practice. You'll notice a difference in your attitude as you minister to fellow saints. And as unbelievers see your love for other believers in action, you'll make a greater impact for the kingdom of God.

THE EARLY CHURCH: YOU DON'T HAVE TO BE A STAR

*Then Peter said unto them, Repent, and be baptized every one
of you in the name of Jesus Christ for the remission of sins,
and ye shall receive the gift of the Holy Ghost. . . . Then they
that gladly received his word were baptized: and the same day
there were added unto them about three thousand souls.*

ACTS 2:38, 41 KJV

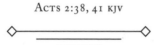

Though Jesus taught that His followers should be "servant of all"
(Mark 9:35, 10:44), our culture encourages and celebrates stardom.
To be considered a success, you must be at the top of the mountain
with plenty of other people looking up to you.

Sometimes, this attitude even colors our Christian lives. If we
don't lead an organization, speak in front of crowds, or find ourselves
in some other notable public position, we might feel like we're failing
God. Or, perhaps, failing ourselves.

But the birth of the Christian Church in Acts 2 provides a good
counterbalance to these fears. Notice that Peter—who was certainly
in a notable position—preached a message that led to the salvation of
three thousand people. Though it's possible that some of their names
appear throughout the New Testament letters written in following
decades, we really know almost nothing about these early believers.
Their average, everyday Christian lives, though, lived out in a very
hostile culture, caused others to accept the Gospel message, and that
pattern repeated itself down to the current day. Your own salvation is
likely part of a long chain of testimony dating to this moment in Acts 2.

You don't have to be a star to be a good Christian. God gave us the
story of these early believers to encourage simple, everyday obedience.

DAVID: MORNINGS WITH GOD

My voice shalt thou hear in the morning, O Lord; in the morning will I direct my prayer unto thee, and will look up.

PSALM 5:3 KJV

When David penned these words, he was probably surrounded by his enemies (verses 6, 8)—perhaps during the reign of King Saul. No matter his circumstances, David made sure to meet with God every morning. He was intentional in turning his face toward heaven and directing his voice toward God, confident that the Lord would hear him.

On this day, he reminded God about His character—how He doesn't take pleasure in nor tolerate wickedness (verses 4-5). But David also acknowledged his own imperfections. He was resolute in communicating with God every morning, not because he was without blemish or fault but because he knew God was merciful (verse 7). So he approached Him in the morning with a healthy dose of fear, knowing he deserved judgment but trusting in God's mercy.

What does your morning routine look like? Do difficulties, business, or laziness keep you from meeting with Him? Or do you approach God daily with a proper amount of reverent fear, knowing He will hear you?

Make your morning prayers an unbreakable habit, just as David did, and see just what God will do in your life.

CLASSICS: CHARLES SPURGEON

PAUL: THANKFUL FOR EVERYTHING

*But my God shall supply all your need according
to his riches in glory by Christ Jesus.*

PHILIPPIANS 4:19 KJV

Paul is exceedingly delighted because he has been, in his deep poverty in prison, kindly remembered by the little church at Philippi, and they have sent him a contribution. Probably the gift does not come to very much, if estimated in Roman coin; but he makes a great deal of it and sits down to write a letter of thanks abounding in rich expressions—"I have all things, and abound: I am full, having received of Epaphroditus the things which were sent from you." His heart was evidently greatly touched; for he says, "I rejoiced in the Lord greatly, that now at the last your care of me hath flourished again."

See how little a gift may make a good man glad! Is it not worthwhile to be free with our cups of cold water to the prophets of the Lord? Instead of a little money, the brethren and sisters at Philippi are enriched by the fervent prayers of the apostle. Hear how earnestly Paul invokes benedictions on the heads of his benefactors. Some would grumble over a roasted ox, and here is Paul rejoicing over a dinner of herbs.

URIAH: FOCUSED ON FIDELITY

David sent someone to find out about her. The man said, "She is Bathsheba, the daughter of Eliam and the wife of Uriah the Hittite."

2 SAMUEL 11:3 NIV

Uriah the Hittite was not an Israelite, yet he proved more upright than the Jewish king he served. This foreigner was part of David's royal guard, carefully picked men who were much more than common soldiers (2 Samuel 23:18–39). But while Uriah was on a military campaign, King David glimpsed Uriah's lovely wife, Bathsheba, as she bathed on her roof, and he lusted for her. He brought her to his palace, slept with her, and returned her home. Then she discovered she was pregnant.

David wanted to make it appear that the child was Uriah's, but though his dedicated soldier returned to Jerusalem at David's command, he would not give in to the comforts of home when his comrades were on the battlefront. So David placed Uriah in the heat of battle, and he was killed. After he died, the king married Bathsheba.

Uriah, a foreigner who served the Lord by protecting the king, had a focus on fidelity that escaped his master. The most unlikely person may serve God faithfully, while a much-honored one fails. Remember, God is no respecter of persons, and even the humblest may do His will.

Do we recognize the importance of humble belief over social standing? Are we looking to the things of God's kingdom or to earthly importance?

CLASSICS: ANDREW MURRAY

JESUS: THE MODEL OF HUMILITY

Even as the Son of man came not to be ministered unto,
but to minister, and to give his life a ransom for many.

MATTHEW 20:28 KJV

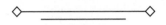

Jesus brought humility from heaven to us. It was humility that brought Him to earth, or He never would have come. In full accordance with this, just as Christ became a man in this divine humility, so His whole life was marked by it.

He might have chosen another form in which to appear; He might have come in the form of a king, but He chose the form of a servant. He made Himself of no reputation; He emptied Himself; He spoke, and His life confirmed what He said, "I am among you as one that serveth."

Beloved, the life of Jesus upon earth was a life of the deepest humility. It was this gave His life its worth and beauty in God's sight. And then His death—His death was an exhibition of unparalleled humility. "He humbled Himself, and became obedient unto death, even the death of the cross."

SAMSON: RELYING ON GOD'S STRENGTH

Then Samson prayed to the LORD, "Sovereign LORD, remember me. Please, God, strengthen me just once more, and let me with one blow get revenge on the Philistines for my two eyes."

JUDGES 16:28 NIV

Samson was a judge over Israel for twenty years. During his leadership, he demonstrated his great strength time and time again, routing the Philistines many times in multiple ways.

Judges 13–16 detail the life of Samson, known throughout history as both a hero and a deeply flawed man. Yet one recurring theme about Samson appears throughout these chapters: the presence of God's Spirit. "The Spirit of the LORD began to stir him" (Judges 13:25 NIV) first when he was a young man. Then, three other times in Judges (14:6, 14:19, 15:14), that same Spirit would become evident right before Samson performed another great act of strength.

But today's passage leads us to Samson's final stand. As with Joshua and Gideon, Samson's prayer of reliance on God came at a critical time—a time in which Samson had the opportunity to demonstrate God's power and strength and strike a major blow against God's enemies and their false religion. God, through Samson, destroyed their temple and killed thousands.

Samson's strength flowed from the same Spirit that empowers us. Strength, courage, honor, and the ability to demonstrate God's power—all of this comes from the Holy Spirit living within us as believers in Christ.

Be ready to follow His leading today.

JOB: A COVENANT WITH HIS EYES

*"I made a covenant with my eyes not to look
with lust at a young woman."*

JOB 31:1 NLT

During an era when polygamy was acceptable, Job still had only one wife. Wealthy men who didn't want the complication of extra marriages could simply take concubines. Job, however, was the richest man in the East, yet he was satisfied with *one* woman. Judging by the beauty their daughters inherited (Job 42:15), we can surmise that Job's wife was lovely. But *most* men's eyes still would've wandered. Why didn't his?

Job realized that unless he determined ahead of time not to look lustfully at beautiful women, his eyes would naturally wander—and one thing would lead to another. So he made a covenant (a commitment or promise) *not* to allow his eyes to linger. Then, when faced with temptation, he refused to lust.

In modern times, we are constantly bombarded with sexually provocative sights, both in the media and in real life. Even if you don't go looking for it, it can ambush you. If you haven't given thought to the matter ahead of time and determined your reaction, you almost can't help but gawk. But this can be very habit forming and addictive.

The secret to victory is to gain control of your thoughts beforehand, determining not to look in lust, even if someone deliberately tempts you. "Do not lust in your heart after her beauty or let her captivate you with her eyes" (Proverbs 6:25 NIV). Look away if necessary. Ask God to help you. And don't give in.

◇— *Day 328* —◇

CLASSICS: D. L. MOODY

JOHN THE BAPTIST: JESUS MUST INCREASE

He that cometh from above is above all: he that is of the earth is earthly, and speaketh of the earth: he that cometh from heaven is above all.

JOHN 3:31 KJV

The last of a long line of prophets, John was beheaded for his testimony and buried in the land of Moab, just outside the promised land, near to where Moses, the first lawgiver, was buried. His ministry was very short. It lasted only two years. But he had finished his course; he had done his work.

Dear friend, you and I may not have that time to work. Let us consecrate ourselves and get the world and self beneath our feet; and let Christ be all and in all. We must "stoop to conquer." Let us be nothing and Christ everything. Let the house of Saul wax weaker and weaker, and the house of David wax stronger and stronger. Let us get to the end of self and adopt as our motto, "He must increase, but I must decrease."

JESUS: SOURCE AND RECIPIENT OF OUR GOOD DEEDS

"The King will reply, 'Truly I tell you, whatever you did for one of the least of these brothers and sisters of mine, you did for me.'"

MATTHEW 25:40 NIV

Have you ever passed a homeless person on the street corner, avoiding eye contact and continuing on your way instead of offering food, drink, clothing, shelter, or money? Would you ignore that person if it were Jesus Himself?

Jesus specifically says that whatever you do for someone else, you do for Him. Whether you give a drink to someone thirsty, food to someone hungry, clothing to someone who needs it, company to someone in prison, or care for someone who is sick, you are giving to the Lord. He's watching you.

Be thankful for all your blessings, realizing that others may not be so fortunate. Don't take what you have for granted. Share what God has given you with someone who has less than you. Even if you don't have much to give in the way of food, money, or clothing, it doesn't cost anything to visit an elderly person and lend a listening ear. It's free to visit someone in prison and offer a word of encouragement.

Consider doing something selfless today.

MALACHI: LEAVING A LEGACY

A prophecy: The word of the LORD to Israel through Malachi.
MALACHI 1:1 NIV

The author of the last book of the Old Testament is a bit of an enigma—we know very little about him. Malachi was probably born in Judah and prophesied in Jerusalem. His book seems to have been written around 465 to 430 BC. Some scholars have even concluded that because *Malachi* means "my messenger," it was a title and not a proper name.

Ezra and Nehemiah were contemporaries of this minor prophet and likely overshadowed him in popularity. However, as the Israelites—having just returned from exile—began doubting and disobeying God by marrying into pagan families, Malachi's message grew more relevant than ever.

Though we don't have a lot of information about Malachi, it doesn't matter. The prophet had a revelation from God, so he called these hurting people back to obedience to their King and Creator.

Even if no one remembers the details of your life, wouldn't you want others to benefit from your faithfulness? May God's message become your legacy to the future, even when your personal story fades.

CLASSICS: D. L. MOODY

JESUS: WORKING IN THE DAYTIME

*I must work the works of him that sent me, while it is
day: the night cometh, when no man can work.*

JOHN 9:4 KJV

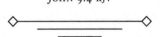

Do you look for that rest here, Christian? There is none. If you are resting, you are neglecting your duty; you are shirking your work and will never enjoy heaven thoroughly. It's the weary only who know what true rest is.

"Work while it is called today"; be up and doing. That which your hand findeth to do in your Master's vineyard do it with all your might. "Be not weary of well doing, for in due time ye shall reap if ye faint not." Blessed be God, "there remaineth a rest."

No rest here below, nothing but toil and labor; but you will enjoy your rest all the more when you do come to the beautiful land above. "Blessed are the dead which die in the Lord from henceforth; Yea, saith the Spirit, that they may rest from their labors; and their works do follow them."

SIMON THE ZEALOT: SERVING WITH PASSION

Jesus went up on a mountainside and called to him those he wanted, and they came to him. He appointed twelve that they might be with him and that he might send them out to preach and to have authority to drive out demons. These are the twelve he appointed: Simon (to whom he gave the name Peter), James son of Zebedee and his brother John (to them he gave the name Boanerges, which means "sons of thunder"), Andrew, Philip, Bartholomew, Matthew, Thomas, James son of Alphaeus, Thaddaeus, Simon the Zealot and Judas Iscariot.

MARK 3:13–19 NIV

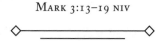

Because Jesus had two disciples named Simon, He seems to have devised meaningful nicknames to distinguish them. The better-known Simon became Peter, while the other was called "Simon the Zealot."

Some scholars say the descriptor *Zealot* indicates that Simon had been a member of the radical anti-Roman fighters, the Zealots. But it's unlikely he would have walked around Roman-ruled Israel identifying himself with such militants.

More likely, the nickname simply referred to his zeal. Simon was no doubt passionate about his faith, purposeful in his walk, and trustworthy with the work God gave him to accomplish.

Zeal can demonstrate itself as "loud and proud," though it doesn't need to be. Some of history's most zealous Christians have been quiet and reserved. Whatever your personal style, simply be faithful to the life God has called you to live. Love the Lord with passion and watch how He'll use you for His purposes.

MELCHIZEDEK: KEEPING OUR THEOLOGY HUMBLE

Then Melchizedek king of Salem brought out bread and wine.
He was priest of God Most High, and he blessed Abram, saying,
"Blessed be Abram by God Most High, Creator of heaven and earth."
GENESIS 14:18–19 NIV

How little we know of this mystery man, who appears briefly in Genesis and receives more explanation in the New Testament than in the Old.

Melchizedek emerged when Abram returned from rescuing Lot from the clutches of the king of Elam. This king of Salem (or "king of peace") came to Abram, carrying a banquet with him. He blessed Abram, using words that indicated he was speaking not of a Canaanite deity, but of the Lord God. And Abram responded by giving Melchizedek a tenth of the plunder he'd gained from the king of Elam and his allies.

If there was any question about whom this king-priest referred to, Hebrews 7 clears it up. The New Testament passage compares Salem's ruler with the Son of God—priest and king and superior to the Levite priesthood.

If nothing else, Melchizedek keeps us and our theology humble. We wonder just where this king came from and how he relates to Jesus. Is he Jesus, or just a picture of Him? Let's remember not to be too secure in our private interpretations. God doesn't tell us everything about Himself—or about mystery men like Melchizedek.

CLASSICS: MATTHEW HENRY

SOLOMON: BLESSING GOD

And he said, Blessed be the L<small>ORD</small> God of Israel,
which spake with his mouth unto David my
father, and hath with his hand fulfilled it.

1 K<small>INGS</small> 8:15 KJV

Solomon began his account with a thankful acknowledgment of the good hand of his God upon him hitherto: *Blessed be the L<small>ORD</small> God of Israel.*

What we have the pleasure of God must have the praise of. He thus engaged the congregation to lift up their hearts in thanksgivings to God, which would help to still the tumult of spirit which, probably, they were in. "Come," says he, "let God's awful appearances not drive us from Him, but draw us to Him; let us bless the L<small>ORD</small> God of Israel."

Thus Job, under a dark scene, blessed the name of the L<small>ORD</small>. Solomon here blessed God for His promise which He spoke with his mouth to David. And for the performance, that He had now fulfilled it with His hand.

We have then the best sense of God's mercies, and most grateful both to ourselves and to our God, when we run up those streams to the fountain of the covenant and compare what God does with what He has said.

PAUL: A PASSION FOR CHRIST

*Whatever you do, work at it with all your heart, as
working for the Lord, not for human masters, since you
know that you will receive an inheritance from the Lord
as a reward. It is the Lord Christ you are serving.*

Colossians 3:23–24 niv

The question is not whether we pursue our passions: we all do, and they inevitably drive our lives in some direction. The real question is—what are those passions?

Sadly, according to theologian Carl F. H. Henry, many men settle "for grime when [they] could reach for glory." Their passions burn for power, possessions, pleasures, and pride. They settle for paths that give temporary pleasure but are ultimately unfulfilling and destructive.

Paul made it clear that the only passion worth living and dying for is an all-consuming passion for God and His work in the world. Nothing can take its place. Nothing is as satisfying or rewarding. Most Christian men wouldn't disagree—yet many of us hang back, distracted by this world's baubles.

In the early 1900s, the rich and handsome William Borden was studying at Yale when he found his passion for Christ. Leading a great Christian student movement, he turned his back on his family's wealth and pursued his call to serve God in China. Borden died on the way and is buried in Cairo, Egypt, but some of his words live on. In his journal, he had written, "No reserves. No retreats. No regrets."

Whatever you do, work at it with all your heart. Remember, you're not working for any human boss, but for the God of the universe.

◇— *Day 336* —◇

JAMES: FROM SKEPTICISM TO FAITH

*"Isn't this the carpenter? Isn't this Mary's son and the
brother of James, Joseph, Judas and Simon? Aren't his
sisters here with us?" And they took offense at him.*

MARK 6:3 NIV

When the truth that Jesus was more than an ordinary man suddenly hit the people of Nazareth, they were astounded. How could He be more than an everyday fellow? After all, wasn't He just like His brother James? An admirable person maybe, but nothing more.

The truth is, at first James didn't believe in his half brother's claims either. Perhaps he couldn't get away from His teaching, but that didn't mean he had to agree with Jesus.

But a change came over James. In the book of Acts, he appears as a Church leader: He spoke for the Jerusalem council that heard Paul's objections to circumcision for the Gentiles, and Paul reported to that council on his missionary experience when he returned to Jerusalem.

James probably wrote the biblical book that bears that name, which is filled with guidance for living an effective Christian life. Within the early Church, he was known as James the Just because of his upright character. He was martyred in AD 62, after being thrown down from the Temple.

If you've read through this entire devotional to this point, it's likely because you have come to the point—like James—of true faith in Jesus. But if you haven't, why not make that decision now? He's just waiting for your call.

CLASSICS: ANDREW MURRAY

JESUS: HIS POWER STRENGTHENS US

And Jesus came and spake unto them, saying, All power is given unto me in heaven and in earth.

MATTHEW 28:18 KJV

When our Lord was about to take His seat upon the throne, one of His last words was: "All power is given unto me in heaven and on earth." Just as His taking His place at the right hand of the power of God was something new and true—a real advance in the history of the God-man—so was this clothing with all power.

Omnipotence was now entrusted to the man Christ Jesus, that from henceforth through the channels of human nature it might put forth its mighty energies. Hence He connected with this revelation of what He was to receive, the promise of the share that His disciples would have in it: When I am ascended, ye shall receive power from on high.

It is in the power of the omnipotent Savior that the believer must find his strength for life and for work.

ESAU: BROTHERHOOD WINS

*And the first came out red, all over like an hairy
garment; and they called his name Esau.*

GENESIS 25:25 KJV

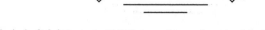

Rebekah didn't just give birth to twins—she gave birth to two nations destined for conflict. The firstborn was Esau, a simple but rough man of the hills. His descendants would become the nation of Edom. Holding onto his heel was the second twin, Jacob, the patriarch of Israel.

As they grew up, Esau would have plenty of reasons not to like Jacob. The younger brother sold him food in exchange for Esau's birthright. Then he pretended to be Esau to get his father's blessing.

Jacob went out into the world and made his fortune; then, in a time of need, he turned back for home. Expecting his brother to fight against him, he divided his people and flocks (so at least some of them might survive) and prepared peace offerings. Instead, Esau ran up to Jacob declaring that he needed nothing else—he had his brother back.

If only we Christians could remember what Esau taught Jacob—that despite our disagreements, we are still brothers!

CLASSICS: CHARLES SPURGEON

DAVID: GOD CARES FOR THE DESPISED

Thou hast also given me the shield of thy salvation: and thy right hand hath holden me up, and thy gentleness hath made me great.

PSALM 18:35 KJV

David, as the youngest of the family, contrary to the general rule, appears to have been despised by his parents, so that when Samuel came to keep the feast they sent for all their sons except David, who was left in the fields keeping the sheep. I should suppose, judging from the conduct of his brethren to him in the valley of Elah, that they held him in very small esteem.

He was the despised one of the family, a reproach unto his mother's children; nevertheless, the Lord had chosen him in preference to all the rest, for the gentleness of God delighted in David the shepherd boy. What a balm must that divine love have been to his wounded spirit! How often, sitting alone with his flocks, must he have sung to his harp, "When my father and mother forsake me, then the LORD will take me up"!

The gracious gentleness of his God to him must have encouraged his broken spirit when he felt the untenderness of his father and the scorn of his brethren.

BARNABAS:
STRENGTHENING THE WEAK

Barnabas wanted to take John, also called Mark, with them,
but Paul did not think it wise to take him. . . . They had such a
sharp disagreement that they parted company. Barnabas took
Mark and sailed for Cyprus, but Paul chose Silas and left.

ACTS 15:37–40 NIV

It's easy to assume that perfect harmony existed among the apostles during the New Testament era. But Acts 15 records a disagreement so serious that two people parted ways.

Paul and Barnabas traveled and worked together during Paul's first missionary journey (Acts 13–14). The two men were also accompanied by John Mark, Barnabas's cousin—but Mark left them and returned home to Jerusalem after a short time.

As Paul and Barnabas planned their second journey, it became apparent that Paul hadn't forgotten Mark's desertion. Paul wanted to leave Mark behind, but Barnabas wanted to give the young man another chance. The two parted ways over the disagreement, and Paul left for his second missionary journey without him.

But Barnabas didn't give up on his cousin. In fact, he spent time mentoring him and encouraging him. In time, Mark became such an effective minister of the Gospel that Paul himself later acknowledged that he had become helpful to him in his ministry (2 Timothy 4:11).

In encouraging young John Mark, Barnabas exemplified the sacrifice it takes to help those who are weaker in their faith. How can you show this love to someone you know?

CLASSICS: D. L. MOODY

SHADRACH, MESHACH, AND ABEDNEGO: UNPOPULAR IN THIS WORLD

Nebuchadnezzar spake and said unto them, Is it true, O Shadrach, Meshach, and Abednego, do not ye serve my gods, nor worship the golden image which I have set up?

DANIEL 3:14 KJV

Now, mark you, no man can be true for God and live for Him without at some time being unpopular in this world. Those men who try to live for both worlds make a wreck of it; for at some time or other the collision is sure to come.

Ah, would all of us have advised Daniel's three friends to do the right thing at any hazard? Are there not some of us with so little backbone we would have counseled these three just to bow down a little, so no one could take notice—to merely bow down, but not to worship?

Daniel and his friends, when they first came to Babylon, perceived that the two worlds—the present world and the world to come—would be in collision: and they "went for" the world to come; they "went for" things unseen. . .even if it cost them their lives! It would only hasten them to the glory; and they would receive the greater reward.

PAUL: EXPERIENCING "PARENTAL" JOY

For we wanted to come to you—certainly I, Paul, did, again and again—but Satan blocked our way. For what is our hope, our joy, or the crown in which we will glory in the presence of our Lord Jesus when he comes? Is it not you? Indeed, you are our glory and joy.

1 THESSALONIANS 2:18–20 NIV

Paul's enthusiasm for the Thessalonian believers bursts forth in today's verse, using language usually reserved for God Himself. Imagine: Paul's "hope" and "joy" and "glory" are tied to this small group of people into whom he has poured his life. When Jesus returns, Paul plans on showing them off.

When we come to Christ, we begin our experience as children of God. We are adopted (Romans 8:15) and begin reshaping our lives as one of His offspring. Then, as we share our faith and help people grow in Christ, we begin to see the *other* side of the relationship— the parental side. God's side. This is why Paul speaks so joyfully: he's displaying the same excited attitude toward the Thessalonians that God has toward all of us—pride and joy!

Paul reflects God's joy toward his own "children" in the faith because God's parental joy is contagious. Like Paul did with the Thessalonians, God rejoices over us, brags about us, dotes on us, and takes pride in us—and He's preparing unimaginable things in heaven for those who love Him (1 Corinthians 2:9). When we see Him face-to-face, we will truly understand what an extravagant parent God is. We will rejoice in Him, and He will rejoice in us.

JESUS: WE MAY ABOUND IN HOPE

Now the God of hope fill you with all joy and peace in believing,
that ye may abound in hope, through the power of the Holy Ghost.
ROMANS 15:13 KJV

◇———————◇

If you look around at the unbelievers in your life, all of them are lacking one thing: eternal hope. Some find earthly hope in their work, wealth, or family. Others have false hope in their good deeds. But most of the people you know outside of the Church have no real assurance or peace about their standing before a holy God.

In Romans 15, Paul explains that Christ is the great hope for Jews and Gentiles alike. In fact, in today's verse, Paul calls Him the God of hope—a title no Gentile could have dared believe before.

We know that Christians sometimes fall into despair and feel genuine sadness. Even Jesus, God's Son, felt sorrow on occasion. But beyond the tears and grief is the great hope of heaven. Not hope in the sense of a child wishing for ice cream, but rather an earnest expectation for ultimate deliverance.

Jesus is the long-awaited Messiah, and belief in Him leads to joy and peace in the believer's heart—both now and throughout eternity.

CLASSICS: ANDREW MURRAY

MOSES: SEPARATE FROM THE WORLD

By faith Moses, when he was come to years, refused to be called the son of Pharaoh's daughter; choosing rather to suffer affliction with the people of God, than to enjoy the pleasures of sin for a season.
HEBREWS 11:24–25 KJV

How wonderful is the place Moses occupies in the kingdom of God. A pattern of Jesus as a prophet, as a mediator, as an intercessor, in his meekness and his faithfulness, there are few of God's servants that stand higher. And what fitted him to take this place? Just this—the choice to give up everything for the reproach of Christ.

Christian, wouldst thou live in the favor of God and enter into His tent to meet Him as Moses did? Wouldst thou be an instrument and a power of blessing, a man strong in faith? Seek to be perfectly separate from the spirit of the world, refuse its pleasure and honor and riches; count the contempt of God's people and the reproach of Christ thy treasures. Ask for the enlightening of the Holy Spirit to teach thee what true conformity to Christ is, in thy relation to the world, its culture, its possessions, its friendship. Beware of judging of what is lawful by any human standard: Christ alone can teach thee what it means to forsake all. . .and follow Him.

JESUS: ANYONE CAN COME

There is no longer Jew or Gentile, slave or free, male and female. For you are all one in Christ Jesus.

GALATIANS 3:28 NLT

Jesus came with a radical and unexpected message: God loved all mankind without discrimination. Women had equal standing in His plan, and the sick were never considered unacceptable.

Social status meant nothing to Jesus. Each person had a gift to share and a role in His plan. Where women and children were once treated as disposable property, God told men, "Love your wives and never treat them harshly" (Colossians 3:19 NLT) and "Fathers, do not provoke your children to anger by the way you treat them. Rather, bring them up with the discipline and instruction that comes from the Lord" (Ephesians 6:4 NLT).

Part of Jesus' plan was to equalize humanity. No one was less important to Him than another. He didn't come to save a few. His rescue plan was for all, and His love was accessible to everyone.

Jesus introduced a new pledge, and He didn't change His mind. This generous pledge challenged tradition and opened new opportunities. When it comes to a relationship with Him, God doesn't erect barriers. Similarly, Christian men should remove every barrier that prevents someone from meeting Jesus or loving others the way Jesus loves.

JOSEPH: FAITHFUL IN DISAPPOINTMENT

"Because the patriarchs were jealous of Joseph, they sold him as a slave into Egypt. But God was with him and rescued him from all his troubles. He gave Joseph wisdom and enabled him to gain the goodwill of Pharaoh king of Egypt. So Pharaoh made him ruler over Egypt and all his palace."

ACTS 7:9–10 NIV

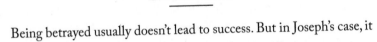

Being betrayed usually doesn't lead to success. But in Joseph's case, it was an essential step.

His brothers hated him because he was their father Israel's favorite (Genesis 37:4). Matters only got worse when he began having dreams in which they all bowed down to him. They considered killing him (Genesis 37:18) but then settled on selling him into slavery. However, Joseph ultimately rescued his entire family from famine, having been put in charge over all Egypt by Pharaoh. Betrayal was part of God's plan for Joseph.

In the Lord's hands, our toughest experiences can be tools for His use. Disappointment can clarify our expectations by stripping away false hopes. Tragedy can work its painful service to show us the reality of a world that isn't our home. Pain, as C. S. Lewis once wrote, can be "God's megaphone" to cut through the world and the flesh's noise and temptations.

Despite his afflictions, Joseph remained faithful to God until God's timing was complete—and all of us are called to do the same. Hard as it may be at the time, know that there will be a reward. And the reward will be more than worth the struggle.

CLASSICS: D. L. MOODY

JOHN THE BAPTIST: BE READY FOR PERSECUTION

*And the Lord said, Whereunto then shall I liken the men of this
generation? and to what are they like? They are like unto children
sitting in the marketplace, and calling one to another, and saying,
We have piped unto you, and ye have not danced; we have mourned
to you, and ye have not wept. For John the Baptist came neither
eating bread nor drinking wine; and ye say, He hath a devil. The
Son of man is come eating and drinking; and ye say, Behold a
gluttonous man, and a winebibber, a friend of publicans and sinners!*

LUKE 7:31–34 KJV

John was beheaded for his testimony, the first martyr for the Gospel's
sake. He sealed his testimony with his blood. He rebuked the king and
told him that it was not lawful for him to live in adultery. He was not
ashamed to deliver God's message just as it had been given to him.

And no man has lived from the time of John but has enemies,
if he be a disciple of Christ. Christ said this, "For John came neither eating nor drinking, and they say, He hath a devil." Think of
saying that John the Baptist had a devil! Such a man! That is the
world's estimate. They hated him. Why? Because he rebuked sin.

DAVID: AVOID PRESUMPTUOUS SINS

*Keep back thy servant also from presumptuous sins; let
them not have dominion over me: then shall I be upright,
and I shall be innocent from the great transgression.*

PSALM 19:13 KJV

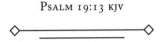

In today's verse, David asked God to keep him from presumptuous sins—that is, deliberate, intentional sins. He knew that willfully indulging in disobedient acts would end up becoming unbreakable habits. It's not that unintentional sins cause less harm than intentional ones, but they don't flow as readily from a person's heart and mind.

The last thing David wanted was to be guilty of "the great transgression," which some believe meant pride or even apostasy.

David knew his wicked heart well. He was a murderer and adulterer, and he lied to cover up both. He might have even been considered slothful, given that he chose to stay behind in Jerusalem while the other kings went out to battle (2 Samuel 11:1). That's when he spiraled out of control.

How about you? How well do you know your own heart? What sort of gross, presumptuous sins might it be capable of? Do you fear being guilty of the great transgression? Use David's prayer in today's verse. Ask God to intervene, to rule your heart, and to keep you from stumbling.

PETER: CALLED TO REJOICE IN SUFFERING

Dear friends, do not be surprised at the fiery ordeal that has come on you to test you, as though something strange were happening to you. But rejoice inasmuch as you participate in the sufferings of Christ, so that you may be overjoyed when his glory is revealed.

1 PETER 4:12–13 NIV

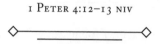

As Peter wrote these words, Jerusalem was facing impending destruction. Rome considered Christianity a threat, and therefore, persecution was heavy. But Peter didn't want believers to lose faith. Instead, he wanted them to see such hardship as an opportunity to participate in the sufferings of Christ.

Trials and sufferings have a way of causing disillusionment, especially when our expectations include a life of comfort. But one day, our boss or a coworker might see a Bible on our desk and bring a complaint against us. Or we might risk losing our job or business for refusing to honor a sinful practice.

In Acts 5, the apostles were arrested, imprisoned, beaten, and told not to teach about the name of Jesus, but that didn't stop them. Neither did it make them bitter or angry. Verse 41 (NIV) says, "The apostles left the Sanhedrin, rejoicing because they had been counted worthy of suffering disgrace for the Name."

When you face fiery ordeals, are you bewildered? Or do you rejoice, knowing that the world needs to see the power of Christ in you?

CLASSICS: ANDREW MURRAY

MANOAH: QUICK TO PRAY

And Manoah said, Now let thy words come to pass. How shall we order the child, and how shall we do unto him?

JUDGES 13:12 KJV

Manoah's sense of need at once found expression in prayer. He believed in God as the living God, as the Hearer of prayer. He believed that where God gave a charge or a work, He would give the grace to do it right; that where God gave a child to be trained for His service, He would give the wisdom needed to do so aright.

Instead of the sense of unfitness and feebleness depressing him, or the sense of his obligation setting him to work in his own strength, he simply prayed. Prayer to him was the solution of difficulties, the supply of need, the source of wisdom and strength.

Let Christian parents learn from him. Each child is a gift of God as truly as Manoah's, and has as much as his to be trained for God and His service. Let us only pray, pray believingly, pray without ceasing, at each step of our work; we may depend upon it: God hears prayer.

JESUS: THE HOPE OF GLORY, IN YOU

*The mystery that has been kept hidden for ages and generations,
but is now disclosed to the Lord's people. To them God has
chosen to make known among the Gentiles the glorious riches
of this mystery, which is Christ in you, the hope of glory.*

COLOSSIANS 1:26–27 NIV

◇————◇

God reveals mysteries in His own time and His own way—for our benefit and for His own glory.

In the Old Testament, God used prophets to reveal mysteries for His purpose. For example, when Daniel interpreted Nebuchadnezzar's dream, the king fell on his face, confessing, "Surely your God is the God of gods and the Lord of kings and a revealer of mysteries" (Daniel 2:47 NIV).

However, when the time was right to reveal the mystery of salvation through grace, God did not rely on a prophet: "But when the set time had fully come, God sent his Son, born of a woman, born under the law, to redeem those under the law, that we might receive adoption to sonship. Because you are his sons, God sent the Spirit of his Son into our hearts, the Spirit who calls out, 'Abba, Father'" (Galatians 4:4–6 NIV)

The mystery of mysteries—Jesus Christ living in us—had to be delivered face-to-face. Jesus revealed it the very night He paid the price to make it possible: "At that day you will know that I am in My Father, and you in Me, and I in you" (John 14:20 NKJV). In us, Christ turned the mystery of the ages into the message for the world.

ABRAHAM: GREAT FAITH

By faith Abraham, when God tested him, offered Isaac as a
sacrifice. He who had embraced the promises was about to
sacrifice his one and only son, even though God had said to him,
"It is through Isaac that your offspring will be reckoned."

HEBREWS 11:17–18 NIV

Other than Moses, no character from the Old Testament receives more New Testament ink than Abraham. Considering the life of faith Abraham lived, it's no wonder that the New Testament has so much to say about the father of Israel.

The New Testament reports that Abraham did the following by faith:

- obeyed God and left to settle in the Promised Land, even though he had no idea where he was going (Hebrews 11:8–9).
- became a parent of a promised son, even though he and his wife were both well beyond childbearing years (Hebrews 11:11–12).
- passed God's test of his devotion to Him (Hebrews 11:17–19).
- was declared righteous before God and called God's friend (James 2:23).

God inspired the authors of the New Testament to focus on Abraham. Why? Because He wants us to live our lives with the kind of faith Abraham demonstrated over and over again.

Abraham's faith inspired Him to trust the One he knew would keep His promises. While Abraham was far from perfect, he shows us what a man who takes God at His word can accomplish.

ELKANAH: HOW TO SHOW LOVE

*And when the time was that Elkanah offered, he gave to
Peninnah his wife, and to all her sons and her daughters,
portions: But unto Hannah he gave a worthy portion; for
he loved Hannah: but the Lord had shut up her womb.*

1 Samuel 1:4–5 KJV

Elkanah loved his wife nevertheless for her being barren. Christ loves
His church, notwithstanding her infirmities, her barrenness; and so
ought men to love their wives (Ephesians 5:25).

To abate our just love to any relation for the sake of any infirmity
which they cannot help, and which is not their sin but their affliction, is
to make God's providence quarrel with His precept and very unkindly
to add affliction to the afflicted. Elkanah studied to show his love so
much the more because she was afflicted, insulted, and low-spirited.

It is wisdom and duty to support the weakest and to hold up those
that are run down. He showed his great love to her by the share he
gave her of his peace offerings. Thus we should testify our affection
to our friends and relations, by abounding in prayer for them. The
better we love them, the more room let us give them in our prayers.

PAUL: STRENGTH IN CONFESSION

*I thank Christ Jesus our Lord, who has given me strength to
do his work. He considered me trustworthy and appointed
me to serve him, even though I used to blaspheme the name
of Christ. In my insolence, I persecuted his people. But God
had mercy on me because I did it in ignorance and unbelief.
Oh, how generous and gracious our Lord was! He filled me
with the faith and love that come from Christ Jesus.*

1 TIMOTHY 1:12–14 NLT

Confession is a difficult thing. Telling people about our sin means
admitting we were wrong. And for men, admitting any kind of failure
is tough. Showing weakness is not something we naturally enjoy, but
it is essential to growing as a man of God.

The apostle Paul's confession in today's scripture is a great sign
of strength, both in his walk with Christ and his ministry to the
people around him. Paul admitted his own weakness and failure, but
he gave thanks to Jesus Christ for calling him to serve, in spite of his
past. Though he was a highly educated, God-chosen leader of the
early Church, Paul emphasized his own weakness over any success
he'd had. In fact, in another passage he said he took pleasure in his
weakness and trouble since those things allowed God to be strong in
him (2 Corinthians 12:10).

Like Paul, let's speak more of Christ than ourselves. If we ever
boast, let it be in our own weakness and in the strength that only
Jesus gives.

DAVID: CONTINUALLY CASTING CARES ON GOD

Cast your cares on the LORD and he will sustain you; he will never let the righteous be shaken.

PSALM 55:22 NIV

This passage of scripture has been a source of great comfort to millions of believers, yet some people protest. "When huge problems come," they say, "I just calmly hand them to God and He takes care of everything? I *wish!*" This is a valid objection, so let's look at this verse in context.

Earlier in the psalm, David spoke of serious threats, conspiracies, battles raging against him, and the stinging betrayal of friends. (This likely happened during the civil war that accompanied his son Absalom's revolt.) David confessed his fear, saying, "My heart is in anguish within me; the terrors of death have fallen on me. Fear and trembling have beset me" (verses 4–5).

David was eventually able to cast his cares on God and experience peace, but it wasn't a quick or easy process. He also had to plan, strategize, and lead his forces against his enemies' attacks. And he had to pray desperately day after day, several times a day. He said, "Evening, morning and noon I cry out in distress" (verse 17). David *continually* cast his cares and fears upon God until he finally received assurance that God had heard him and would answer.

Yes, you *can* just calmly hand small problems over to God. But when huge problems assail you, you may have to desperately and repeatedly cast your cares on Him. And He will answer.

GOLIATH: PRIDE IS DEADLY

He looked David over and saw that he was little more than a
boy, glowing with health and handsome, and he despised him.
He said to David, "Am I a dog, that you come at me with sticks?"
And the Philistine cursed David by his gods. "Come here," he said,
"and I'll give your flesh to the birds and the wild animals!"

1 SAMUEL 17:42–44 NIV

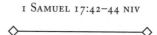

When the Israelites saw the massive Goliath and his impressive armor, their mouths must have gaped. It's not hard to understand why no one wanted to fight the huge Philistine champion. Who could win against a man with Goliath's battle experience and mighty weapons?

Only one Israelite believed he had a chance of winning. David, a shepherd boy who had defeated wild animals with his slingshot, saw Goliath as a wild man—one who had the nerve to defy God. The youth didn't think much about his opponent's size or armor; he was too busy thinking about his own powerful God.

David's confrontation with the giant made Goliath an example of "the bigger they are, the harder they fall." As David trusted God, his slingshot aimed accurately. A stone hit Goliath squarely in his forehead, and the huge fellow collapsed, dead. Quickly, David grabbed Goliath's giant sword and cut off the giant's head while the rest of the Philistines ran for their lives.

And Goliath's insulting trash talk comes down through history as a warning against pride. Though if you don't want to take his word for it, how about Solomon's? "Pride goes before destruction, a haughty spirit before a fall" (Proverbs 16:18 NIV).

CLASSICS: D. L. MOODY

DANIEL: WHAT MAKES ONE GREAT

Humble yourselves therefore under the mighty hand
of God, that he may exalt you in due time.

1 PETER 5:6 KJV

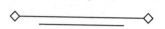

Daniel becomes a great man. He is set over the province of Babylon: he is lifted right out of bondage, right out of servitude. He was a young man, probably not more than twenty-two years old: and there he is—set over a mighty empire; is made, you might say, practically ruler over the whole of the then known world.

And God will exalt us when the right time comes. We need not try to promote ourselves; we need not struggle for position. Let God put us in our true places. And it is a good deal better for a man to be right with God, even if he hold no position down here. Then he can look up and know that God is pleased with him: that is enough.

ASAPH: TOO DISTRESSED TO PRAY

I think of God, and I moan, overwhelmed with longing for his help. You don't let me sleep. I am too distressed even to pray!

Psalm 77:3–4 NLT

Have you ever been so upset, depressed, angry, or overwhelmed that you couldn't even pray? If so, you're in good company.

Even Bible writers struggled like that, as Psalm 77 proves. Asaph, a Levite assigned by King David to lead music when the ark of the covenant was moved to Jerusalem (1 Chronicles 15), came to prominence in a time of joy. How different his outlook when he penned today's psalm.

"I cry out to God; yes, I shout," Asaph began. "Oh, that God would listen to me! When I was in deep trouble, I searched for the Lord. All night long I prayed, with hands lifted toward heaven, but my soul was not comforted" (Psalm 77:1–2 NLT). And then Asaph wrote the words of today's scripture, recording his moaning, longing, and sleeplessness. He found it impossible even to pray.

Happily for Asaph—and instructively for us—he discovered a way out of his morass. By verse 11, this talented musician had decided to "recall all you have done, O LORD; I remember your wonderful deeds of long ago." And that proved to be enough. Today, let's follow Asaph's example, praying as he did, "You are the God of great wonders! You demonstrate your awesome power among the nations" (Psalm 77:14 NLT).

JESUS: RECOGNIZING THE VALUE OF CHILDREN

But Jesus called the children to him and said, "Let the little children come to me, and do not hinder them, for the kingdom of God belongs to such as these."

LUKE 18:16 NIV

Have you ever noticed that some grown-ups love to be around kids? Jesus was one of those people. During His three and a half years of ministry as an adult, Jesus gave an amazing amount of priority to ministry to children.

Jesus talked with children, something only parents and grandparents usually did in that culture. Jesus commended the faith of little children, who in that culture were sometimes considered unable to truly embrace religious faith until they were almost teenagers. Not only that, but Jesus blessed children and fed them. He even used a little boy's sack lunch to feed the multitudes.

Beyond that, Jesus healed boys and girls who were demon possessed and cured others who were sick and dying. He even resurrected a twelve-year-old girl who had just died and an older boy who had passed a few hours earlier. In His teaching, Jesus said that children are a strategic, essential part of His kingdom in heaven and on earth. In other words, Jesus proclaimed, "Listen! My kingdom belongs to kids!"

Are there kids in your life who could use a bit of Jesus' love?

DAVID: MEMORIZING GOD'S WORD

*I have hidden your word in my heart that
I might not sin against you.*

PSALM 119:11 NIV

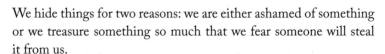

We hide things for two reasons: we are either ashamed of something or we treasure something so much that we fear someone will steal it from us.

David knew great sin, but he also knew great forgiveness. In his experience, hiding the Word of God in his heart was the only way to combat his sinful nature and to keep him from falling even further.

To say that he hid the Word in his heart implies several things. First, he went beyond simply owning a copy of God's Word. Owning a copy isn't transforming. Second, he went beyond hiding the Word in his mind. Our memories can fail us. Third, he went beyond simply reading God's Word on occasion. Reading it is helpful, but possessing it in our hearts is transformative.

If you find your faith lacking the power to overcome sin, consider a Bible memory program. It doesn't have to be elaborate—index cards will work just fine. Find verses that speak of the sin you are struggling with and jot the verses down on the cards. Carry them with you everywhere, referring to them throughout the day.

If you meditate, study, and recite the verses often enough, they'll soon become embedded in your heart—the perfect place for the Holy Spirit to access them for your spiritual breakthrough.

JESUS: HE UNDERSTANDS OUR WEAKNESSES

This High Priest of ours understands our weaknesses, for he faced all of the same testings we do, yet he did not sin. So let us come boldly to the throne of our gracious God. There we will receive his mercy, and we will find grace to help us when we need it most.

HEBREWS 4:15–16 NLT

Sometimes, it's hard to acknowledge our need for help. We live in a self-sufficient culture, so it may shock us to read that Jesus spent time on earth in order to feel our weaknesses and show mercy to us.

If you struggle with sin or don't think you can set your life right, remember that Jesus felt your fears, inadequacies, and even weaknesses. He knows your temptations, struggles, and tendencies to make poor choices.

Jesus was tested in all of the ways you have been tested, and while it may be hard to believe, He is merciful to you. And He wants you to come to Him in your weakness and failure.

Do you need to know today that Jesus is merciful and ready to help you? He desires that you have no fear when you approach His throne. And take note that this throne is not one of judgment, but of grace.

Acknowledging your weaknesses and failures is the first step toward restoration.

CLASSICS: D. L. MOODY

PAUL: FINISHING WELL

Thou therefore endure hardness,
as a good soldier of Jesus Christ.

2 TIMOTHY 2:3 KJV

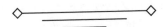

On the page of history the name of Paul is written down as a good soldier of the Lord Jesus, who could endure hardness like a true soldier should. As one of God's faithful ones, who feared not the face of man, he could say, "I have fought a good fight, I have finished my course, I have kept the faith; henceforth there is laid up for me a crown of righteousness, which the Lord, the righteous Judge, shall give me at that day; and not to me only, but unto all them that love His appearing."

Ah! He could say, "I have kept the faith." Blessed be God!

Paul is not dead; he lives up there; and at the day of Christ's appearing he shall receive an unfading crown of glory, beautiful, bright and new, from his Savior.

DAVID: THIRSTING FOR GOD

*You, God, are my God, earnestly I seek you; I thirst
for you, my whole being longs for you, in a dry
and parched land where there is no water.*

PSALM 63:1 NIV

Physical thirst is tangible. Your throat is dry. Your muscles begin to cramp. In extreme cases, confusion or hallucinations will set in. No matter how severe the case, nobody needs to tell you that you're thirsty. You instinctively know all the signs.

You also know the signs of other types of thirst. You know the longing to finally watch a movie you've been waiting to see. You know how it feels to yearn for the presence of a spouse. You know the urge you feel to hit a fitness goal when you're getting close.

But do you know the signs of spiritual thirst? Bible commentator John Gill suggests that spiritual longing will include a deep desire for the Bible, worship, church ordinances, communion, greater knowledge of God, and more grace from Him. That's what David felt as he penned today's verse in the wilderness of Judah. Even in such extreme circumstances, his whole being longed for God.

If you have this type of longing, go straight to God. He will slake your spiritual thirst.

JONATHAN: FIRM IN
THE FACE OF TROUBLE

Saul boiled with rage at Jonathan. "You stupid son of a whore!"
he swore at him. "Do you think I don't know that you want him
to be king in your place, shaming yourself and your mother?"

1 SAMUEL 20:30 NLT

◇———————◇

Today's scripture contains a father's words to his son. We can only imagine the hurt King Saul's insulting accusation caused for Jonathan.

At issue was the deep friendship the royal heir had with the up-and-coming hero, conqueror of Goliath. The account of that contest is in 1 Samuel 17; the next chapter begins, "After David had finished talking with Saul, he met Jonathan, the king's son. There was an immediate bond between them, for Jonathan loved David" (18:1 NLT).

Three verses later, Jonathan seems to recognize that he will not succeed to Saul's throne, and gives David his royal robe. Their friendship was sealed by a vow of protection made before "The LORD, the God of Israel" (1 Samuel 20:12 NLT).

Jonathan's devotion was tested by Saul's angry response—which included, as David had also experienced, the king hurling a spear at him (20:33). But Jonathan, whose name is synonymous with true friendship, could stay firm in the face of trouble because of his prior, intentional commitments.

Today, we will face opposition and insults for our friendship with Jesus. Have we made a firm, intentional decision to stand with Him regardless of anyone's reaction?

Day 365

JESUS: WORTHY OF ALL HONOR

*Saying with a loud voice, Worthy is the Lamb that was
slain to receive power, and riches, and wisdom, and
strength, and honour, and glory, and blessing.*

Revelation 5:12 KJV

We have got on record what heaven thinks of Christ. Here on earth He was not known—no one seemed really to understand Him; but He was known in that world in which He had been from the very foundation thereof; for He was there before the morning stars sang together, before Adam was placed in this world. We are told that John was in the Spirit on the Lord's day, and being caught up, he heard a loud shout around him, and looking, he saw ten thousand times ten thousand angels, who were shouting, "Worthy is the Lamb that was slain, to receive power, and riches, and wisdom, and strength, and honor, and glory, and blessing!"

Yes, Jesus is worthy of all this. That is what heaven thinks of Him; would that earth also would take up the echo and join with heaven in singing, "He is worthy to receive power, and riches, and wisdom, and strength, and honor, and glory, and blessing!"

SCRIPTURE INDEX

Genesis

1:26	Day 1
4:4–5	Day 280
4:6–7	Day 89
5:3	Day 189
5:21–24	Day 60
5:22–24	Day 256
5:27	Day 248
6:9	Day 41
6:13–14	Day 84
7:1, 7	Day 100
7:5	Day 143
11:31	Day 132
12:1, 4	Day 14
12:4	Day 74
14:18–19	Day 333
15:6	Day 91
17:1	Day 127
18:22	Day 221
19:29	Day 254
21:17	Day 165
22:16–18	Day 284
24:12	Day 99
24:63	Day 198
25:25	Day 338
26:24	Day 297
31:36–37	Day 18
32:10	Day 87
32:24–26	Day 229
32:26–28	Day 294
34:25	Day 122
35:23	Day 39
39:1–3	Day 25
39:12	Day 62
39:19–20	Day 85
39:20–21	Day 142
40:9–10	Day 241
45:26	Day 179
48:20	Day 111
50:24–25	Day 215

Exodus

3:4–5	Day 46
3:11	Day 86
14:15	Day 137
17:10–13	Day 159
18:17	Day 224
24:12–13	Day 40
32:25–26	Day 147
34:30–33	Day 164
35:30–31	Day 68
40:18–19	Day 214

Numbers

13:30–31	Day 76

Joshua

6:2	Day 235
11:18–20	Day 292
14:8	Day 154
14:9, 12	Day 212
15:14	Day 310

Judges

3:27–30	Day 272
4:8–9	Day 269
6:16	Day 9
8:22–23	Day 23

11:32–33	Day 176
13:12	Day 350
13:24	Day 71
14:8–9	Day 133
15:18–19	Day 196
16:22	Day 277
16:28	Day 326

Ruth

2:4	Day 8
2:8	Day 112
2:12	Day 148
3:10	Day 232

1 Samuel

1:4–5	Day 353
3:12	Day 107
7:12	Day 222
9:21	Day 58
15:10	Day 27
16:13	Day 34
17:32–33	Day 47
17:36–37	Day 66
17:37	Day 81
17:42–44	Day 356
17:45–46	Day 101
20:4	Day 145
20:30	Day 364
22:1	Day 131
23:4	Day 144
24:6	Day 162
26:23	Day 195
29:6	Day 205

2 Samuel

2:4–5	Day 216
3:1	Day 233
5:24	Day 239
7:27	Day 246
8:6	Day 262
9:3	Day 274
9:8	Day 275
11:3	Day 324
12:1	Day 44
19:32	Day 285
22:30	Day 286

1 Kings

2:28, 30	Day 188
2:45	Day 5
3:5	Day 104
3:11–12	Day 177
4:20	Day 236
8:15	Day 334
11:4	Day 311
11:26–28	Day 155
14:4–6	Day 140
15:9–11	Day 45
15:11, 14	Day 116
17:2–4	Day 26
18:17–19	Day 94
19:4	Day 226

2 Kings

2:1	Day 169
2:13–14	Day 141
5:17–18	Day 319
7:3	Day 301

15:32, 34–45 . . . . Day 97
18:3 . . . . Day 15
20:5 . . . . Day 138
22:1 . . . . Day 22

1 Chronicles
1:10 . . . . Day 151
4:10 . . . . Day 245
21:24 . . . . Day 24

2 Chronicles
14:8–11 . . . . Day 178
26:5 . . . . Day 268
29:3 . . . . Day 210
32:6–8 . . . . Day 265
33:13 . . . . Day 184
34:27 . . . . Day 257
35:14 . . . . Day 63

Ezra
1:2 . . . . Day 96
3:8 . . . . Day 161
5:1 . . . . Day 42
5:5 . . . . Day 119
7:17–18 . . . . Day 38
9:3–4 . . . . Day 197

Nehemiah
2:4–5 . . . . Day 73
2:11–12 . . . . Day 259
4:4–5 . . . . Day 65
9:7–8 . . . . Day 316
10:29 . . . . Day 130

Esther
2:21–22 . . . . Day 266
2:23 . . . . Day 50
10:3 . . . . Day 208

Job
1:1 . . . . Day 7
1:4–5 . . . . Day 103
2:9 . . . . Day 173
4:1–2 . . . . Day 296
5:8, 27 . . . . Day 187
29:19–20 . . . . Day 201
31:1 . . . . Day 327

Psalms
5:3 . . . . Day 322
18:35 . . . . Day 339
19:13 . . . . Day 348
55:22 . . . . Day 355
63:1 . . . . Day 363
77:3–4 . . . . Day 358
119:11 . . . . Day 360
143:2 . . . . Day 202

Ecclesiastes
1:2 . . . . Day 258

Isaiah
6:8 . . . . Day 53
60:2–3 . . . . Day 166

Jeremiah
15:16 . . . . Day 291
33:2–3 . . . . Day 93

Ezekiel

2:4–5 . . . . Day 80
16:60 . . . . Day 249

Daniel

1:8 . . . . Day 11
3:14 . . . . Day 341
3:17–18 . . . . Day 230
4:34, 37 . . . . Day 238
5:29 . . . . Day 75

Amos

7:14 . . . . Day 223

Jonah

1:9–10 . . . . Day 13

Micah

3:8 . . . . Day 170

Habakkuk

1:12 . . . . Day 182
3:17–18 . . . . Day 120

Zechariah

1:1–2 . . . . Day 217

Malachi

1:1 . . . . Day 330

Matthew

1:19–20 . . . . Day 244
2:1, 10 . . . . Day 10
3:8 . . . . Day 12
3:13 . . . . Day 113
4:1–2 . . . . Day 307
4:21–22 . . . . Day 17
5:1–2 . . . . Day 20
5:3 . . . . Day 36
5:44 . . . . Day 98
9:9 . . . . Day 56
10:29–31 . . . . Day 206
10:39 . . . . Day 209
11:11 . . . . Day 243
11:28 . . . . Day 237
17:1–3 . . . . Day 281
17:4 . . . . Day 28
19:21 . . . . Day 79
20:28 . . . . Day 325
25:40 . . . . Day 329
27:54 . . . . Day 306
28:18 . . . . Day 337

Mark

1:16–18 . . . . Day 51
2:3–4 . . . . Day 64
3:13–19 . . . . Day 332
5:15 . . . . Day 302
6:3 . . . . Day 336
6:31 . . . . Day 106
7:20–23 . . . . Day 124
9:24 . . . . Day 163
10:48 . . . . Day 123
14:51–52 . . . . Day 117
15:21 . . . . Day 125
15:43–46 . . . . Day 168

Luke

2:20 . . . . Day 43
2:27–28 . . . . Day 59
4:42–43 . . . . Day 139
5:4–5 . . . . Day 172
5:17 . . . . Day 121
5:23 . . . . Day 109
6:12–13 . . . . Day 146
7:6–7 . . . . Day 19
7:12 . . . . Day 278
7:22 . . . . Day 192
7:31–34 . . . . Day 347
7:36 . . . . Day 48
8:41–42 . . . . Day 185
11:29–30 . . . . Day 276
12:14–15 . . . . Day 264
12:20 . . . . Day 295
17:15–16 . . . . Day 16
18:16 . . . . Day 359
19:2 . . . . Day 32
19:8 . . . . Day 135
19:9–10 . . . . Day 293
19:16–17 . . . . Day 263
22:15–16 . . . . Day 288
23:42 . . . . Day 160
24:30–31 . . . . Day 82

John

1:40–41 . . . . Day 240
1:49 . . . . Day 57
3:2 . . . . Day 72
3:30 . . . . Day 78
3:31 . . . . Day 328
5:8 . . . . Day 158

6:8–9 . . . . Day 102
6:27 . . . . Day 167
7:37 . . . . Day 175
9:4 . . . . Day 331
9:6–7 . . . . Day 309
10:28 . . . . Day 225
11:1, 3 . . . . Day 69
11:16 . . . . Day 157
11:22 . . . . Day 231
11:35 . . . . Day 251
11:39 . . . . Day 181
12:27–28 . . . . Day 150
12:35–36 . . . . Day 260
13:1 . . . . Day 270
14:6 . . . . Day 267
14:18–20 . . . . Day 282
14:26–27 . . . . Day 299
17:15 . . . . Day 31
17:26 . . . . Day 304
18:10 . . . . Day 114
18:40 . . . . Day 313
19:38 . . . . Day 289
21:15 . . . . Day 152

Acts

1:8 . . . . Day 49
1:13 . . . . Day 174
1:21–22 . . . . Day 183
2:14, 17 . . . . Day 203
2:38, 41 . . . . Day 321
3:2 . . . . Day 67
4:13 . . . . Day 252
4:36–37 . . . . Day 33
5:38–39 . . . . Day 220

6:3, 5 . . . . Day 149
6:8 . . . . Day 55
7:9 . . . . Day 287
7:9–10 . . . . Day 346
7:55–56 . . . . Day 228
8:2 . . . . Day 92
8:29–31 . . . . Day 110
8:34–35 . . . . Day 300
9:11–12 . . . . Day 128
9:17–19 . . . . Day 312
9:26–27 . . . . Day 190
9:27 . . . . Day 303
10:44–45 . . . . Day 317
11:21 . . . . Day 70
12:5–8 . . . . Day 279
13:12 . . . . Day 90
13:22 . . . . Day 30
15:19 . . . . Day 52
15:37 . . . . Day 3
15:37–40 . . . . Day 340
16:2–3 . . . . Day 4
16:22 . . . . Day 6
16:30–34 . . . . Day 153
17:34 . . . . Day 105
18:24 . . . . Day 77
18:26 . . . . Day 37
20:9 . . . . Day 199
20:24 . . . . Day 35
21:11 . . . . Day 108
21:14 . . . . Day 54
24:6–7 . . . . Day 298
28:1–2 . . . . Day 250
28:23 . . . . Day 83

Romans

1:9–11 . . . . Day 21
1:16 . . . . Day 95
5:3–5 . . . . Day 61
8:38 . . . . Day 115
11:3–4 . . . . Day 315
15:13 . . . . Day 343
15:20 . . . . Day 126
16:17–18 . . . . Day 134

1 Corinthians

1:10 . . . . Day 156
1:14 . . . . Day 207
1:27–29 . . . . Day 171
4:9 . . . . Day 180
4:12–13 . . . . Day 186
4:16 . . . . Day 194
9:20–21 . . . . Day 204

2 Corinthians

4:8–9 . . . . Day 227
4:17 . . . . Day 234
12:7–9 . . . . Day 242
12:9 . . . . Day 314

Galatians

1:10 . . . . Day 255
1:15–17 . . . . Day 261
3:28 . . . . Day 345
4:28 . . . . Day 29
6:9 . . . . Day 218

Ephesians

4:1–3 . . . . Day 271

Philippians

1:29	Day 283
3:17	Day 290
4:6–7	Day 308
4:13	Day 318
4:19	Day 323

Colossians

1:26–27	Day 351
3:23–24	Day 335
4:12–13	Day 136
4:14	Day 253

1 Thessalonians

2:18–20	Day 342
5:18	Day 247

1 Timothy

1:12 –14.	Day 354
6:12	Day 213

2 Timothy

1:7	Day 118
2:3	Day 362

Titus

2:2	Day 88

Philemon

1:10–11	Day 200

Hebrews

4:15–16	Day 361
11:7	Day 273

11:8–10	Day 219
11:13	Day 191
11:17–18	Day 352
11:24–25	Day 2, 344

James

1:2–3	Day 129
1:21	Day 211

1 Peter

3:9	Day 305
4:10	Day 320
4:12–13	Day 349
5:6	Day 357

Jude

1:20–21	Day 193

Revelation

5:12	Day 365

More GREAT DEVOTIONS _for_ GUYS

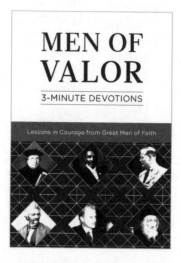

You'll find powerful lessons in courage in _Men of Valor: 3-Minute Devotions_. These 180 meditations pack challenge and encouragement into just-right-sized entries for guys of all ages, highlighting worthy Christian leaders who served God with courage—men like St. Augustine, Dietrich Bonhoeffer, Frederick Douglass, Jim Elliot, and many more.

Paperback / 978-1-64352-645-4 / $4.99